09/11 8:48 AM

Documenting America's Greatest Tragedy

09/11 8:48 AM

Documenting America's Greatest Tragedy

Edited by
BlueEar.com: Global Writing Worth Reading

with
the faculty and students
of the New York University
Department of Journalism

Foreword by
Jay Rosen
Chair of the Department of Journalism
New York University

Introduction by
Ethan Casey
Editor-in-chief, BlueEar.com

BOOKSURGE.COM • SEPTEMBER 2001

Published by BookSurge.com

Cover Photograph by
Terry Schmidt

Cover Designed by
Jon M. Taie

Book Design by
Jeff Schwaner

Composed in Hoefler font

09/11 8:48 AM

Documenting America's Greatest Tragedy

CONTENTS

Foreword by Jay Rosen / v

Introduction by Ethan Casey:
"Remembering Ed" / ix

Part One: September 11

3

i

Part Two: Aftermath

93

Part Three: Angles of Vision
223

Contributors / 309

Foreword

Jay Rosen

Early on in the crisis that followed the terror of September 11, it became clear that the destruction in New York and Washington was a new kind of international event. Not only did it concern people around the world; but in some way we are still trying to understand, it happened to people around the world. The very networks we had been celebrating as embodiments of a global age ran in reverse, so to speak.

Because we're all connected, we could all feel personally terrorized, even if it was not your own city left smoking and stunned the next day. The night the Berlin Wall fell, we all celebrated—and were right to do so. The day the World Trade Center fell, we were all crushed—and right again. If there is a dark side to the information age, we never knew how dark until those planes crashed and the networks lit up with the news, "completing" the act of terror by enlisting our emotions in its spread.

Before glasnost, it would have been possible to hijack an Aeroflot jet. But it would not have been easy to terrorize the people of the Soviet Union, for the simple reason that the state could smother news of the event and contain its spread. Back then, the authorities could prevent public discussion of a proper response to terror, like the one that started almost immediately, worldwide, on September 12, 2001. That discussion is actually part of the terror, and provoking it part of the criminals' intent.

In the Hollywood movie *Die Hard* (1988) the hero cop played by Bruce Willis makes a monstrous error when he establishes radio contact with a shadowy gang who have taken over a skyscraper, holding fifty people hostage, including the woman he loves. Once they knew he was listening, the criminals could threaten her life and force Willis to take actions he did not want to risk. He got connected, and they informed him of facts that fed his terror, drew him into a personal hell. This is what I mean by networks that ran in reverse. Over the same lines that carry information goods came a shocking information evil.

About ten days after the catastrophe in lower Manhattan, the city of Los Angeles paid for a full page ad in the New York Times declaring LA's common cause with the people of New York. The Netherlands brought itself to a halt for three minutes, so that the Dutch could think together about what had happened in the United States. Candelight vigils spoke to each other across oceans and continents. Parliaments passed resolutions. Writers took up their pens. Musicians took out their instruments to sing an American tune.

These poignant expressions of fellow feeling showed that something else had happened, after our terrible lesson in how globalization and the media age really work. The free peoples of the world began to shout their outrage at the crime on United States soil, their solidarity with the inhabitants of New York and Washington, their grief at the more than 6,000 lives wasted, their resolve not to let the terrorists "win," their acute awareness that the attack was aimed not only at its immediate victims, their emotional involvement in everything that happened that day—and also, in the U.S., their war fever and desire for payback, mixed with raw fear, public confusion, open prejudice and spontaneous national unity.

The free peoples of the world also began the arguments they knew they had to conduct in the aftermath, a lesson-learning that will last for years. Warnings not to over-react were heard as soon as the pattern in reactions was felt. And so the global networks almost instantly lit up with information goods again, now so easy to recognize. Which brings us to this book.

The writing collected here includes eyewitness accounts, on-the-ground reportage, personal essays, political argument, public debate, oral history, and a number of other genres. But there is a single theme: how to make human sense of what happened, especially in the City of New York, especially to the people of that city, thousands of whom died in the space of an hour. We use words like "unimaginable" and "unbelievable" to describe the devastation and loss of life in Manhattan, yet there is something not quite right about such terms—not right for this book.

The most basic act of journalism, by no means limited to journalists, is when someone says to us, "I was there, you weren't, let me tell you about it." Or equally often: "I'm there now, you aren't, so let me tell you." Information changes hands, but it is equally a moment where the mind begins to imagine. Television (and all terrorism is for television) appears to pre-empt this drive to conjure with reality. The images are "there," as in right there. You can—in fact you did—point to the screen and say: look! But how often have we asked one another in the days after Black Tuesday, "Can you imagine?..."

Actually, it's a great question.

We trust the answer is yes, those who edited and authored this book. But we're not taking any chances. Something about a book invites reflection, more than just reaction. We're counting on ordinary book-ness to work its effect here. Life has not even returned to normal as this volume goes to press, and that is one reason it went to press, nineteen days later. The extraordinary global moment that followed upon the attacks is still with us. The writings and reports published here are part of that moment, and they are sent out into it. Each is the work of a struggler, and many of the strugglers were also witnesses to New York City's waking nightmare. The faculty and students in New York University's Department of Journalism were there, so we can tell you about it. NYU is the closest journalism school to what is called Ground Zero. As chair of the program I thought it proper that the Department itself help edit and author this volume of reports. Any time you can offer students the role of worldwide witness, you must—even if some are not quite ready. Any time you have the chance to be writing precisely what they are writing, from the ground of a similar emotion, you should. Among the student accounts published here, most of them are saying: I was there, with my generation, you weren't. Please let me tell you about it. And so you should. We sent them out to document the destruction, but the reason we sent them out had as much to do with repair.

Finally, this is a book of the Internet Age. Most readers will buy it by the Net or learn about it on the Net. All of the work here originated on the Net, grew from exchanges on the Net, or got sent through the Net to make publication possible. I know that for myself as author, the Internet has never seemed more miraculously human than in the two weeks following the attacks. Being connected is such a mysterious good, I don't think we understand a tenth of it. All I know is that I had more people with me than ever before, and every New Yorker felt something similar. No, civic solidarity doesn't follow from pushing Send. But when people actually feel it, they send it with ease now. Counter-terrorism begins there.

Introduction:
Remembering Ed

Ethan Casey

When I lived in Thailand in the mid-1990s, I came to know Clyde Edwin Pettit, a fascinating man who had written, in Bangkok in January 1966 after spending several weeks in Saigon, a prescient letter to his state's U.S. Senator, J. William Fulbright. At that early date in the Vietnam War, Ed had dared to use the phrase "the unlikely but ever-present possibility of catastrophe," and had written: "I am very frightened. ... The road from Valley Forge to Vietnam has been a long one, and the analogy is more than alliterative: there are some similarities, only this time we are the British and they are barefoot. ...I would rather America err on the side of being overly generous than on the side of military miscalculation of inconceivable cost. For what, the world might well ask should we win the gamble, have we won?" Fulbright caused the letter to be published in the *Congressional Record* (much to Ed's alarm at the time) and publicly credited it with forcing him to reverse his position on the war.

Later Ed compiled a book, a tour de force of editing and a forgotten classic titled *The Experts: 100 Years of Blunder in Indo-China* (alternate subtitle: *The Book That Proves There Are None*), consisting of nothing but 439 pages of quotations from politicians, generals, and journalists, all claiming to know what was going on and coming next in Vietnam, arranged chronologically. Read from cover to cover, as Ed insisted it should be read, *The Experts* is an engrossing, horrifying narrative. In the book's Foreword, Ed wrote:

> The Vietnam War is a textbook example
> of history's lessons: that there is a tendency
> in all political systems for public servants to
> metamorphose into public masters, surfeited
> with unchecked power and privilege and
> increasingly overpaid to misgovern; that war
> is necessary to any elite corps, which has
> no reason to exist without it; that even free
> peoples are inevitably led to death and maiming
> because they do not have the intelligence to
> realize that all wars are against their interests;
> that there may be some dark and perverse
> tropism in our very natures that makes us turn
> toward the senseless destruction of war; that
> wars, once started, may become inundating
> forces of nature, inexorable and beyond the
> control of any of the participants.

"You would hear constantly, 'Napalm will win the war for us,'" he told me over whiskey in his hotel room. "Fucking napalm was the greatest thing ever to come down the pike, you woulda thought. It was always *something* was winning the war. They were always surrendering in six months. It was always 'these *little* gooks,' with the emphasis on how diminutive the people were—and are—not perceiving that that was an advantage."

To have one's pessimistic prescience confirmed is a bitter vindication, and Ed was a bitter guy. Much of the time he cloaked his bitterness, thinly, in gallows humor, joking for example about a new disease he had diagnosed called "mass Alzheimer's—nobody remembers anything!" Once, quoting Gandhi, he greatly amused an Indian friend of mine with his attempt to mimic the Mahatma's accent: "It is wrong to kill.

But if you must kill, you should kill in your own village. What is most wrong is to go to some other village and kill someone there to whom one has not even been properly introduced." But his bitterness was real. When, brimming with ambition, I said I might do for Bosnia what he had done for Vietnam, he was dismissive. "You could do a sequel to *The Experts* about anything," he said. What he meant was that once was—or should have been—enough to make that book's point.

The book you're holding is intended as a record of what a wide range of people in New York and Washington, around the United States, and worldwide saw, felt, believed, and wanted on and soon after September 11, 2001. The very nature of the event and its aftermath calls into question the moral authority of the long-reigning punditocracy—the Experts—because we're so obviously all in this together. It's fitting—nay, it's urgently important—that this book has many authors, and that many, perhaps most, of them are claiming no authority but that of unmediated personal experience. The events of September 11 called forth a deluge of writing, much of it very good, some of it astonishing in its honesty and prophetic quality. The pieces in this collection are by professional journalists and highly credentialed academics as well as proverbial "ordinary people," and what's most impressive to me is the bracing blend of audacity and humility they exhibit. Many academics' and journalists' contributions are strikingly different in every literary trait from what their authors might ever have written otherwise. This is, I think, because the event itself transformed them instantly back into ordinary people, not least because so many academics and journalists live or work in Manhattan. The writing in this book is above all *honest* writing.

Ed Pettit was in several ways my most important mentor. He taught me the value of courage, and its price. He taught me why self-awareness and honesty are crucial in writing as in life, and *The Experts* showed me how even the most elegant prose dates and taints itself when it lacks these. Ed also taught me the hard necessity of seeing history whole and with clear eyes, and the freedom to be found in understanding and living life in this world on one's own responsibility, whatever the personal cost.

When I last saw Ed, in December 1997, I asked for his take on the Asian economic crisis that had begun right there in Bangkok half a year earlier, which at the time was the focus of the world's fickle attention (how soon we forget, as global crises follow swiftly on each other's heels).

The author of *The Experts* and The Fulbright Letter furled his brow for a long moment—it was what he called going into a trance. Then, he imparted his vision. They can make all the multilateral pacts and groupings they want, he said, but something is always going to be left unaccounted for; every system falls apart. "Don't make any bets about the future of the world economy," he said. "All I know is that the next five years is going to be the goddamnedest merry-go-round, the goddamnedest ferris wheel. It's going to be a *fantastic* time to be alive."

This book's editorial incubator was the Blue Ear Forum moderated email community (http://www.blueear.com/forum) edited by my colleague Tim Walker, where a stunning number and variety of eyewitness accounts were posted on September 11 and in the days following. I remember well my own momentary paralysis after I first heard the news; I even considered staying offline entirely that day. Then Robin O'Brien posted his eyewitness account (published here as "I just watched the second tower collapse"), and the floodgates were opened. The Forum had received praise in the past, but we really knew we were onto something when, on September 16, member Dorothy Jane Mills posted a message that included these words:

> During this appalling week, the Blue Ear
> Forum has fulfilled its purpose in full measure.

It served as a college course in contemporary affairs by furnishing us with a breadth of information that we could not have found in any university because of its amazingly wide membership among intelligent people around the world.

Then Mitchell Davis of BookSurge (http://www.booksurge.com) approached me with an idea for a book. I felt confident enough to undertake such an ambitious project, on such a schedule, because we already had in hand so much excellent material from the Forum. Articles in this book by the following authors all were first published on the Blue Ear Forum: Helga Ahmed, Aung Zaw, Brian Calvert, William Davis, Alex M. Dunne, Larry Hartsell, Donna Headrick, Lydia Lakwonyero (as part of the Kampala, Uganda-based Africa Speaks initiative: http://lifeinafrica.com/africa_speaks), Blake Lambert, Challiss McDonough, Robin O'Brien, Jeff Rigsby, Jay Rosen, Roger Tatoud, Alexandra Walker. Steve Lanier posted "Humvees in D.C." to our separate Blue Ear Travel list (http://www.blueear.com/travel), and J.R. Lankford sent "Quiet in America" to Blue Ear Books (http://www.blueear.com/books).

Then we started sending out calls via e-mail for other material, and submissions and suggestions began coming in thick and fast. The first challenge was simply to read it all, and we had to make some difficult decisions about what to leave out; I apologize to everyone who generously offered material that we were unable to include. I also am delighted to thank Philippa Neave and Sinead Donohoe of Correspondent.com (who went above and beyond the call), Darren Campbell, Steve Klein, Mary Kay Magistad, Scott McLemee and Liz McMillen of *The Chronicle of Higher Education*, Najam Sethi, Laurel Sheppard, and Sharon Spiteri for suggesting and/or finding a number of the book's contributors, and Annie Hedges for last-minute proofreading help. Thanks also to Scott McLemee for his editorial pinch-hitting in the ninth inning. Jay Rosen and his colleagues and students in New York University's Department of Journalism—the J-school nearest "Ground Zero"—caught the vision and produced an array of fine reporting and essays on very short notice. NYU-affiliated contributors are identified as such in the Contributors section below, and some of their pieces were first published on the Department's website "Dispatches from Ground Zero" (http://journalism.fas.nyu.edu/wtc/). The idea for this book belongs to Mitchell Davis and Jeff Schwaner of BookSurge.com, the publisher, who had not only the vision but also the wherewithal to make it happen using innovative technology and marketing methods.

The following articles are republished here with kind permission: "'Oh my God, people are jumping'" and "A Terrible Absence" by Conor O'Clery, from *The Irish Times*; "'They were playing nicely together'" by Constance Daley and Gene Albertelli, from *The Weekend* of St. Simons Island, Georgia; "Intangible but Oppressive" by Preston Peet from Freedom News Network (http://www.wizardsofaz.com/freedomnewsnetwork); "A Priest's Diary" by Fr. Julian Cassar, from *The Times of Malta*; "Stranded Airline Passengers Count Their Blessings" by Jaclyn O'Malley, from the *Garden City Telegram* of Garden City, Kansas; "A Pakistani Woman in New York" by Humera Afridi, from *The Friday Times* of Lahore, Pakistan (where it ran in different form); "A Ragged, Determined Army of Volunteers" and "A Lone Sneaker" by Dawn Shurmaitis, from the *Wilkes-Barre Times Leader*; "Don't Understand America Too Quickly" by Todd Gitlin, from OpenDemocracy.net; "Coyles Know What Americans Are Going Through" by Jeffrey Cohen, from the Meriden, Connecticut *Record-Journal*; "Personal Lessons" by Gary Gach, from *The American Reporter* (http://www.american-reporter.com); "The Long Way Back Home" by Cynthia G. La

Ferle, from *The Daily Tribune* of Royal Oak, Michigan.

"A Complex God" by Stanley Hauerwas, "Toward the 'New Normal'" by Edward T. Linenthal, "Why We Shouldn't Call It War" by Christopher Phelps, and "Giving Meaning to Survival" by Robert Jay Lifton all appeared in the issue of *The Chronicle of Higher Education* dated September 28, 2001.

Finally, special thanks to my BlueEar.com colleagues Jim Austin, Leah Kohlenberg, Steve Lanier, Hugh Martin, and Tim Walker for holding down the fort; to Blake Lambert and Lenny Miller for coming through in the clutch; to John Bebow, Mindy Feldman, and M.J. Rose for their generosity to and support of this project; and to Lucy and Stefan for their love and indulgence.

Ethan Casey
Editor-in-chief
BlueEar.com: Global Writing Worth Reading
editor@blueear.com
September 29, 2001

Editor's Note: During copy editing and proofreading, mindful that much of the material in this book originated as e-mail, we've made sometimes arbitrary decisions concerning stylistic consistency in a conscious attempt to retain the immediacy of the writing.

For those who died on September 11, 2001

Part One

September 11

On the Beach

M.J. Rose

Tod's Point, Greenwich, Connecticut—When you are jogging in this 147-acre park, there is a spot you pass at the halfway mark when you come around a bend and on a clear day—like today—you can see the whole gleaming skyline of Manhattan.

Except this morning there was something that seemed wrong.

There were two smokestacks on the horizon in a place there never had been smokestacks before. And it took a minute—a long minute—to figure out that the smoke was billowing out from the World Trade Towers.

About twenty yards up ahead, a few people had congregated, and I stopped to ask what had happened.

Their news was swift and delivered in short sentences.

At that point, both Towers were still standing. And so we stood. All strangers gathered on an outcropping of rock, watching a scene that did not make sense.

And then a woman ran up and began to climb those rocks. She was crying, and her movements were frantic. She could not get close enough to their edge—to the water. She was in tears. A few steps behind her another woman followed who tried to keep the first from climbing down the rocks to the water.

"But he's in that building," the crying woman said as she fought off her friend.

The crowd grew as the minutes passed. And some of us stood back to let the war widows past. You could tell who they were: the women and men who came—some alone, others with friends—who had loved ones in those two towers.

Ashamed to watch their grief, to see their trembling hands and smell their fear, I kept my eyes on the sky.

"It's collapsing," a man shrieked. And the wailing started.

In this suburb that sits on the outskirts of New York, we watched the Twin Towers fall. But we didn't hear the sirens or the explosions. We only heard the gulls screaming and the widows weeping.

"Time was like years"

Peter Wong

Subject: Right under the elevator lobby of WTC 1
between the two ID checkpoints

I heard the sound of broken glass, smelled burning gas, a door blown off about twenty feet in front of me, heat was coming my way. I stepped back and hid myself at the middle elevator of the Blue Cross/Blue Shield section when the strongest wave of explosion passed by with chunks of glass and debris flying around. I was lonely and desperate. When things turned quiet, a piece of big metal the size of a chair was just ten to fifteen feet away on the floor.

My God, I thought it was a car bomb from the garage where I normally park my car. Would there be a second one coming? For a while I was frozen and didn't know what to do. This is the second time I was caught in a bomb blast. February 26, 1993 was so close. "Get out! Get out!" My brain was so numb that I just followed the instruction of the security person to run up the moving stairs leading to the concourse where the fountain was, only to find out there is no way out already. Glass was all broken and I joined two other people and ran back down and rushed through the lobby of the Marriott Hotel. I saw women lying on the floor, faces covered with blood and blackened, being attended by people. Outside the hotel were policemen guiding us, running diagonally across West Street to the other side of the street at Financial Center.

I was safe!? The street was full of people trying to call on the handphone but in vain.

People started to cry when we saw individuals jumping from the burning floors. There came the roaring sound of a plane. I stared up and witnessed the plane (bluish and big) hit fiercely into the building. My God, it's not a movie, I saw that over my head.

People were so panicked and started running to the south. I saw women fall on the ground and I had to steer aside to avoid being hit and fall myself. Where should I run?

I could not get near to any high-rise again and could not stay outside anymore. I didn't know where I was, I didn't want to see the burning towers, I came to a stop at a two-floor building where a woman was crying near the door and I went in. I am the Asian man who broke down in tears. The staff in that building's management office were so nice and helpful in letting us call to our family members. There were about eight of us there. Twice we hid under the table when we felt a rumbling of the floor when the two towers fell. It was as dark as if we were in a cave and we didn't know that we were at the mercy of God had the towers fallen in our direction instead of going straight down. Time was like years, no one in the office knew what we should do but to stay. We were finally guided to the nearest waterfront and shipped to the other side of Jersey. My sympathy to all who suffered or lost their life or loved one! May all blessings be with you.

I'd like to thank the lady and the four kids who drove me to Journal Square, and also Bill and Lucy Comerford, and finally Tom and Kelly, who provided me the soda and sandwich which were my breakfast and dinner. Thank you.

On September 23, 2001, Peter Wong e-mailed the following to the editor of this book:

Please I would like you to include my e-mail to my daughter, which I sent out with my pager during the collapse of the two towers. I just want people to know how desperate were people like me in this situation. And for those who vanished in this incident, I know your anger, your helplessness, and how unwillingly you had to leave behind your loved ones without being able to convey any message. Mr. Ethan, please don't edit any word or spelling here, as this was the true and identical message as appeared on my pager even now.

QUOTE "Iam in abldg called milford mamagement corp If anythong happenibg u know how tp retrieve me. Take care of mom n patrick" UNQUOTE

Sincerely, Peter Wong

Loss, Panic and Helplessness:
Three New Yorkers Speak

Karmann Ghia

Sean Geraty

"My sister Suzanne is missing. She's 30. She worked for Cantor Fitzgerald on the 103rd floor. The last we heard, she called our Mom and said there was just a fire. We don't think she made it, but we're still hoping."

Tuesday, 7:40 a.m.—Sean Geraty, 33, a commodities broker, boards a crowded train in Princeton, New Jersey, headed for the World Trade Center. He eventually gets off and boards another train headed toward the ferry.

9:03 a.m.—Geraty's train arrives in Jersey City, across the river from the World Trade Center. He's about to board the ferry when he sees the north tower on fire. A plane crashes into the south tower. Geraty is stunned. Crowds watch in disbelief. Many cry.

9:10 a.m.—Geraty's mother receives a phone call from her daughter. She says she's okay and she's going to make her way down. That was the last anyone heard from her.

"We heard on television that people who called their families were told to go up. Smoke was thick and black, the ceilings were falling in, and they were told to go up. She gave me the impression she was going down. She's been trained in fire safety. She had been trained in lifesaving measures. She would know not to go up. Smoke travels up."

Geraty's mother tries to call her daughter back. There is no answer. Throughout the day she tries to call her cell phone. There is still no answer.

10:20 a.m. — Geraty goes back to Princeton to see his wife and contact his mother. He waits for news and watches television all day.

Wednesday, 5 p.m. — Geraty goes to the Cantor Fitzgerald crisis center at the Pierre Hotel in uptown Manhattan.

"Everybody there was in the same water as us. The company had 1,000 employees. 270 are accounted for — through vacation, staying home sick, or getting out. 730 employees are missing, including the brother of the CEO of the company. No one at the crisis center knew where they were."

7:30 p.m. — Community prayers are held at the family parish. Congregants light candles for Suzanne Geraty and several other parishioners who are missing.

Thursday afternoon — Geraty's mother appears on the Fox News Channel pleading for the rescue of her daughter. Later friends, family and strangers call to exchange information.

"People were calling up saying they were sorry to hear about what happened. People calling up who had missing relatives. No one had heard anything. Everybody's hoping and praying they're in an air pocket somewhere and they'll come home. We're all waiting for them."

10 p.m. — Geraty is down the block from Bellevue Hospital posting his sister's missing person flyers at a bus stop. He wears a flyer taped to his t-shirt. Then he files a missing person's report a couple blocks away at the Armory.

"It's been real hard. Just not knowing. Even just to get a body, to get closure. My father just passed away last October, and now my baby sister. My mother is just breaking down. She's hysterical sometimes. Numb sometimes. We're trying to keep people around her. Yesterday, we were just dealing with

Mom. She kept thinking about how much fear her daughter felt. That she was all alone, without her family."

Friday, 10:51 a.m. — Geraty leaves home to file a missing person's report with the Mayor's office. He has a friend there and is hoping for some luck.

12 p.m. — A Mass is held in the family's parish in Brooklyn. Suzanne's mother, siblings, aunt's, and cousins attend.

"Our prayers go out to everyone else in the same position as we are. And we thank everybody for all they've done for us. New Yorkers are great people."

Rahaman Khan

"I've been a nurse for 33 years. This is my job. I knew what I was coming into. I worked here for the other bombing at the trade center in 1993. Of course this was much, much worse."

Tuesday, 9:30 a.m. — Rahaman Khan, 56, a registered nurse at Bellevue Hospital in Manhattan, watches the events on television in horror at his home in Queens.

"I was anxious to get in to work, even though my shift ended several hours earlier. The subways weren't running, and all the tunnels and bridges were closed. I called the police and asked them if they could take me to the hospital. Then I called the hospital and asked if I could come into work early. I was told they had enough staff. People that lived close by, whether it was their shift or not, came in."

10 a.m. — World Trade Center victims arrive in ambulances at Bellevue Hospital. Khan watches television throughout the day and rests up before his twelve-hour shift starts.

"My family was worried about the whole situation. My

wife was crying all the time. I had a friend that was supposed to be in a building next to the World Trade Center. She saw it fall. I had another friend that was supposed to be in the first building that fell. She was late for work because she was getting her breakfast."

6 p.m.—Khan arrives to work one hour early and works until morning. Most patients at the ER now are suffering from heat exhaustion and smoke inhalation. They are not office workers, but firefighters, emergency service workers, and police.

"Ambulances were coming in all the time. Three or four people in each car. But they were just the people helping to find the victims."

2 a.m.—A team of doctors and nurses ride down to the site of the tragedy, responding to a trauma call.

"A Port Authority cop was trapped under debris, and we tried to see if we could get him out. We went to assess the situation. The whole team went down. He had already lost one leg from falling debris. His other leg was fractured, and he had abdominal injuries. But we were able to save his other leg. We had to transfuse him with blood down there. That's the worst I saw."

4 a.m.—The ER slows down.

"We were very disappointed. Of course, you don't want people to be hurt, but this is what we do."

Wednesday, 8 a.m.—Khan goes home.

"I keep thinking about it. It's on my mind all the time. So many people lost their lives. There's so much suffering. This is depressing to everybody. They keep talking about it, looking at the television, asking if there's anything they can do."

Thursday, 10 p.m.—260 patients have been admitted since Tuesday's tragedy. Ambulances rarely arrive at the hospital. But a school bus filled with trained experts in chemical warfare sent down from Albany, New York are expected at any moment.

10:15 p.m.—A crew of men arrive dressed in puffy white suits at the emergency center entrance. They line up one by one to shower outside the emergency center before they are de-contaminated and can go back to their hotel. Khan goes inside and waits for them.

Mary P.

"I've never believed in God less in my life—ever."

Thursday, 10:45 p.m.—Mary P., 46, owner of an arts and educational film/video production company in Manhattan, walks home from Bellevue Hospital dressed in borrowed clothes and carrying her possessions in two shopping bags. She clutches a map of lower Manhattan.

"I need it. I need it to talk to people and tell them what happened."

Monday, 1:30 a.m.—Mary rides home in a cab after visiting a friend. As she heads to her apartment across the street from the World Trade Center, she talks about religion with the driver, a Pakistani Muslim. Both feel religious wars are idiotic and that people should be free to worship as they wish.

Tuesday, 8:45 a.m.—"I was woken up by an Islamic Jihad across the street. Flying paper, charred and burnt things were raining down. I threw my clothes on, grabbed my wallet, keys and cell phone, and was about to run out of my apartment. I wanted to look before I left. From my kitchen window, I saw the next building being hit by a giant orange fireball." The phone rang. It was her roommate's friend. "'Kristina,' I said, 'I'm really scared. Wait five minutes and call me back to see if I'm still alive.'"

She ran out soon after the friend called back.

"One of my neighbors latched on to me and held me. I told her to leave. I was telling everybody to leave."

10:05 a.m. — She heads for the East River and tries to call her mother, but her cell phone doesn't work. She hides in a friend's apartment one block away. Another blast sounds, as the south tower of the World Trade Center collapses. She dives for the bathroom, the only room with no windows. Four people and four dogs hide inside. She has no idea how long they are in there.

"It was the worst noise you ever heard. You don't ever want to hear that sound. Eventually, we opened up the door. The bedroom windows were black. We went back into the bathroom and stayed there for a while. When we came out again, the windows were gray. Dust, debris and fine soot covered the windows. The TV was still on, covering the tragedy."

Mary puts a wet towel on her head and sunglasses and runs out of the building. She figures she can jump in the water. No one in the building would come with her. The soot is ankle deep on the street. Mary, a native New Yorker with an expert command of its geography, gets lost, but she keeps running. The second building starts to come down. Someone hands her a mask, and she runs under the Brooklyn Bridge into Chinatown. Hundreds of Chinese stand in the streets, looking up at a huge smoke cloud in disbelief.

Tuesday afternoon — She calls her landlord, and they make a list of building residents.

Thursday, 3 p.m. — Mary hears everyone in her apartment building is accounted for, except for one person. She hopes he left the city and just didn't think to call the landlord.

"I won't watch television, but I've heard my building has refrigerator-sized holes. The front windows are blown out, too."

9 p.m. — "Oh God, the e-mails I've received. And phone calls. There have been so many. I've heard from all over the world. But I had to get out and get away from everything. I started walking to Bellevue."

10 p.m. — She arrives at Bellevue to get sleeping pills.

"I heard they were giving them out free to victims, but there aren't a lot of survivors. I have survivor guilt. There are so many people dead."

"I don't compare this to Pearl Harbor. These are people who aren't evil capitalists. It's not the military-industrial complex. This was just sick and evil. I worry that we have an idiot for President. I'm afraid governments are going to start throwing around missiles. We do have to clamp down on terrorism, but I have little hope our government is going to be smart about this.

"All I can think of is to start working for the Justice Department on Monday. I want to work for families whose loved ones were killed. I'm going to Long Island this weekend. My aunt, uncle and cousins want to hug me. And I think it's important that they get to. Luckily, my husband was in California. He tried to talk me to sleep the other night. It didn't work. Hopefully tonight, I'll get to sleep in the bed, rather than re-run it.

"Life is really different today for me, but I want to be here in New York, and I want to say 'Fuck You.' I want to say we're not destroyed by this."

"Oh my God, people are jumping"

Conor O'Clery

The first bang came at 8.50 a.m., shaking the windows of my 42nd floor office which has a clear view of the two World Trade Centre towers three blocks to the southeast.

I looked out and saw a huge ball of flame and black smoke billowing out of the north-facing side of the nearest tower.

As the smoke cleared a massive hole 10 stories high became visible just below the top 10 floors and flames could be seen encircling the building behind its narrow slit-like windows.

Ten minutes later a passenger plane appeared from across the Hudson River heading straight for the second tower.

I didn't notice it until the last minute.

It was tilted so that the flight path took it straight towards the second tower.

It hit and simultaneously a gigantic ball of flame emerged from the east side of the second tower as if the plane had crashed right through the heart of the 110-storey building.

Debris fell in chunks onto West Side Highway followed by a blizzard of shards of glass and paper where ambulances and fire engines were beginning to congregate.

Flames began to leap from the side of the Marriott Hotel just across from where the tiny white Greek Orthodox church stands incongruously in a car park.

People by this time were streaming from the bottom floor of the World Trade Centre, which stands on top of a shopping mall and wide marbled corridors containing airline offices, shops, and a subway station.

Some 50,000 people work in the seven-building complex and many would have been in their offices by now.

Tourists would have begun arriving to queue for the lifts to the top of the tower with its famous Window on the World restaurant and wonderful views over Manhattan.

Watching through binoculars I could see people hanging out of the windows beside and above where the fires were raging.

One man waved a white cloth as he clung to a window strut.

Then a body fell from a window above him with arms and legs outstretched and plummeted some 100 stories onto Vesey Street.

Two other people fell in the succeeding minutes.

I ran down to the streets where office workers and traders, still wearing their red jackets, were milling around.

Some women were screaming "Oh my God, people are jumping, Oh my God."

Some of the residents of my building, where many members of the financial district live, were sobbing uncontrollably. I returned to the office.

As I watched, the top of the second tower suddenly fell outwards onto West Side Highway, the main thoroughfare along the western side of Manhattan which passes right by the World Trade Centre.

Massive jagged pieces of the tower the size of houses crashed onto two fire engines and onto rescue workers on the roadway.

A huge cloud of dust and ashes rose from the impact, enveloping the Embassy Suites Hotel across the highway and the 50-storey buildings of the World Financial Centre which house Merrill Lynch and stands between the towers and the Hudson River promenade.

I shifted my eyes upwards to the first tower that had been

hit and was still standing, and saw that several more people had appeared in the upper stories where they had smashed windows.

The man with the white cloth was still there, hanging precariously by one hand with his body out over the abyss.

I wondered why there was no attempt to rescue them by helicopter as part of the roof of the 1,350-foot building was clear of smoke.

But then the tower began to sway slightly and two people fell in quick succession from the windows as if unable to maintain their grip, falling down onto West Side Highway into the dust and smoke from the first collapse.

Then the tower simply slid in on itself, imploding with a huge roar, leaving the lift-shaft like a stump of a blasted tree with twisted metal arms.

This time the clouds of dust and smoke were so huge they enveloped the whole of southern Manhattan.

Thousands of tons of rubble fell onto Tobin Plaza, where open air concerts are sometimes held and onto the annex housing Borders giant book store.

A westerly breeze kept it about a hundred yards from my building. As it cleared, the scene around the towers was like one from a war zone, which it truly was.

The roadway and pavements and bicycle path, all the streets, cars, fire engines, pavements, traffic lights, awnings and police vehicles, were coated with dust. The green park between my building and the towers where kids play American football had been transformed into a grey field, as if covered with a toxic snow.

About 20 cars in the open air car park between it and the disaster scene were on fire.

As the dirty grey and brown smoke cleared around midday I could see that the Marriott Hotel had taken the full force of the falling tower.

All its windows were shattered and long strips of jagged metal hung over the awning.

The wide, covered pedestrian bridge from the mezzanine level of the financial centre and the Winter Gardens, with its palm trees, was a twisted mass of wreckage.

Out on the streets again, people who had been standing aghast in Battery Park by the river were now streaming uptown on foot.

"Go north, head north," shouted a police officer. The police and firemen remained mostly calm but their faces reflected the horror of the certainty that they had just lost many comrades.

Before the collapse dozens of firemen and police had rushed into the twin towers to try to help with the evacuation.

What had become of them? It was too horrible to contemplate.

Or to think of the thousands of people trying to escape from both towers, executives in suits, receptionists at polished desks, secretaries, traders, messengers, choking in their offices or racing down smoke-filled emergency stairwells below the destruction line.

It was just 10 minutes before nine when the first plane crashed into one of the towers and the offices were undoubtedly all either doing business or preparing for another working day.

The two gift shops at the top and the food court would have been almost ready to open up.

In the mall below thousands at that time of day criss-cross through the wide corridors past designer stores and coffee shops and newspaper vendors.

Shocked and weeping people trotted down Greenwich Street and west Broadway and Broadway with their hands to their eyes, obeying the arm-waving police officers, and fleeing in the direction of uptown.

Others crowded onto the cross-Hudson ferries at the harbour surrounded by the financial centre buildings.

The ferries had borne workers from the New Jersey shore to their work in the financial district just two hours before. The clothes of those caught in the explosion of dust were coated with grey; some had dust-covered hair and eyebrows.

Between midday and one o'clock there were three more muffled bangs from the vast area still hidden by thick acrid smoke as more sections of the two towers collapsed.

As the smoke drifted eastwards further scenes of immense destruction came into view: The twisted metal and piles of rubble and crushed dust-shrouded emergency vehicles which filled Vesey Street and West Side Highway.

There among the rubble, coated with dust, were many bodies, some of those who had jumped, and some of firemen caught beneath the heavy, deadly cascade of falling concrete and metal.

Another plane appeared overhead, causing a frisson of panic, but it turned out to be a military jet, arriving one assumes to shoot out of the sky any further suicide pilots. It was too late to save downtown Manhattan.

A Day of Horror

Niamh Early

My train suddenly stopped halfway into the station and my ears popped and we heard a loud noise. After a few minutes the train operator said there was a problem with some smoke at the station and we were not stopping there but going onto the next stop. I exited the subway a block away and saw the tower on fire surrounded by a lot of smoke. At first I couldn't even work out which building was on fire—it didn't look like the WTC from the angle I was at due to all the smoke—couldn't see the top of the building nor the second tower. Then it dawned on me it was the WTC because of the windows. I stopped in shock and just stared—people were upset on the street—paper was floating in the air down to the ground.

Everybody was staring in total disbelief. I had no idea at this stage that a plane had hit the tower. I decided to go straight to my office on Wall St—to get away from the WTC—I am down by the water so I knew I would be safe(r)—5 blocks away. I reckoned that it had to be a bomb by the way various floors were damaged—it was not a regular fire. I got to the office as the second plane impacted and immediately called my parents.

In the next 15 minutes we were no longer able to make any outside calls only receive them. Our cell phones weren't working either. I felt my building shake when both towers collapsed. We were unable to see outside our windows—we had paper and debris blowing up against the windows. We were unable to get out of our building due to all the smoke so we waited for the worst of the smoke to lift. I looked up to the top of Wall St and couldn't see anything but a big bellow of thick black smoke. I knew I was safer inside the office than on the street due to possible smoke inhalation, falling debris etc. The ground was completely covered with ash and our building had the foresight to have face masks in the basement—must have been from Y2K I imagine. The whole downtown area looked like an apocalypse- the movies—like a nuclear fallout. I was very fortunate to get a ferry to Brooklyn where I went to a friend's apartment. People were very calm just walking around stunned. It was surreal. I have never seen the streets of NY so quiet—little to no traffic in Brooklyn and Queens and people were all very quiet. It is the same today.

I couldn't get a cab home until 7 p.m.—the subways weren't running. I went down to my local bar to catch up with some friends. Everyone was in a state of shock and disbelief with one more horror story after another. Luckily enough I know of no one missing among my friends. However a lot of my clients had offices in the Towers so no doubt will—everyone will know someone or have a friend who has lost someone in this tragedy.

Tonight when I was parking my car I saw cops guarding some mosques in my neighborhood fearing attacks on the Arab community in my neighborhood. Similarly last night I witnessed a fight between a young Arab and an American. My neighborhood is predominantly Greek but there are lot of different ethnic groups here. However it is a very safe neighborhood so I am not worried about this.

The downtown area was closed today and am sure will be for the rest of week. We have closed our office until Monday for the moment. I am not looking forward to the thought of going downtown next week and seeing the space where the towers used to be. It is a very eerie feeling to look over to Manhattan now and not see the towers particularly as I know they should be there and exactly where on the skyline.

"I just watched the second tower collapse"

Robin O'Brien

A quick report from the 12th floor of an office building in Jersey City, directly across the river from lower Manhattan:

I just watched the second tower of the World Trade Center collapse. The first imploded into a cataclysmic cloud that quickly enveloped lower Manhattan. The ferries scurried from the piers as we watched in disbelief. Just as the smoke was clearing, Tower 2 just disintegrated, I-beams flying like matchsticks, an even greater cloud rushing out into the river, obscuring the downtown once more.

On the street below a crowd is gathered, a throng of anxious faces. I waded through the crowd as I came up from the PATH (the subway that links Manhattan and North Jersey). Many are on cellphones, most in vain. The circuits are overloaded. The buildings here contain satellite offices for companies based right across the river, some in the very buildings that until two hours ago dominated the Manhattan skyline.

I was on one of the last trains out of the city. Everything is now sealed off. We wait, wondering where the next strike will come from, worrying about those we know and love.

As others hurry by, two people, 12 stories below, are locked in the longest embrace I remember. I watched them run toward each other before they connected. I've called my wife and Dad, I've emailed my friends (many of whom are in Washington, DC. I pray that they're OK).

Now, we wait, and watch. It's a helpless, helpless feeling. Most folks here are cried out now. Some are talking in low, incredulous voices, trying to make sense of what appears to be a coordinated, devastating, deliberate attack. The radio dominates the hushed room of cubicles and offices. We'll probably be here for some hours yet; the bridges and trains into the city are closed, all air traffic in the country is grounded, the roads are clogged with people trying to get back to home base.

Hollywood meets Manhattan. What a terrible day.

Things Change

Kevin Barber

I'm in Brooklyn Heights, New York, safe, uninjured and have no idea when I'll get out. You've seen the news.

I watched in a surrealistic swirl of emotion, horror and morbid fascination as two icons of global stability and power were erased. This day has been the longest in my life, and yet each time I look at my watch I'm amazed another four hours has passed. Time is not a concern here.

No one had any idea what was going on. An airplane had hit the World Trade Center, how bizarre. We went to the rooftop to get a view, then watched as a second jet flew into the second tower. What was going on? I left my friend Rochell's apartment and headed toward Manhattan to see what was up. By the time I stopped at the deli for coffee and ambled to the Brooklyn Bridge I was clear that whatever was going on was bigger than what I'd thought or could ever imagine.

People came across the bridge by the thousands. A sea of people, some crying but most were expressionless and quiet. Then the rumble, then the screaming, then twelve seconds later the first tower had fallen. I looked up to the bridge and saw a thousand twisted faces watch as the mammoth building crumpled before them in a puff of smoke. They flooded off the bridge in a cacophony of screams and police sirens. Some talked to themselves, some wailed, a guy covered in soot guided a woman along the sidewalk as she cried uncontrollably into her hands. Hundreds of cell phones were dialed and re-dialed with no chance of connection.

I hurried to the Brooklyn Heights Promenade to get a view of the Lower East Side. Instead I found a ball of gray smoke a mile high and forty blocks wide heading right toward me. People were gathering by the hundreds but no one spoke; we just watched. Moments later from inside the smoke we heard another roar, more screaming, and I feared the other had fallen. I hurriedly made my way to the apartment as papers and ash and the dirty smell of fire and grief rained down on my head.

My walking became brisk, and I wanted out of here. I caught bits of conversations and radio announcements as I passed: "Four hijackings," "the Pentagon," "Pennsylvania," and "one plane still missing, maybe headed toward Chicago." I heard jets above my head, my blood ran cold and I frantically searched the sky for the source of the sound but never spotted it. I heard later that it was a military jet guarding the city.

I passed a hospital with fleets of gurneys and wheelchairs staged on the sidewalk next to the loading dock. Blank-faced people in green hospital gowns and paper booties stood in small groups and furiously smoked cigarettes. They didn't seem to see me as I passed. I saw two firemen standing in an open doorway guarding their empty firehouse. They looked like scared ten-year-olds hiding from the school bully, and I realized I was scared too.

I get to the apartment, open the door and run upstairs. The television was out, the phones were out, Rochelle was at work in SoHo, I'm in a town on the other side of the country, the airports are closed, I don't know if the airline I work for is involved, and I'm freaked out. I look out the window and watch the morning light dim as smoke and ash swallow the neighborhood.

After twenty tries I get a long distance phone line and call my phone service to change the outgoing message to let everyone know where I am and that I'm all right. I hang up and dial and dial and dial and dial and dial and dial and after what seems like days finally get through to a friend in San Francisco. I fall apart and sob into the receiver. She assures me I'm all right and tells me all there is to do at this moment is to continue to breathe. I do and feel connected to the world again.

I go back to the roof to look around and find a nearly pristine piece of paper that tells me how to "Renew The World Trade Center's physical infrastructure and systems to meet tenant needs and expectations by achieving timely implementation of the capital program and of short- and medium-term improvement programs." Who knows what page two had in mind, because the page I held was blown from its staples and shot to me across the East River.

I imagine a broad man in a starched white shirt and wide tie sitting at his desk reading all about "Making it Easier to do Business with the World Trade Center," as he watched a United Airlines jet fly into his office. Maybe the nameplate on his desk reads "Dave."

About noon Rochelle made it back in from Manhattan. We ate a sandwich, then went out and watched people roam like zombies from one point along the water to the next, watching the city. Watching what I don't know; there wasn't anything to see but smoke. Maybe we silently needed to be with people, and this was the only way we knew how. We were silent, separate but together.

We get to a television at 7:30 p.m. and see our first images. I can't speak. By midnight we find a pub and watch more television reports. The Mayor looks like he was soaked with a hose then wrung out by the hands of some invisible giant. His face has collapsed, and his eyes look vacant. I wonder how many people he knew died today. I wonder how many times he's cried.

At 4:00 a.m. EST on Wednesday, I still hear the sirens

and helicopters. The smell of burning styrofoam cups is everywhere, and I push away the notion that I've been breathing people. It was one of the best days I ever saw this morning. Sitting under crystal clear blue skies, the city looked clean and fresh from the rain the night before. I was supposed to have gone to see the Empire State building, hang out with some friends, and shop for guitars in Times Square that day. Then I was going to the World Trade Center to have a hot dog. Things change.

No More Enticing a Target

Grant Barrett

While reading *My Antonia* by Willa Cather at 8:40 a.m. this morning, the radio was on, tuned to WNYC AM. My brain slowly focused on the manic voice of the announcer, strained and high, and the rough sound of the broadcast. It sounded like a rebroadcast of the 1993 attack on the World Trade Center. Only it wasn't.

As the minutes passed, it became clear that a small two-engine commuter plane had hit the north tower of the World Trade Center in lower Manhattan, presumably killing everyone on board. The WNYC FM broadcasts, as well as those of any other radio or television broadcast that uses the top of the World Trade Center as a high point from which to send signals, was off the air. The WNYC studios are very near the World Trade Center, so the station dropped out of normal programming to have producers and other staff members, most of them eyewitnesses, report what they had seen.

One staff member, sounding foreign, and a bit frightened, reported that he had just seen a second plane hit the south tower. How could that be? That would mean it wasn't an accident, that the attacks were pre-meditated.

The sweet innocence of the Cather novel was a poor introduction to the fire and death of the morning.

I rushed to the shower, threw on my clothes, grabbed the digital camera, and headed for the streets. The Twin Towers dominated the skyscape of New York, so they were visible, even from Greenpoint, Brooklyn, across the East River and miles away.

First I saw the smoke. Long streams of thick, gray smoke, blowing to the east with the normal sea-bound prevailing winds. I sped up to a jog and turned down a side street, in the opposite direction of the subway. I was supposed to be in school. I had classes and a paper due today. But school is on the island of Manhattan, to the north, and that meant using public transportation. Would it be open? Would it be safe?

I sped down Berry Street in Brooklyn, passing the warehouses. I could now see the towers. Two tall monoliths of smoke. Pinpoints of red flame on the south tower, the upper half of the building charred, smoke streaming to the top. The north tower looked like a candle that had just been put out.

Along the side of one warehouse, three Hispanic men were talking in Spanish, discussing the events. Nearby a ladder rested against the building, pointing to the roof. I asked for permission to climb. "The boss is up there. Ask him."

On the roof, Isaac, a Hasidic Jew who ran the construction materials depot, gave me permission. From there I could see news helicopters flashing in the distance as they kept to the north of the building, out of the path of the smoke.

Isaac said he had been on the phone with a friend at the time the second plane hit. His friend, on the other end, was watching the first building burn, and saw the second plane dive into the tower.

"He said to me, 'Here comes another plane. Oh my God. It's coming!' Then I heard it explode. He said there were people jumping out of the windows. Bodies falling, anyway."

On the subway were drawn faces and tense grimaces. Everyone talked about it, but quietly. The day's newspapers, with yesterday's most important news, were still in-hand but they seemed like trifles, uninteresting and irrelevant fluff puffed up to seem important, to fill space. There would not be that difficulty tomorrow.

The train service was slow and jerky. Long stops at each

station, endless announcements by the conductors and the public address system. No trains running to Brooklyn, no express service on certain lines. No trains of any sort going to downtown Manhattan. A lot of the announcements used the euphemism, "Due to a police investigation…" but some alerts, belted out by announcers more interested in passing on information, said, "Due to events at the World Trade Center…" This was an hour and a half after the horrifying events. Already it was safe to assume that everyone knew, that eyes and ears and minds were tuned to the buildings where 50,000 people worked on a given day. How many of them had been there? What were the casualties? At what point would we stop hearing about buildings and airplanes and start hearing about humans, bodies, husbands, wives, children?

A number of people had managed to catch trains headed uptown from downtown before the service was interrupted. They worked in buildings nearby the twin towers. Many had witnessed the second plane attack, a few the first. They had been watching the first fire, thinking it a horrible accident. Rumors abounded. One woman said the Supreme Court was hit, and the White House, but that the president was safe because he was in Florida. Another said that the Pentagon was hit. One said there was a third airplane that had hit the towers, kind of a finishing number. A number said the buildings had fallen. There's no radio in the subway, no television, no mobile phone service. Word of mouth was the only news. Had the two buildings fallen? How could that be? And attacks in Washington? That would mean it was pre-meditated.

One man just started speaking. He was hanging on the stainless steel bar, as the express train thrummed along the tracks, away from the death downtown. He was sweaty. A darkness was in his eyes. "I saw it. I saw it happen. They were jumping. Just jumping. Like they thought they could fly. Bodies in the air."

Another man: "The second plane swooped around and went right in. The building just swallowed it up." That was an echo of the first reports on the radio, when a producer for WNYC reported that the second airplane had just vanished into the building. Went right in and didn't come out the other side.

On campus at Columbia University, the rumor was that classes were cancelled and that administrative buildings would be shut. People went to class anyway; this is a competitive school, after all, and you can't afford to miss a lecture. Mobile phones were in everyone's hand, but no one was talking because a signal was near impossible to get. Maybe one out of a hundred calls went through. Cell phones were cursed, and pay phones were sought out. "Mom, I'm fine" was the refrain.

I tried in vain to reach my parents, to tell them the same. I managed 15 seconds to a friend before I was cut off. A mutual friend, Melissa, lives one block south of the World Trade Center. Where was she? Was she safe? She's a photographer, so the thought ran through my mind that she was there, on the scene, when the towers fell, when the clouds of dust rolled through the streets.

Now the Europeans can never say, "You wouldn't know what it's like to be bombed..." We now know.

In the computer labs at school, every workstation was in use. News stories, photos, video flashed on every screen. "MSNBC is down!" someone would shout. "Try the BBC!" or "What about Reuters?" came back. Sites were swamped. The university's own fat pipe, capable of handling even the worst MP3-traders and warez hogs, became saturated. Text was allowed to pass, but images were given second priority. What we needed most, though, was images.

The televisions in the lobby of the business school were tuned to CNN, with all the images we would need. Replay after replay, reporter after reporter. There is, after all, no town more media-saturated than New York. Multiple angles, still shots, man-on-the street interviews. Home video footage and talking-head experts would come soon. From the sky and from the ground, from the tops of buildings near and far, from neighboring buildings with unobstructed views of the mayhem and chaos, we watched the buildings burn and fall again. In that lobby, watching those televisions, were students from around the world. People who had known bombings at home, war, murder, genocide, death. They were here to move beyond that life, to strike out on new paths, to seek non-violent, educated answers to the problems that their home countries faced. Now they were not so sure. There were tear-stained eyes and tear-streaked faces. Heads on shoulders, hand-holding, arms in arms. Students with a wispy grasp of English, unable to understand the audio and incapable of keeping up with the fast-flowing subtitles, sought translation. Where were these pictures taken? In New York City? Here? How could that be?

I have my laptop with me, and I am plugged into the Internet. I am swimming in a sea of information, in visuals, and my head is straining to grasp the enormity of these events, in much the same way I spent years getting my mind around the size of the city itself, of realizing that its parts were connected, and that I was just one ant among many.

Melissa, the photographer, called. She was on a bus headed up town. "Do you know if I still have a home?" she asked me. I said that I thought she did, but I really did not know. Even if it still exists, she may not be able to go back for weeks. It is well within the danger zone, and above the rabbit-warren of tunnels and passages of the subway that merge in lower Manhattan before they dive under the rivers and harbour.

So I am here, at the University, cut off from my home. Manhattan is an island, and I am an island upon it. The tunnels are closed, the bridges blocked. My cell phone has signal, but I cannot get a connection. School is indeed cancelled, at least for the day. I am here for the duration.

Like others, I seek answers. We are aware of our vulnerabilities now. We knew these things before, but we didn't feel them. We knew about the security tests at airport after airport that exposed shortcomings, in which laughably underpaid and undertrained personnel were expected to protect us. Now we see those shortcomings in action. We feel them. We knew about the arrogance and the cock-strutting of our military and police, who were convinced and convinced us they were the best in the world. Now the prideful boasting looks suspiciously like that of Britain at the end of its empire, losing wars against poorly armed and under-trained armies in the bush, in the same way they had lost against the irregular new Americans before them.

There is, perhaps, no more enticing a target than that which has been paraded in front of the world as invincible, and no people more likely to feel the sting of their own hubris than those who scoff at others. That is us.

The View from Queens

Jeff Rigsby

I overslept my alarm clock today and didn't get out of the apartment until around 9:05, just a few minutes after the World Trade Center towers were hit. I came very close to boarding the #7 subway train and riding obliviously into town—the trains had not yet been shut down at that early stage. Then I happened to notice a little crowd of people on the street across from the front door, and when I looked across to Manhattan (I live in Long Island City, with an excellent view of the financial district), it was pretty obvious what had happened.

My building is right at the entrance to the Queens-Midtown Tunnel, and at that point, around ten minutes after the initial explosions, the area was already being cordoned off so that fire and police vehicles would have exclusive use of the Manhattan-bound lanes. Apparently the city's rapid-response plan really is pretty rapid in situations like this.

Call me stubborn, but I decided the thing to do was to try and get a little closer to the action, if not actually into my office (I'm temping for a financial company near South Street Seaport, a few blocks east of the towers—and my boss is not answering his phone). I made it into Brooklyn and as far as the on-ramp of the Williamsburg Bridge before the police turned me back: by 9:30 or so there was no unofficial traffic on any of the bridges or tunnels.

I made it back to my apartment around 10:00 and managed (again through bad timing, or maybe good timing) to miss one of the more dramatic moments of the morning.

The little crowd was still standing across the street from my building, and people were looking aghast and shaken ... this is an hour or so after the initial attack, so I knew something worse had just happened. By the time I parked my bike and joined the crowd, it was too late to see anything. The South tower had vanished in a huge plume of dust.

I bike two blocks to what was once my favorite intersection: Jackson Avenue and 50th Avenue, where depending on which direction you face you have beautiful lines of sight to either the Empire State Building in midtown, the Citibank Tower here in Queens, or (until this morning) the Twin Towers in lower Manhattan. The crowd here is a little bigger, not surprisingly. The dust over the financial district has now become much thicker, and it's clear that the South tower isn't there behind it; the dust is the tower. There are a few moments of panic when someone sights a low-flying aircraft overhead. But it turns out to be a jet fighter scrambling, one of ours.

Back at the apartment, I log onto the Internet, for lack of anything better to do. I don't own a television, and at the moment I don't even have any means of transportation—as I was carrying my bike upstairs, some stranger offered me his credit card and asked to borrow it. His brother works in one of the towers. I told him to head north and try the Queensboro Bridge, but I have no idea if he even made it into the city.

The initial coverage is annoying. The wire services are filing stories from Washington about a simultaneous plane crash and car bombing near the Pentagon ... this when thousands of people have evidently just died in lower Manhattan. Talk about an inside-the-Beltway mentality. At any rate, I can't get any Internet radio connections, and most of the major news sites won't load.

I send out a few high-priority e-mails (including one

responding to a worried friend who's working late in Singapore) and then head back outside to get a better view. Once again I've missed the dramatic stuff; the second tower fell down while I was indoors.

I walk up to the overpass of the Pulaski Bridge, which connects the westernmost districts of Queens and Brooklyn, and spend half an hour or so with the crowds of rubberneckers on the observation decks. This must be one of the best places in the five boroughs to view the destruction, and people have already begun to realize it. I suppose bridges are not the best place to stand during a massive terrorist assault, but everyone seems to be operating on the assumption that nothing in the outer boroughs is worth attacking, so here we are.

The wind is coming from the west, and downtown Brooklyn is now under a huge pall of smoke. Lower Manhattan must be in complete chaos now. My mobile phone is working only sporadically, but well enough that I manage to reach another close friend in Shanghai—who's already seen the explosion on TV, as it turns out.

What else is there to say? Fifty thousand people work in the towers, and just after the first one fell down I overheard something on a policeman's radio about the evacuation having been "too slow". It's been three hours now, and I'm still hearing sirens outside as the ambulances try to get through the Midtown Tunnel. I don't think I know anyone who works in the WTC, but I'm pretty certain that friends of friends, at least, are among the dead. It doesn't look good.

In Manhattan, September 11

Jay Rosen

For so many people in New York, today will forever be the day their world ended.

Millions of lives intersect in the area where the World Trade Centers were. Merely to say that—"were"—stuns and repels the mind. I am about 50 blocks away now. Offices are deserted, people criss-crossing the streets, smoke where downtown used to be. Military jets can be heard overhead. Gone from the sky are the towers that were the all-time symbol of New York, the beacon for hundreds of miles around. Unimaginable devastation on the streets, and in the seven stories that exist below those streets.

The Twin Towers, as every New York kid called them, were part of the stable world of my daughter, Sylvie—only four and too young to know where she is on the map. Except when she saw those Towers. In some way I can't explain, I felt proud of the city when it was able to orient my little girl.

So I ran home to explain to her, but television already had. New York will never be the same for us now, for anyone who loved it the way it was: proud, tall, unconquerable. It seems time is more flexible than we thought. There are so many hidden ways it can end.

"They were playing nicely together"

Constance Daley

When I write "Skyline to Shoreline," I'm creating images meant to be timeless postcards, scenes of the ever-present, never-changing, like Mount Rushmore or Niagara Falls. America ... from sea to shining sea, here is where you start, this is what you'll see. Yesterday, the majestic skyline of New York crumbled at her feet with the twin towers of the World Trade Center folding inward at the insult, not keeling over in defeat. Not only New Yorkers knew workers in the buildings, but the tourists in the city had family all over the world concerned about someone who could be there ... then.

My nephew Jonathan was my worry, working at Deutsche Bank in the WTC complex, and not reachable. In a network of calls to all our family in New York, we learned he was safe. He was the last one out of his office. At the back door, it became "every man for himself, and oh, Aunt Connie, you won't believe what I saw. Bodies all over, people jumping from buildings, it was horrible, horrible. I got hysterical. We all ran toward the East River and headed home," he wailed, beginning to sob anew.

"People were running to each other and hugging, tighter and tighter, and not letting go." While still near the tragic scene, he made his way to a coffee shop, found a phone and called his mother. We learned he was safe. I sent a brief e-mail to a young friend from the Upper East Side of New York. "Tell me where you were and what you saw." Here is his response:

World Trade Center I & World Trade Center II

by Gene Albertelli

I left my apartment late, as usual, and crossed Third Avenue at 88th Street. As I looked south, I saw a white-gray cloud hanging very low. I thought it was strange, but it had rained a lot last night. Maybe it was a remainder of the clouds. I thought of the bombing at the World Trade Center—when was that, 1995? I took the train at 86th Street, my usual routine: the express to the local to 28th Street and, again as usual, into the local Le Croissant shop for an iced tea. The woman at Le Croissant was looking past me through the window and saying: "A plane has hit the World Trade Center." I looked at her, confused, not understanding what she said. I spun around to look out the window as the man next to me said, "Yeah, both towers have been hit." Stunned, I paid for the tea, thanked her, and went to my office. My co-worker was on the phone, and said: "It's your sister." When I got on the phone with Amy, she filled me in with what little she knew but really just wanted to be sure I was fine. My co-worker told me, "I was on the el [elevated train] coming in from Queens, and I saw one of the towers in flames, and then a fireball coming off the other."

We snapped on the radio in my office and heard a woman reporter screaming: "Oh my GOD, OH MY GOD!" She didn't seem to realize we couldn't see what she was seeing as she continued, "The building is collapsing. The Tower is crumbling." One look at my co-worker, and we both knew we needed to get out of our office immediately. Our telephones were not working. We thought the electricity would go out and strand us in an elevator—which would not place us as a top priority—so we walked down the 20 floors to the ground.

The two of us started walking toward my brother's flower shop a few streets away. I needed to know that he was well. I hoped we would see my sister there, too. The buses were not running, and both my sister and my co-worker would have to find a way home to Long Island on the train. Traffic was light compared to any other day. Sirens were everywhere: racing up Sixth Avenue, down Seventh Avenue, bouncing off the cavernous streets of midtown. A sign on a telephone pole had a photograph of Mark Green—"Vote for me in the Primaries on September 11." "I want to be your next Mayor." This was not a good day for a primary election.

People walked hurriedly with cell phones to their ears, passing many others who stood on long lines for payphones. I overheard someone saying, "This is like the day that J.F.K. was shot." Walking to the West Side, along 28th Street, we stopped at every avenue looking south just as every other person was doing. At Sixth Avenue, we saw the one remaining twin tower in flames. We stopped. We watched. We continued to walk, and by the time we got to our destination just beyond Seventh Avenue, we were told that the second twin tower had collapsed. Like sand castles built by the shore. Eroded sand. Dust.

We reached the flower shop. My brother was there; his bosses were there—he was not at the World Trade Center where they work regularly. They were all very emotional. They know people who work in the building, but they don't know how they are. I knew I could not stay there. I needed to walk around. I needed to be alone. I walked out to Sixth Avenue to look and see for myself that the single building I saw in flames was, in fact, gone. I walked passed a man who wore a gray T-shirt with the black letters "vendetta." Did he know what was going to happen today? Did he have some foresight? I wondered, knowing that, like anything else, he could not have known. His face was serious, as was everyone's. It was a day where eyes met eyes softly, without the toughness so common to New Yorkers' faces: a toughness that is, in reality, a façade. When our eyes met, there came a familiarity of the tragic event just experienced. It was still in his eyes, still in mine: fear, imprinted at seeing two buildings, beacons of the southern tip of our island, melt into the ground. Our eyes held uncertainty and devastation, overshadowing the pride we New Yorkers take in our city—believing always each and every piece of our New York will last forever. I passed a group of Asian women just leaving a building, speaking loudly in their native language, which I do not know. Their words, their expressions, the motioning of their hands told me they were speaking of the twin buildings.

Around Pennsylvania Station at 34th Street were large groups of people waiting for trains to Long Island and New Jersey. Manhattan was closed down; New York City was forced to stop. On the Eighth Avenue side of the train station, the main branch of the U.S. Post Office stood silently proud with its strong columns. The Postal Police were everywhere. Along the 31st Street side where the trucks park, there were bright yellow cords. This area was off limits to everyone. Were they protecting the mail? Or were they protecting the train tracks that sit below the post office? A further walk toward the river showed me the Postal Police blocking the entrance to the Lincoln Tunnel. A single Postal Police officer stood there guarding the tunnel. His car radio was screeching and cracking. Sirens were yelling in the background—continuously. At the West Side Highway were garbage trucks parked along the river's edge, again probably protecting the underground trains. Outside O'Farrell's bar on Eleventh Avenue was a man who looked like an Irishman, holding a large American flag. He just stood outside the bar stoically. People passed by on their way to the West Side Highway to hop a ferry to New Jersey.

There were no trains or buses leaving.

A man was saying, "I was in Battery Park when the first one went." And another man responded, "I saw it hit—on the opposite side." A woman, standing still, spoke with a Jamaican accent, "I don't know how this happened," she said. Car doors were open and radios were played loudly to let passersby hear recent developments. I overheard a woman with a gum-cracking voice say, "This is the weirdest thing—like a mass exodus. I kinda wanna have a camera." I had a camera with me, but I could not take photos. Taking photos seemed "hard" to me. I did not want to "take" anything; I wanted to give. What should I do? Where should I go? I heard a woman speaking into her cell phone, "Happy Anniversary. You won't forget this one. I love you." I continued Southbound on the West Side Highway; I passed the Emergency FBI/NYPD outpost. I saw someone I knew at a job I worked twelve years ago. I did not say hello. Across the street, parked on the Southbound side of the West Side Highway, were ambulances.

For as far as one could see, following the curve of the West Side Highway which mirrors the island and passes the Chelsea Piers Sports Center, the ambulances sat waiting, like vultures, I thought. Normally the view down the West Side Highway would be rewarded with the Twin Towers, but they were gone. There was smoke billowing upward. The ambulances had the names of hospitals from all over New York, Long Island, New Jersey and Westchester. People stood watching the smoke rise from the rubble. They were just watching in disbelief. A screech of a fighter jet, an F-15, was above. It was an eerie sight to see above New York. I walked past two men at 21st Street and the West Side Highway. They asked, with a European accent, how to get to Soho. I stood for a moment as they gave me the two cross streets—saying that they could meet a friend who lived there. I gave them the directions and asked them if they were on vacation. They were from Italy. They were very upset about the devastation of the twin towers. We spoke briefly: unbelieving. One of the men asked, "How could this have happened?" We stood there without words to explain. We parted, shaking hands and wishing each other well. Coming towards us as we parted was a couple in-line skating. The windows were open at a bar on 23rd street. A man stood aside so I could poke my head in the window to see a CNN newscast with films of the twin towers in flames before they fell and then images of the buildings falling. Repeating the images over and over again, as the CNN news people continued to repeat the same information over and over. On the bottom of the screen in red, white and blue were the words in uppercase letters: AMERICA UNDER ATTACK.

People were parting. There were long hugs and instructions, "Call me as soon as you get home. I need to know that you get home OK." I wanted a quick bite. I didn't feel callous; I was hungry. It was 3:00 or so, and I stepped into a bar where there were many TV screens. We were forced to watch CNN. Throughout the report on NY, we were on our best behavior watching and listening. As soon as they went to the Pentagon, we all looked at each other and started to drink our drinks, as if Washington did not matter. We ordered grilled cheese sandwiches: comfort food. The trains started running, and everywhere were people hugging and saying the same thing: "Get home safe." I continued to walk to my apartment on 91st street. I walked through Central Park. I wanted to be in Central Park, to see the green and not have to hear the sirens. I walked past the carousel with the horses rising and falling and found the pipe organ music annoying. There were children and tourists on the carousel. I stopped and watched. I saw some German-speaking tourists speaking in their native language. I could not understand a word, but their hands motioned in a crumbling motion. I knew what they were talking about. I continued on my journey home. The park was solemn. I could still hear sirens. I could still hear the fighter jets above. I could still hear people on their cell phones. I overheard one side of a cell phone conversation by a man sitting on the grass: "Yes ... I walked ... Giuliani told everyone to go to the Upper East Side." I thought that was pretty funny.

New Yorkers follow instructions, and when the Mayor says, "Go..." we go where he says. I got close to 86th Street and, needing reassurance, passed by the Metropolitan Museum of Art, one of my favorite places. It was still there. It was unharmed. I stopped at the Church of Heavenly Rest and said a prayer. There was a woman there, sniffling. I walked through the streets of the Upper East Side, and there was hardly any traffic; eerie for 5:30 PM. There was lots of silence. And, of course, the ever present sirens in the distance. I crossed Third Avenue and could still see the smoke billowing above lower Manhattan. Just a few streets from home now, I walked past a park and saw children playing. They did not know what was happening. There were children of different colors and different religions. They were playing nicely together.

Going Nowhere

Mindy Diane Feldman

Outside my kitchen window, the late summer sky was a cross of cerulean and cornflower, and the air was fresh, with the promise of warm, on the morning that day became night in New York.

I was easing into my morning when I first saw the headline on CNN.com. "Plane Hits World Trade Center, " it said, and above it was a small photograph of the building, dark, dense smoke oozing to the right. I glanced at the top of the page, looking for the familiar maroon banner that signals breaking news on CNN, and found none. Comforted at the implication, I drifted back to the paragraph below the picture: a few lines of scant information and a promise of more details to come. " It must be a wayward pilot," I thought, "or that crazy Frenchman who climbs national monuments and walks tightropes between skyscrapers".

I turned on the TV, curious but unalarmed, and sat on the sofa over breakfast, still thinking it was a poor piper cub that had lost it way. A camera was trained on the first tower, from an angle reminiscent of the postcards on sale at the observation deck.

I listened with three-quarters of an ear; there was no new news. The anchors were improvising and repeating the same facts over and over, the way they do on an election night with a foregone conclusion.

For a split second, I was disoriented when the second plane sliced into the second tower on live TV, and I was not alone. "Wait a minute. Is this live or a tape?" screamed an anchor in a voice filled with anguish and disbelief. I did not like the sound of that voice; it was a violation of the rule that doctors, fathers, and journalists must never sound scared.

I started to shake. I stood a foot in front of the TV, as if my contacts were fogged or my ears were plugged. I grabbed the phone and punched in seven digits. Busy. Again. Busy. Again. Busy. Again. I kept punching at the same seven keys, desperate for a physical outlet that last number redial would not provide.

"Turn on the TV," I whispered into the phone, when my sister answered. "I know," she said. "I saw." We watched together, forty blocks apart, side by side on our psychic sofa: the same channel, the same horror, the same shock.

When they announced the evacuation of the UN, I started to cry. I live in its shadow, on a block with a park named after a secretary general who died in a plane crash on a mission to bring peace to Central Africa.

We debated in sisterspeak:

"Come here."

"But what if?"

"I know."

"But you can't stay."

"Well, maybe ..."

Finally, I remembered.

"Actually, I'm going away today," I said, "to visit a friend in Westchester." I was looking forward to cuddling with her baby and snuggling with her kindergartner.

And like a lid closing on a coffin, my sister whispered across town: "You are not going anywhere.

"The bridges are closed.

"The tunnels are closed.

"The borders are sealed."

The Only Home They Know

Aisha Khan

I switched on the television as a second plane crashed into the second tower. And then the Pentagon.

Please God let this not be Muslims.

Even before there were any suspects, many Americans seemed to have made up their minds about the face of the enemy, or at least its rough description. For Muslims in America, and for the approximate 3.5 million Arab American citizens, this knee-jerk assumption was all too familiar, referencing the anti-Muslim sentiments that erupted in the hours following the Oklahoma bombings—too recent a historical event to conceive of their being forgotten. We were victims then to an irresponsible media and a revenge-hungry public.

By 9.30 a.m., my husband had been evacuated from his building and was heading north, feeling terrified as the towers collapsed, but also because the crowd he walked with was chanting, "Death to Arabs, Death to Muslims." Someone in the crowd pointed at him: "He's a terrorist." A man asked, "Did your people do this?" One man got a police officer to ask my husband to show the contents of his bag. My husband refused and walked away.

On the television, long before the FBI had come up with any leads, news channels had already begun talking of Islamic terrorism. Although the last major carnage in America was carried out by one of its own—one of our own—none of the channels even explored this possibility. Everyone had latched onto the bin Laden story.

Experts streamed in and out of TV stations, purporting to explain the "Muslim psyche." I watched from my living room as the religion practiced by more than a billion people worldwide was reduced to the fanaticism of one man and his associates. In consequence, Arab Americans currently live with a distinct, immediate fear in addition to the collective and grave fear of unknowns that all Americans feel. The fear and tension of my friends and family in New York is palpable. We are all being lumped into the same category, assumed guilty on the basis of our religion. It doesn't matter that we were born here, or that on the basis of speech and dress we are practically indistinguishable from other Americans. My friend's mother, a 70-year-old Pakistani, was recently heckled and cursed by a man in Queens. Even Sikhs are being harassed. The Sikhs! Do Americans think that turbans and beards alone imply involvement with the Taliban?

I am a South Asian Muslim who grew up in India, a country with its own issues of religious hatred and violence. In India, as a member of a minority that was thought to have extra-territorial loyalties, I had my patriotism questioned time and again. And now I see the older generation of South Asian Muslims, who have been here in the United States for nearly 30 years, forced to prove their loyalty again. They feel a deep sense of loss, of agony. In a sense, they belong nowhere. Many fled India at the time of partition for Pakistan. They fled Pakistan to come to America.

The younger generation of South Asian Muslims is largely experiencing a sense of bewilderment. They have known no other land but America. They grew up just like other young American kids, listening to the same music, hanging out at the same spots, wearing the same clothes, cheering the same teams. Now, as they are being told to go home, they are in the only home they know.

Silent Village

Robyn Shepherd

Looking south on LaGuardia Place by Washington Square—out of range of the explosions, screams, and falling debris—the Twin Towers still lorded over the landscape in the minutes following the attack. The sight of the smoking, mutilated monoliths looked like a scene out of a hackneyed summer blockbuster, but for the silence. It was the silence that was most unsettling.

As the denizens of Greenwich Village staggered into the park and into the intersections to gawk at the scene unfolding two miles before them, there were moments when I almost wanted the scene to be more chaotic. That's what would happen in the movie. People would flee from whatever terror they were facing. There would be screams, and sobbing, and pandemonium. That's how the scene ought to be directed. Hysteria would have been an expected, forgivable reaction.

But there was no panicking in the street on University Place. It was too early for tears. The sight was too shocking, too real, for exclamations. Occasionally someone, just rounding a corner and seeing the burning towers for the first time, would gasp, but the primary sound was that of the newscasts emanating from the cars parked along the sides of the road. Each car seemed to be tuned to a different station. When one news report would fade away, another one would come into earshot, right on cue. "...say that there could be more hijacked planes..." "... White House has been evacuated and the President taken..." "...unconfirmed reports that a car bomb in front of the State Department..." By the time I got to my dormitory on Union Square, I was able to piece together the whole story.

Dozens of people had staked out a spot on either the stone plaza on the southern side of the park or the area on the western side reserved for the farmers' market. Here, as opposed to the small crowd at Washington Square that I had left 15 minutes earlier, there were more people watching the towers from behind the lens of a camera or camcorder. But still, silence reigned.

The vigil by the Union Square subway station continued as the first tower was enveloped in a cloud of dust, which eventually cleared enough to reveal a pristine blue sky where the building once stood. Shortly thereafter, the quiet was broken by a fighter jet screaming its way south. It was the only time that a ripple of fear ran through the crowd, but still very few people spoke. Some pointed up to the sky. Everyone seemed to communicate telepathically. Is there another plane that needs to be shot down? Is that plane even one of ours? The jet passed without incident, and the crowd's attention settled back on the remaining tower.

Behind me, someone emerged from the subway, apparently a passenger who had been detained on a train since the time of the attack. He came blinking into the harsh sunlight of an otherwise beautiful autumn day. His voice sounded like a bullhorn as he looked up and saw the plume of black smoke reaching heavenward, and the white cloud of dust dominating the street level.

"What the hell happened here?"

I tried to serve the same purpose that the car radios had shown to me.

"They were hit by planes. One of the towers collapsed," I offered.

But the man didn't seem to hear. He walked past me, mouth agape, and was lost in the crowd of people bearing silent witness to the disaster.

Never Leave the Dead Girl

Aman Batheja

During the last week of August, NYU's Resident Life Department put its newly-appointed Resident Advisors through a vigorous week of training. I had been assigned as an RA to the school's Water Street dorm in the heart of the financial district just a month earlier. During those seven days, we were taught how to handle every situation we could possibly come across throughout our employment as guardians, caretakers, watchdogs, and babysitters for the university's 19 dormitories and their more than 10,000 residents.

Toward the end of training week, the new RAs spent a day participating in a role-playing exercise called "Behind Closed Doors." The program consisted of the returning RAs pretending to be residents and creating difficult situations for the new RAs. The situations ranged from a depressed student having just taken a bottle of pills to a drunken guest becoming belligerent with a resident's roommates.

For the most part, the new RAs were consistently overwhelmed by the situations and tended to handle them irrationally. I myself left a girl passed out on a bed in the middle of a raucous dorm party so I could deal with the candles another resident had lit on the other side of the room.

"Rule #1," the unconscious RA awoke to tell me. "Never leave the dead girl."

The point of the exercise had not been to destroy our confidence, but rather to shake it up a bit. It taught us that the best way to handle overwhelming situations is to keep them from overwhelming us. Remember to keep calm and use your common sense. Above all else, if you ever find yourself in a potentially dangerous situation, leave.

September 11, 8:45 a.m., a Boeing 767 crashes into the north tower of the World Trade Center less than a mile from my dorm, and I am a sound sleeper. In fact, I am completely clueless of the apocalyptic horror occurring in my neighborhood until my alarm clock wakes me up at 10 a.m. I look out my second story window to see hundreds of confused bodies walking down Pearl Street covered in soot.

A moment later, there is a knock on my door.

It is two of my residents. One of them appears calm. The other is hysterical.

They tell me one of the Towers has collapsed and the Pentagon has been hit. I am also told the Sears Tower has been evacuated and there might be a bomb in the White House. "What should we do?" they ask me.

I tell them to stay in their rooms with their windows closed until I give them further instructions. "And try and keep calm," I add, praying that I am able to practice what I preach.

I take the elevator to the Manager's Office. There are already several RAs there when I arrive. I soon discover that out of the dorm's 29 RAs, we are the only ones not in class at the moment. There are fewer than ten of us, and we have to notify 1,200 residents to stay in their rooms until we alert them otherwise. As we quickly divvy up the floors in the largest dorm in the country, a television twenty feet away informs us that the second Tower has just gone down. Lisa, one of our superiors, curses briefly, then tells us to get moving.

Twenty minutes later, about six of us have covered most of the building. We find Lisa in the stairwell. She tells us we are evacuating due to all the smoke, and we must leave immediately. We all refuse. We had just told hundreds of panicked students to stay in their rooms. Lisa declares that our safety cannot be compromised just because we are RAs, but by this time, we have already run back up the stairs.

As I make my way down the floors, banging on doors and shouting down hallways, the smoke becomes thicker. My heart is racing and my breaths are shorter. I can't stop moving. I am in a dangerous situation, I tell myself, so therefore I should leave. On the other hand, I can hear ringing in my ears ...

Never leave the dead girl.

After we get through the entire building, praying that we have reached all of the people inside, we leave through the emergency exit on Fulton Street. We walk in a herd through smoke and ash and victims and bits of paper flying through the air. We make our way through Chinatown's chaos to campus, where we all regroup in safety at the school's sports center.

During the trek, everyone keeps turning back to see the towers, now a memory. I look back once and assume all the smoke must be clouding my view. "I thought they'd last forever," I hear someone say. I figure everyone is being much too melodramatic. They have to still be there. They're enormous. Where could they have possibly gone?

That afternoon, several of us are lying on wrestling mats breathing quietly. Craig, another member of our staff, walks over to us. Amidst all the talk of war, Arabs and evil throughout the morning, his opening remark is the most profound thought I have heard yet.

"Next year," he begins, "'Behind Closed Doors' is going to be really twisted."

Our laughter sucks up the tension like a mellow antacid. I remain in hysterics until tears begin to stream down my face. I don't know whether I am happy or insane. Be prepared, I think to myself. How could anyone ever be prepared for this?

Radio Waves

Kate Bolick

I don't own a television. When the World Trade Center went down I heard it on the radio, play by play, like a baseball game. Sitting on the couch, listening, trying to conjure images to match the words I was hearing, I added yet another instance to my peculiar store of pre-visual experiences, and drove yet another nail into the culture bubble that might some day prove to be a sort of coffin.

I didn't tune in until the second plane had sliced through the second tower—I'd been drinking my morning coffee, unsuspectingly, during the first attack, and then, once the news arrived by phone, had climbed to the roof of my midtown apartment building to see what I could see, which was only a great black mushroom of smoke. It wasn't until I had hurried back down the fire escape and through the bedroom window that I turned on the radio to catch, more or less, the third inning.

The announcers' grave pronouncements crackled with something like hilarity. There were three of them—one woman and two men. Their agitation was unseemly, and they knew it, but they couldn't help it. Who could? They were somber one moment and then virtually athletic the next, clambering over one another with their breathless, repetitive descriptions— "Huge plumes of fire!" "The flames are enormous!" Every so often a sober voice emerged from the hubbub to offer up a fact—"Downtown subway service has been suspended"— before being subsumed again by the clamor. They were beholden by an extraordinary vision.

But I couldn't see a thing. I was relying on my ears to guide me, and ears are such inert appendages. We say we "prick" them, or "strain" them, but in fact we do nothing of the sort. Their action is passive. They "receive," they "catch." What use are these weird whorls, I kept thinking, if I can't make a picture with them? I sat listening for a while, wishing I could see what the announcers were seeing, trying to piece together an accurate picture, but all I came up with was some cobbled-together comic of Godzilla climbing the Empire State Building. I couldn't even remember what the World Trade Center looked like.

Suddenly, before my very ears, there was a great intake of breath. The radio fell silent. I stared at it. It is one of those Bose radios, oddly humble and arrogant. The way it sits on the nightstand like a squat, beige wedge of cheese couldn't be more reticent, but its voice is startlingly resounding and confident. For one long moment the radio did nothing but blink its green numbers: 9:50 a.m.

And then it exploded. Words flew out like shrapnel. The announcers nearly babbled. "Gone!" "Obliterated!" "The air is glittering! Is it glass?" The woman regained her composure and pronounced the verdict, heavily, as if each word were a heavy stone she was reluctantly moving: "The ... World ... Trade ... Center ... has ... collapsed." One of the men interjected— "The south tower, ladies and gentleman, has fallen." "We are witnessing history," the other man said. There was a rustle, an off-stage voice, a correction—"No, no, that was the north tower." The first man laughed ruefully, "What does it matter?" "But people might know people in one tower and not the other," the woman said. The fact that there were people in there hit everyone like a revelation. They fell silent again. And then, "People, this is an historical moment."

I loathed them right then. I loathed them for emoting on the airwaves. For talking too much. For re-stating the obvious. For cluttering the silence with words. For rushing to brand this history-in-the-making.

But only for a moment. Because in that moment I saw more than I had all morning. I still couldn't quite envision the spectacle of these collapsing towers, but I could feel the bewildered panic of human voices. It didn't take much more than that to imagine the awful welter of emotion that had been underway inside each elevator and boardroom and hallway in the World Trade Center, and inside each airplane cabin that crashed into it: confusion, terror, generosity, hatred, homesickness, denial, bravery, blind urgency, horrible sadness. I remained as stunned and numbed as the next person, but for that one moment I was able to put a face on the terror in a way that might have been eclipsed by witnessing the explosion on television.

On September 6, a friend I hadn't seen in ten years visited me from his current home in Amsterdam. He flew home on September 9. On September 10 he peeled an old postcard off his wall, scrawled a thank-you note, and mailed it to me in Manhattan. The postcard was of the World Trade Center. It didn't arrive until yesterday. It felt eerie to pull it from the mailbox and carry it up to my apartment. It was as if this old souvenir from another era, airborne just as the towers were collapsing, was still creepily innocent of what had happened. As if, by simply being en route, its eyes were closed, and hadn't yet opened. How important was it actually to see the attack? I still don't know. I just keep looking at that postcard.

A Lifeline

Doug Nairne

My trip to New York wasn't supposed to be like this.

I came here to cover a press conference held by a software company called Vignette, but I ended up seeing more than 6,000 people die.

I was in Manhattan when terrorists flew two airplanes into the Twin Towers of the World Trade Centre. I saw most of what happened. What I didn't see, I lived through again and again on television and in conversations with survivors.

It's hard to describe how you feel after witnessing such a monumental loss of life. I found that in many ways it was more difficult to watch a single person die than it was to see thousands snuffed out all at once.

In the minutes between the times the planes hit and the towers fell, I watched in disbelief as people who worked in the doomed buildings tried to escape from the spreading flames by leaping out the shattered windows. It took a long time for them to fall 110 stories.

As they floated through the air, tumbling like dolls in the wind, I wondered what they were thinking at that terrible moment. I felt their fear as they neared the earth. Imagine the terror of knowing you are going to die that way, but having to wait so long for it to happen.

I saw a man and woman leap hand in hand to their death. Did they even know each other? Did holding someone's hand at that terrible moment make a difference? I'll never know. But I'll always wonder.

When the first tower collapsed, it dropped 250,000 tons

of steel and concrete onto the people below, many of them firefighters. It pulverized those who were still in the building, running down the emergency stairs trying to escape. Some of them would have made it, but they had stopped to carry others who needed their help.

At that point my brain shut off. I stopped feeling what I was seeing. Professional detachment is a lifeline for journalists and other people who live around disasters, and I grabbed on tightly.

Seeing a solitary person tumble from the sky devastated me. Seeing 5,000 people crushed in an instant was just too much to comprehend. It became a newspaper story that I had to write, or maybe a horror movie I was watching in a theater.

There are other images that will remain with me.

When the flying bombs hit the towers, they at first just disappeared into the side, leaving behind a puff of smoke, a bit of broken glass and a surprisingly precise surgical incision shaped like an airplane.

A fraction of a second dragged past. Nothing happened.

Then the fire suddenly exploded out the far side of the tower, and debris spewed everywhere. It was as if someone had hit the pause button, let us think about what was happening, and then hit fast forward.

When the towers fell, it was surprisingly quiet. I felt a bit of a rumble. Then the ash and debris started to cascade down and shoot quickly through all the side streets, causing even more destruction as it spread. The disintegrating corpse of the World Trade Centre covered everyone with a thick layer of grey dust.

The strange, acrid smell of fallen building began to spread. I never knew there was a unique smell just for that occasion, but there is. It's an unpleasant odour, a bit like the heavy, greasy stench of burned wiring or the remnants of a chemistry lab experiment gone badly.

Then there was the reaction of the people around me. The people who had the heart of their city ripped out. They were angry, and they were defiant. The city and the country came together as one to stand against what had happened.

The powerful symbolism created when people literally rallied around the American flag could only be understood by being here. The Star-spangled Banner flew everywhere and radiated strength and hope in a remarkable way.

I'm not an American. I felt like an outsider when the flags began waving and people sang patriotic songs with their heart on their sleeves. I wanted to share their pain and their anger and be part of the healing, but it didn't feel right.

I grew up on the Canadian Prairies, always within a few kilometers of the U.S. border, so I know more about Americans than most foreigners do. But there I was again, sharing so much in common with these people and still standing on the outside looking in at them.

I joined a candlelight vigil one night on the outskirts of Central Park. Business people in dark suits joined hands with cleaning women in aprons and men in jeans and anyone else who stopped to share the moment of grief. Black, white, Asian, Arab, Jew, Christian, Muslim and Buddhist, they stood side by side and quietly sang "God Bless America."

In a moment, it summed up for me what is right with this country. It told me why America, for all its faults, is strong.

During each day that passes, a little more of the incredible horror I saw escapes from the place deep inside where I locked it away in the moments after the first tower fell. I can tell it is leaking out, because sometimes I just feel like crying for no reason at all.

When I looked around me on the streets of New York, I saw that same feeling in the faces of people everywhere.

The lives of the American people will never be the same after what happened last Tuesday. And neither will mine.

An Eerie Sense of Equanimity

Bill Pfeiffer

On Tuesday morning about 8:50 am September 11, 2001, my friend and colleague Leslie Goldstein and I left the apartment of an old friend in Park Slope, Brooklyn. We were on the second day of a business trip seeking support for the Sacred Earth Network. Just before entering the Union Street station at 4th Avenue, I casually looked over to the World Trade Center in the distance and noticed smoke pouring out of a wedge of floors about 2/3 of the way up the building. I gasped and told Leslie that this fire was big and unprecedented. We walked into the subway, and as soon as we entered the car Leslie and I agreed the best thing to do was pray.

Fifteen minutes later, we were getting out to meet my mother for breakfast at the Marriott Hotel in Brooklyn Heights, closer to Manhattan. Smoke was filling the air, and people were filling the streets, as all commercial buildings over a few stories high were being evacuated. Despite the crisis that was just beginning, there was an eerie sense of equanimity about people's behavior. People were scared, but they were not freaking out. This was a theme that would hold throughout the day.

My mother, who was looking for Leslie and me, decided to go home to her apartment about five minutes away. There were just too many people for her to find us. We quickly went upstairs to her 11th-floor apartment and made a couple of calls to other family members to tell them we were OK. My mother suggested we then go to the roof on the 16th floor to get a better look (as the view of the WTC was obscured by another building). Upon entering the roof, I saw and felt things I will never forget. Both WTC buildings were in flames, and a huge black plume of smoke was blotting the skyline. There were a dozen other people on the roof. While taking in this scene and entering a shock that I was only later able to realize I was in, a Hispanic maintenance man said the Pentagon had been bombed. It was at this moment I entered into an altered state. The end of the world truly seemed to be at hand.

The only thing that kept me from panicking were the thousands of people walking (not running) over the Brooklyn Bridge in steadfast determination to get out of harm's way without hurting others. A man on the roof added another layer of stability when he said, "Let's think about how we can help." When I looked up again, WTC One collapsed. Imagine a mountain disappearing before your eyes. I stared in disbelief. Leslie let out an appropriate scream. I held Leslie and my Mom, and they held me. I thought someone or something was playing tricks on my mind. I then realized that this was a common nightmare everyone was dreaming. This realization and one about non-violence became central teachings for me on this day.

My survival instinct kicked in. Although my stomach was in knots, having not eaten, I knew that I could not face this day without food. We went to a diner downstairs. Walking a block there I ran into a Russian woman, struck up a very quick conversation, and she exclaimed in Russian, "America is supposed to be safe. This should not be happening." I wished her well and went into the diner, sat at the counter with Leslie and my mother, and ordered a cantaloupe and scrambled eggs with toast and home fries. The Hispanic staff was steadily serving the packed house. A man to my right drinking coffee was nervously talking almost incoherently. Others of all ethnic backgrounds around me seemed to be shaking. I was too. I ate quickly, and two young men came into the diner. I thought they were friends. It turns out they both had escaped "ground zero" separately. Frank was a tour guide for the WTC, and Kevin was a broker-in-training at Morgan Stanley from Cincinnati. Kevin was on the 61st floor of WTC One when he felt the impact of the plane hitting the building below (!) him. He managed to get all the way to the street, watching others carrying the elderly and handicapped on their backs.

He was stopped by security on the 40th floor, having been told that the smoke was so intense he might not make it the rest of the way down. When the second plane ploughed into WTC Two, he decided he had to get out of there. Frank, who had not entered the WTC yet, saw burning bodies flying out of the twin towers. Outside the buildings there were crowds gathering at nearby City Hall, trying to make calls on pay phones to their loved ones. Like many others, Frank and Kevin were unsuccessful. Most cell phones were not working. Then WTC One collapsed, resulting in a mass exodus over the Brooklyn Bridge. We invited Kevin and Frank to make phone calls at my mother's apartment. We finally felt like we were able to help.

Later on, we went to the roof again and spoke with other Brooklynites to see what else could be done. Later, Leslie and I went to the nearest hospital to try to donate blood and volunteer. Upon arriving, there were hundreds in line to do the same. Again, there was this steadfast calm that pervaded the scene. There was enough medical and volunteer help, and they sent us home. Before leaving, we stopped at the chapel/ crisis counseling room to see a woman EMT with a broken arm who had lost all her colleagues. All the streets were getting cordoned off into different sections. The Manhattan and Brooklyn bridges were closed off. Martial law was in place.

After resting at my mother's apartment and taking Kevin back to his father's friend in Park Slope and Frank back to the just re-opened subway back to Manhattan, we headed to the Unitarian Church to be part of an interfaith service where a rabbi and a priest moved us to tears. They spoke of "remembering the goodness," "loving the people close to you," "cherishing the moments of celebration," and choosing peace and non-violence. We listened to the words of Gandhi. They also spoke of the appropriateness of feelings of rage and grief. Leslie and I went to the hospital for the second time, making our way through choking smoke and wondering if more wounded would be there this time. They were not. The consensus was that people were either dead, still trapped, or miraculously alive with minor injuries. We went back to my mother's apartment for the last time that day, made a few phone calls, and fell into a rocky sleep. It seemed I saw a million faces come into my hypnogogic view.

Now you know my "Terrible Tuesday." What is my response? I want to change the 5,000-year-old conversation that says if you hurt me I must hurt you back. I've devoted my life to humans living in harmony with the Earth. We humans are part of the Earth. If we do not disarm our hearts and put away our swords of revenge, I'm afraid we will not be able to live on the planet for another 5,000 years (maybe not even 50), and we will destroy another massive portion of the biosphere in the process. I'm going to write to my congressman, President Bush, and the media and say, of course we need to find the perpetrators and ensure they are not able to roam freely throughout our world and hurt our children, but what about peace? I also will say that we need to take all sensible actions to ensure that this kind of terror does not happen again, but if we bomb other cities, other innocents, who are so much more like us than different, how will that help us achieve the security we so long for? Can we do it differently this time? Can we actually try to use our economic might to rebuild the economies of the "have nots" so they hate us a little less? Can we show them we care? Can we learn that fundamentalism and fanaticism are minority opinions? Can we learn that darkness is not "over there" but something each country and individual must wrestle with. I want us to do what the rabbi said is what the Torah commands: "Choose life, so that you and your children may live." I hope you will make a commitment to non-violence part of your conversation, not only with people that agree with you, but also with those that do not.

Finally, and this is more subtle: On the roof, I felt as if we were in a nightmare that we could wake up from. I believe we can use our imaginations to "dream a different dream," a dream that does not believe that violence is a solution. Einstein said, "Imagination is more important than knowledge." He also said that "a problem cannot be solved at the same level of consciousness that created it." Let's use this vast creative intelligence we have been given, like grace, to put an end to greed, exploitation, and punishment as a viable way of relating to the Earth and each other. We are not victims of the past. To quote John Lennon, "You may say I'm a dreamer, but I'm not the only one."

Intangible but Oppressive

Preston Peet

The sense of disbelief I feel when I look out my window while typing reminds me of the smoke plume still rising from the downtown NYC skyline tonight, nearly 60 hours after the first jetliner plowed into the World Trade Center: intangible and hard to grasp, but oppressive and overwhelming just the same. The reality of the Towers was firm, an everyday thing. They were always within view from just about anywhere on the island, but that reality has been eradicated permanently. It is hard to grasp even now, but the silence of the streets outside, the stench of smoke wafting in, and that huge empty hole in the city skyline all slap me with reminders. The World Trade Center is no more.

Just before 10 a.m. Tuesday a message was left on our answering machine. "Please call. I'm worried about you in the city," said my girlfriend's mother. Wondering what she was talking about, my girlfriend got out of bed and strolled to the front room to play back the message, flipping on the TV as she did. Seeing the WTC burning on the screen, she leaned over and took a look out the window. When we moved into this apartment last year, we'd both commented on how great a view we had of the WTC. She called me with an urgency that brought me running. Tower 2 had just fallen, the resultant cloud of dust and smoke nearly obscuring the fact from our window, but Tower 1 was clearly on fire like a giant torch, flames visible through unfathomable, gaping, jagged holes multiple stories large way up high in the sides of the Tower.

Already, as I threw on some clothes, my mind was trying

to wrap itself around what was happening, imagining how odd it was going to look with just the one Tower standing. The TV was blaring alarming reports of a plane or, as I subsequently found out, two planes, striking the Towers, of another hitting the Pentagon, of a car bomb outside the U.S. State Department, a fire on the Washington Mall, and up to a total of eight jets out of contact with air traffic controllers and possibly hijacked by knife-wielding terrorists. President Bush was speaking at a school I attended in my hometown of Sarasota, and it was my birthday. The whole thing was just too surreal, but it got even more so very quickly.

Grabbing a camera, I tore up the stairs to the roof, where the unobstructed view from just south of Houston Street allowed me to begin snapping photos. The crystal clear blue sky had a roiling black wound on it spreading to the south, ugly black smoke that rose into the air from the one remaining Tower and the empty hole beside it, pouring east across the water to cover Staten Island. The scene was something from a dream, a nightmare, so utterly beyond anything that I ever expected to be witness to that I could only stare, snapping away with my camera, thinking of the people on what I now knew to be two planes diving into the Towers, one after the other. Another tenant who witnessed the second jet slam into Tower 2 described it to me, the horror etched on her face as she related seeing the second plane deliberately crash headlong at high speed into the side of the Tower, then explode in a huge ball of flame and debris. After a few minutes upstairs, people from all around me on my roof and many of the surrounding buildings began screaming, "Oh God, there it goes!" Quickly raising my camera, I took pictures as Tower 1 cracked, broke, and began to crumble in what appeared to me from my vantage point slow motion onto downtown Manhattan below. Then all I could say over and over was, "Those poor people, all those poor people," as a writhing cloud of hell on Earth covered the lower part of Manhattan like a living animal, obliterating many of the remaining high-rise buildings from view.

I'm grateful I didn't witness the people falling from the upper floors where I stood, and even more so that I don't live south of Canal Street, now the northern border of a 5-mile crime scene and disaster area cordoned off by police and National Guard units. Until Wednesday night, we couldn't even smell the smoke here. But we sure saw the people fleeing on foot north through Manhattan that morning. Avenue A had more pedestrian traffic than I've seen in almost eight years in New York City. Most had paper masks covering their faces or hanging around their necks with their loosened ties and collars, many were covered in soot and dust, and all had an eerie, somber air to them, tense and confused. Military jets were crisscrossing periodically overhead, adding to the air of siege that permeated the city.

Walking across the island a few hours later, seeing the pall on the lower horizon each time we crossed an avenue affording us a view of the sky formerly hidden by the WTC, it felt like being on the largest movie set imaginable. The massive destruction and the audacity of the attacks both here and on the Pentagon, the loss of life estimated into the tens of thousands, were all so chilling, so abominable, it was almost too much to register, and still is. The scenes of family and loved ones cramming the hospitals and recovery sites in one of the largest, most modern cities in the U.S. and the world, hoping beyond hope to find lost loved ones who somehow managed to survive two 110-story Towers and another 47-floor tower all collapsing on top of them, are heart-wrenching, threatening to rip tears from my eyes as each fiancé, mother, sister, and cousin appears gazing forlornly into the television cameras, plaintively holding out their photocopied, phone-numbered pieces of paper with pictures of loved ones. Is this how the victims of U.S. bombings around the world feel when they begin to realize their neighbors, friends, family and loved ones aren't coming home again?

A Refugee Crisis in Business Casual

Mindy Diane Feldman

I was standing on one leg, shimmying into my pants, still a foot in front of the TV, when the pentagon went up in flames. I fell to the floor in a heap, remembering that the only other time in my life that my knees had buckled was the day my mother died, over twenty years ago.

I had decided to evacuate, or at least to try. After years of feeling claustrophobic and trapped in my midtown apartment, I suddenly felt exposed and vulnerable, avoiding the south-facing windows and the wall that fronted the street.

On the corner of Third Avenue, I turned south to look for a bus and gasped out loud, my hand over my mouth. At the foot of the island, behind an approaching M101, was a massive opaque white cloud that filled the horizon and obscured the skyline of downtown New York.

I rode the bus for six blocks and forty-five minutes. We held the children of strangers on our laps to make room for more passengers. A woman with a Walkman relayed snippets of news to the rear of the bus. We leaned in closer, as if trying to hear through her headphones.

It became obvious that many who were leaving their offices did not know that the city was in lockdown. "I am going to Queens," a young, coal-skinned woman offered, "to find my kids so I can come back to find my baby in day care downtown." We explained that there was no way out of the city save walking, and no way back into the city at all. Her eyes welled with tears. And I started to cry, again.

I got off the bus when the collective tension and terror

became overwhelming, and because I knew that my sister would be frantic with fear if I didn't get to her apartment within an hour or two of our last phone call.

I began to walk.

Manhattan's avenues run north-south, and they were teeming with humanity at ten o'clock in the morning, the sidewalks more saturated than Fifth Avenue in December. It looked like a refugee crisis in business casual, occasionally in suits. Beautiful young women in Gucci and Prada clutched high heels in their hands and walked barefoot on the cold concrete. Handsome young men clutched useless BlackBerrys and beepers and cellular phones. And everyone headed north. Like all refugees, not sure where they were going, but clear that they had to leave.

In the streets traffic was infernal, but drivers did not honk. In pairs and trios, people insane with worry spoke in hushed, muted tones. The sounds of the city had become other-worldly, like a muffled morning after a crippling blizzard or the percussive silence under water.

And in the distance was the indefatigable din of sirens, and the low hum and rattle of fighter jets in the morning sky.

The pace of the crowd was quick and resolute, heads bowed for the most part, some holding hands, many crying. I tried to bob and weave to gain some ground, but it was like the start of the New York Marathon: I was stuck in the pack. When the traffic thinned near Bloomingdale's, we started to walk in the streets, as if the city had become a giant pedestrian mall.

It took two hours to make the forty-block trip.

I stayed with my sister until nightfall, suddenly desperate to sleep in my own bed. She walked me down to the street, and we covered the half-block to the corner in seconds and in silence. I decided not to take a taxi, though there were many on the streets; there was something about being isolated in the back seat behind a plastic partition, like a critically ill newborn in an incubator, whose parents cannot hold or touch her.

New Yorkers rode the buses for free that night, the drivers waving away our metro cards with sad, poignant smiles.

I caught the bus on Second Avenue, riding past sidewalk cafes filled with singles suddenly scared in the night, and under an ebony sky filled with hundreds of stars and too many angels to bear.

In the Bull's Eye, 1

Scott McLemee

You knew immediately that for years to come people would ask where you were when it happened. It would be a coordinate of identity. That instant would become "a defining moment." My God, am I sick of that phrase. It has been used to death these past ten years. (Please excuse "used to death" too.) Anyway, it was by no means certain, at that defining moment, that I would be having leisurely conversations about the topic in the future. Because we were, for all practical purposes, in the bull's eye.

It is still not clear what target was intended for the fourth jetliner bomb, the one that crashed in Pennsylvania. On television, the anchors kept saying Camp David. Exactly how they made that determination was not clear, even then; nor has it come to seem any less like a wild guess in the meantime. Would an adrenaline-fueled commando unit with somewhat rudimentary flight experience have been aiming at Camp David? I mean, symbolic value, sure. But you figure these guys needed to aim at something with the qualities, approximately, of a barn door, preferably a very large barn door, one that had been painted bright red; a target visible, as such, from a considerable distance. With maximum symbolic impact. Meaning the White House, or maybe the Capitol.

Meaning in my case, for all practical purposes, home.

We live about fifteen minutes from the White House, by foot. My wife is a reference librarian at the Library of Congress. I write about ideas and scholarship for a newspaper.

We have two cats and a few thousand books, packed into a one-bedroom condo (two if you count the study) where we have lived for almost seven of the eight years we have been married. Not long ago we started planning to have bookshelves built into the place, floor to ceiling: the sort of decision that embodies a will not to move again for a very long time.

The offices of B'nai Brith are a couple of blocks away from our apartment. A few years ago, the building was quarantined for a day while the authorities dealt with a package that an accompanying note said was full of anthrax. It turned out not to be. Yay.

You always knew that this was one place on the globe potentially yielding maximum ego gratification for somebody with the right weapon. An incredibly troubling range of scenarios sprang to mind. It seemed like a matter of time.

The important thing was never to let such ideas take root. It had always been possible to think: "Well, it hasn't happened. So maybe it won't." Which was not exactly a logical argument, but it dampened the anxiety somewhat.

That Tuesday morning, Rita was working in the Senate Reference Center, answering questions from members of Congress. I was taking the day off. I had just returned from Salt Lake City, where I had spent half a week following a prominent philosopher around in an effort to determine what relation, if any, her ideas might have to the way she carried herself in public. It had been exhausting, and I was glad to be home. The big item on my agenda for the day was laundry.

As usual, I had left the apartment before seven, to get some coffee and "do some writing," a process that involves a lot of what looks to the unaided eye like staring off into space. I also bought some magazines. After three hours, the coffee had provided as much inspiration as it was going to, so I walked back home.

Rita had left a voice-mail message saying to turn on the television because a plane had crashed into the World Trade Center. She had probably called a few minutes before I got in the door. For some reason, I then checked my e-mail. By the time I got to the television, reports were coming in from the Pentagon, about fifteen minutes away by Metro.

Here is what happened next. I could call this a stream of consciousness. But in fact, over the next hour that stream narrowed to a trickle, the world growing dry and brittle, almost ready to shatter:

Flip through the channels. Turn off the sound. Try to call Rita. Busy signal. Try to call my parents in Texas. Punch in the numbers, but there is nothing. No connection. Hang up. No dial tone. Hang up again, try waiting. Again, no dial tone. Repeat. (Supposition: phone lines have been shut down for security reasons.) Eventually a dial tone.

Then: Try to call Rita. Dead silence. Try to call Rita, again. Another busy signal—the kind with extremely fast beeps, usually indicating technical problems. The television stayed on, of course.

Remain very calm. Stop by the bookshelf where we keep all the quarters, in piles of one dollar each, for the laundry. Fill a pocket with quarters, methodically: a number sufficient, judging from experience, given the mass of dirty clothes. Back to the telephone. Dial Rita. It rings!

Everything goes amazingly well. I even actually speak to somebody at the Senate Reference Center, at least until he puts me on hold to go get Rita. During which time we are disconnected. Try again. Busy signal with fast beeps. I am not, repeat not, freaking out. Time to go downstairs to the laundry room. It will take half an hour to do a load.

Heading back upstairs, it seems logical to consider the possibility of (for example) serin gas. To wonder if that, too, is in the works. I decide to stop thinking that way.

The phone rings. It's Rita. The Senate Reference Center is shutting down. She's heard that the Metro isn't running, so she will need to walk home. I tell her to be careful, not sure what that means.

The news reports that a car bomb has gone off in front of the State Department. A second jetliner hits the other tower of the World Trade Center. I reach my father by phone; he says my mother is heading back from her job at the headquarters for mass transit in Dallas. I tell him that Rita is on the way home too.

My wife is walking three miles through downtown Washington, D.C. while car bombs are going off.

We have plenty of change on the bookshelf. I transfer wet clothes to the dryer, then go back to the apartment. They will need one hour to dry. Experience suggests that leaving the clothes there unattended is completely safe.

It turns out the Metro wasn't actually shut down. The part about the car bomb going off in front of the State Department was wrong, too. (The guys on television correct themselves.) You learned these things well after the fact. Or rather after the non-fact. In the meantime they were real, they shaped the world you were in.

Rita appears, safe and sound, at 11:20. Our embrace a defining moment, not through any big cinematic surge of emotion but in its reassuring ordinariness. She tells me about passing big crowds on the way, office workers who carpool from the suburbs, now stranded in front of the buildings where they worked, unsure how to get back home.

We plant ourselves in front of the television for the next twelve hours. After I bring the clothes upstairs, Rita irons. The plane crashes into the tower, again and again and again and again.

Each time, there is a period—one second or maybe two, though it seems to go on forever—between the plane hitting the building and the cloud of fire blowing out the other side. Each time, I have the vague sense, perfectly irrational of course, that time stops; that maybe the cloud of fire won't roll out, maybe someone will walk away.

No comparable images of destruction-in-progress come from the Pentagon bombing. A suitable cultural cliché at this point would be to announce that the World Trade Center (four hours away by Amtrack) seemed a lot closer, that day. How ironic! But that would be bullshit.

Under the unrelenting flow of television coverage, the morning's subdued panic gave way to a state of consciousness that is more difficult to narrate.

After a while, of course, you were numbed from repetition. Later in the day, other cameras provided images of the crash shot from different angles. But the numbness did not fade. It was joined with a visceral, searing pain. Someone had been beating you with a baseball bat for a while, then switched to long strands of barbed wire. The skin of consciousness was being torn away from its limbs.

The reality of it all started to flicker. There were fighter planes overhead. We might die very soon. Our cats needed to be fed. I will never forget my envy for their world, in which it was a wonderful day because Mom and Dad were home, on the bed, watching television. Comfortable laps.

After a few hours, a thought crossed my mind, leaving me sick with shame. "One day," it said, "all this will be on DVD. There'll be a feature where you can see how it looked from, say, the other side of the Brooklyn Bridge."

As soon as it had been formulated, I wanted to disown this idea. It did not come from me. It was, rather, the voice of an ambient cynicism, something I had absorbed, like toxins from badly cooked chicken. It is necessary to anticipate the trends in a society that constantly rationalizes its cultural bookkeeping by reference to the lowest common denominator. Right? Commodifiable images devour public reality. I mean, it's not my fault. Right?

A Priest's Diary, Day 1
September 11

Fr. Julian Cassar

I got up as usual at 4.45 a.m., went for my usual 30-minute fast walk, showered and had breakfast.

I prayed the office, prepared for Mass and practised my flute for the usual hour in church.

After the 9 a.m. Mass, I stopped to see the nursery school children, also to get energised by seeing 15 happy and smiling three-year-olds.

Then I came to my room to prepare for my Communion Calls which I usually do on Tuesdays, visiting the seven elderly home-bound parishioners and giving them Communion.

I noticed my telephone message flashing and checked to see who had called. It was my mother's voice frantically begging me to call back to see if I was OK, after telling me briefly that the World Trade Centre had been bombed.

In a split second I turned the TV on, and the phone rang again. My parents called again. I was speechless as I watched the horrifying collapse of the first tower, and after assuring them I was OK, I hung up, still speechless and in disbelief.

Like the rest of the world, I watched the second tower crash down and followed the unbelievable aftermath.

I could have stayed in front of the TV all day, as most people did, but I had some elderly friends to visit and also to console, as everyone was heartbroken and searching for answers.

Since my parish is 80 miles away from New York City, I could only follow the tragic events like most New Yorkers, through television, but I realised my service would be needed soon to lead people in prayer and console them in the coming days and weeks. We scheduled a Mass in our church in the evening, and the congregation was standing-room only.

We invited the people to mention names of people they knew who were missing, dead, or injured.

We had a dozen names prayed for. People cried and sobbed, still incredulous at what had happened in Manhattan.

They stayed after Mass, sharing stories, reminiscing, praying, and hoping.

"I became the link to the outside world"

Peter Shankman

First off, my prayers are with everyone in the country and around the world today, affected by this tragedy. I want to thank the WWWAC list—You served as my, and the rest of United Flight 425, from Newark to Colorado's link to the outside world for about 20 minutes.

I boarded that flight at Newark at 7:40 in the morning. There were 14 flights ahead of us for takeoff, according to the pilot. I nodded off.

The pilot came back on when we were fourth for takeoff, telling us that something was wrong with the World Trade Center, and we'd be waiting on the runway for a few minutes.

I pulled out my Visor and wireless modem, and instantly checked my email. As I was, the pilot announced that a plane accidentally flew into the World Trade Center. Everyone looked to their left out of the plane, and sure enough, there was smoke coming off the horizon.

That's when I got the first few emails from the list, talking about it. Within two more minutes, I'd found out about the Pentagon as well.

I became the link to the outside world for the next 15 minutes, with the flight attendants and passengers waiting for the 30-second e-mail checks. I read them off as I got them.

The pilot came back on and said we were returning to the gate. We all sat down. In all the time I've been flying, that moment was the scariest time of my life. We barreled back to the gate faster than I've ever seen it before. Something in my mind just told me to get off the plane and turn in my ticket.

At that point, the airport was still open.

We got outside of the gate, and that's when it hit me—I was looking at the skyline, and one of the towers was NOT THERE. That was the first time I realized the magnitude of what happened.

We waited at the outside of the terminal for about three hours—I wound up finding about five people, all of whom didn't know each other but sort of came together as a group. My Visor was overloaded at that point, and I couldn't get a signal. But my Motorola Timeport two-way pager was still on, and I was able to send messages to my parents, finding out that they were both OK.

Finally, we found a bus that was able to take us to another terminal, where we waited. A guy in a van came by and took me and my five new friends to the Marriott, still on airport property. We hung out in their bar for about five hours; it was around 6 p.m. by this time. Somehow I managed to get a room at the hotel, and I grabbed my new friends, and we went and washed our faces for the first time in about twelve hours.

We went downstairs afterwards and sat on the lawn, on the grass. It was surreal—the smell of the grass, a beautiful sunset, and in the background smoke, soot, dust, and a hole where the World Trade Center used to be. Truly, truly surreal. We went back upstairs and just fell asleep. Totally exhausted. Left the television on, and six people, none of whom had ever met before, two of whom spoke Japanese and very little English, all fell asleep on a king-size bed, all holding each other.

Woke up early this morning, and no cars were going in or out of Newark. We gathered our suitcases and started walking. We walked out of the hotel and out of the airport. We walked on the roads, on the ramps, until we got onto Route 9 North. A poultry truck stopped for us and told us he could get us to right outside of downtown Newark. We thanked him and climbed into the back of the truck. Once we got to downtown Newark, we walked a few more miles to the PATH train, which was running to 33rd Street. We got on the train and got to Penn Station. I walked out of Penn Station, looked up 8th Avenue, looked down 8th Avenue, and started crying, as I started walking home to my apartment on 43rd Street.

A Strange Confluence of Events

Donna Headrick

It was by a strange confluence of events that I was on neither the Portland U.S. Airways Flight to Boston nor American Airlines Flight 11 from Boston to L.A.

I had initially planned to leave on the early flights for an extended trip out west. But some documents that had been overnighted to me via FedEx were not delivered on Saturday as promised. Indeed, they did not arrive until 10:00 a.m. Monday.

And instead of a small cardboard mailer, it was a large box filled with far more than I expected. All documents that needed to be reviewed, if the early portions of the trip were to be useful.

I dithered Monday, crabby with FedEx. Annoyed with having to change flights, yet again. Thinking that perhaps I could get documents reviewed and abstracted on the plane west.

And then a phone call came from a close friend. He called to see if I could take care of their three-year-old little guy the next afternoon. I laughingly told him I would prefer to babysit than to be on an airplane, but Tuesday afternoon was out for me.

Coincidentally, he was taking the shuttle from Boston to NYC for a noon meeting in Manhattan and suggested I drive to Boston with him so we could have a chance to "catch up." He is a friend of many years but since his marriage and parenthood we seldom have time alone to be the current-events junkies we are.

It was an easy choice. Who wants to spend a lovely summer day inside followed by a long plane ride buried in documents anyway? So I called to change my flight, made arrangements to have the early part of the trip become the back end of the trip, and went to the beach for the remaining part of the afternoon.

And found garnet-colored beach glass as well as a couple of starfish.

We were a little late in leaving Portland Tuesday morning (actually I was the one who was late, par usual), but his meeting wasn't until noon, the shuttle runs hourly, and I could change flights easily, so we were in no hurry and spent the time talking. I no longer remember any of our conversation.

We were just pulling up to the departure doors at terminal D at Logan when my cell phone rang and a friend from Portland said: "Where are you? A plane just hit the World Trade Cen...."

That was the last of my cell phone until many hours later. It simply didn't work at Logan, and most of the land lines didn't either.

When I relayed the partial information about a plane and the World Trade Center, my friend said he would go to Central Parking and check in to the Shuttle anyway. In comparing notes, we understand that his thoughts immediately went to weather, since he had failed to check it. And since his meeting wasn't until noon, perhaps there would be no problem at all.

My early thoughts were more bizarre. I thought of how large the Trade Center is and wondered what goofy pilot of a small plane could have failed to see it. Then I wondered why that would be a disaster for my flights and concluded it wouldn't. After all, a small plane wouldn't do much more than bounce off the Trade Center, though it would surely terrify some inside.

It seems odd, though now I understand, that I was able

to say good-bye to my friend, have a Skycap take my luggage inside to a ticket counter where I changed my tickets to a different flight, check my baggage, and walk towards my gate, looking for a quick cup of iced cappucino along the way.

Several things began happening at once. First, a loudspeaker with an FAA security announcement telling us not to leave luggage alone and not to approach any luggage that was not accompanied by people. Or something like that.

I'm not sure I'll ever know the exact sequence of events in the minutes and hours after that. Shopkeepers gating their places of business. (They are closing? So early? What's the problem?) And people beginning to stream in another direction. I was still headed for my gate. Others moving toward the sounds of television in skyway taverns. A terrified-looking young girl, holding the arm of an older woman, saying: "A plane has been hijacked from here. Maybe two planes or three ..."

Then an announcement on the PA system that Logan would be closed until noon.

Oh, pooh. Logan closed until noon? That meant I wouldn't be getting to the west coast early enough to have the day be useful. <grumble> Hmmm....solution: Find a hotel for the night and get an early flight the next day.

The buzz in the airport was getting louder. More people hurrying towards exits. Businessmen with worried expressions and cell phones to their ears. More businesses closing.

I did the obvious thing and returned to the ticket counter. Only a lone agent was there, and he rebooked me for a flight at 8:30 the next morning.

On my way down to the baggage claim office to retrieve my checked baggage, the PA system announced that flights were grounded all across the country.

Through the windows I saw a line of police cars, perhaps State Trooper cars, bumper to bumper with lights flashing and sirens roaring, coming down the ramp into the outer perimeter of the arrivals areas and a thickening crowd—people and vehicle gridlock.

Shock, dread, uncertainty, confusion—but the practicalities intruded as well, and my tendency when things are crazy around me is to "continue hoeing the garden," as St. Francis of Assisi said when asked what he would do if he learned the world were coming to an end the next day.

And there was a hotel to be found, baggage to be gotten and transportation to be arranged—in case the world didn't end, you know.

There are kiosks in the airport with phones that connect to accommodations. The one closest to me was crowded with people.

Much that I have read since then talks of how cooperative people were with one another. How calm.

It wasn't true in Boston, where I was. Mostly there was shoving and pushing and a buzz of what little information folks had or thought they had: The Pentagon has been attacked. 800 are dead. The White House and the Capitol have been hit. Many more planes hijacked from airports around the country.

So why are we pushing and shoving to reach the two available phones?

One person says: "I've been waiting on hold for fifteen minutes with the Holiday Inn." Another: "The Hyatt has no rooms!" And another: "The Holiday Inn doesn't answer now!"

Somehow I reached a phone and dialed #24, a Best Western Roundhouse Suites. I asked about rooms, and the person who answered asked if I was okay. It was the only time that day that anyone asked. Seems silly now, but it was such a relief. I said I was fine. What else do you say?

They had rooms. I gave her my name. Hung up the phone. Several people yelled: "Do they have rooms?" I said yes, and a chorus erupted: "How much?"

It hadn't occurred to me to ask.

A flash of thought: "The world is ending, and we want to know how much a hotel room is?"

There was a shuttle somewhere, so I made my way to the arrival doors and moved outside. More gridlock. The fumes were intense, and the heat close to intolerable. I backed against a wall so as not to be pushed and shoved. Thinking things would clear and I could eventually make my way.

They didn't.

Central Parking had been closed. No one could retrieve parked cars, and the panic increased, as did the rumors floating through the crowd. I got very thirsty and woozy from the fetid air. Inside the terminal appeared to be empty, at least from my vantage point. There were only people with walkie talkies and credentials hanging from their shirts. All men, it seems to me now.

It is totally counterintuitive, but I slowly moved to the doors. They weren't locked, so I went back in—expecting to be challenged, but wasn't. No one paid attention to me as they patrolled the hallways and went about their business.

It was cool inside, and there were vending machines with water and plastic chairs in groups of four. Not so comfortable usually, but a godsend then.

Water.

Seldom has plain old water in a bottle tasted so good.

My cell phone wouldn't work. Nor the land lines.

So I sat and read. Got out some of the documents that had come in the mail yesterday and went to work.

Ask me why.

Who knows?

Perhaps because reading requires a concentration that blocks out other stimuli.

So I read. And made notations. And occasionally tried

the cell phone or a land line. And moved from one set of plastic chairs to another until I'd reached a passageway and then a new terminal.

Friends have asked me why I went back inside the terminal when there appeared to be a threat. I'd like to say it seemed to me that the threat was over or that the virtually empty inside seemed a safer bet than the chaotic fume-filled arrivals ramp. It wasn't any of that. I was just thirsty and hot, and the noise and crowd were bothersome. It looked cool in there. And quiet.

It was both.

I'm not sure how long I was there, but my hotel receipt shows a check-in time of 2:37 p.m., so it was easily two hours, probably more. I eventually came to a small terminal with no upper and lower decks and by then very few people standing around. A van came around with a driver yelling out the window: "All Boston hotels!"

I was the only one to get in. There were three members of a flight crew and a passenger who had been taking off and had to do an emergency abort. On another day, that in itself would have been a news story. But not that day.

A young man who looked like he might be a navigator or co-pilot was talking into a cell phone, and the three flight attendants were bemoaning that passengers had been given their luggage back. They looked, to a person, terrified.

Their passenger was an attorney from London. He said he had been to the States for a calming symposium on Japanese Art. He no longer felt calm and wanted to be on any plane headed out of the United States and towards Europe.

My arrival at the hotel was uneventful. It was a few blocks from a hospital complex, on the border between Roxbury and Southie, and the only visible restaurant was a ribs joint across the street.

No matter.

A television was on in the lobby, and it was only then I learned that disaster had not been nearly so thorough as had been rumored at the airport. Funny, what I felt in those first few minutes of watching was tremendous relief.

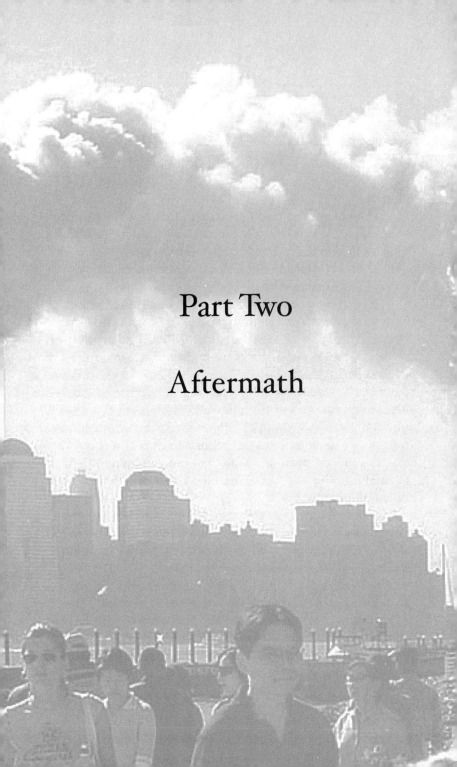

Part Two

Aftermath

A Terrible Absence

Conor O'Clery

The collapse of the World Trade Centre towers created shock waves which registered on seismographs at New York's Columbia University. But the aftershocks of the catastrophe will be deeply psychological. What happened challenges our capabilities of comprehension.

How does one regain a sense of equilibrium when the community in which one lived and worked is destroyed in a hellish day of flames, dust, soot, ash and glass? For the twin towers were not just office blocks. They were the symbols of the world's largest economy, the first sight of New York for passengers arriving on ships passing the Statue of Liberty. They towered over a world beneath in which tens of thousands of people worked, shopped, dined, had their shoes shined, bought newspapers, drank coffee, hurried for subway trains.

It is now a heap of rubble and tangled metal in which thousands of people are entombed and which has been renamed "ground zero" by the rescue workers. And surrounding it, much of southern Manhattan, from Chambers Street and City Hall to the river, the location of the greatest financial institutions of the world, including the New York Stock Exchange, has been reduced to a dust bowl.

Burned-out cars, buildings, grassy parks, canopies, scaffolding, all have a coating of two inches of dust and millions of torn bits of paper, some of which floated on the smoke-choked westerly breeze across the East River to Brooklyn.

Electricity and gas have been cut off in southern Manhattan to prevent more fire and explosions—which meant that the riverside Tribeca Point building, where *The Irish Times* has its 42nd-storey office four blocks to the north-west, had to be evacuated late on Tuesday as its 1,000 inhabitants joined the exodus to uptown hotels.

How long ago it seems now since I sat on the bench outside on Sunday looking over the financial district and telling the building manager, Mr Rosie Rosenstein, how this was such a wonderful place to live.

Walking away from the building through the darkening streets on Tuesday evening, past exhausted firefighters who had watched helplessly all day, grieving for 300 dead comrades, we encountered people standing in groups, too shocked to talk.

They stared south to where the twin towers had stood in all their magnificence at the start of a wonderful sunny day, stunned by the enormity of watching two skyscrapers collapse, imploding in on themselves, exploding floor by floor and slipping down out of sight as if swallowed by the earth.

The towers, they had been told, had been built to withstand hurricanes, earthquakes and ordinary fires, but they could not cope with the impact of a 707 and a 767 passenger airliner, gorged with aviation fuel which burned at 2,000 degrees and warped and weakened the 61 steel support columns in each tower so that they could no longer stand the weight of the concrete floor slabs, the office furniture and banks of computer terminals.

The Trade Centre was in fact seven buildings, the two 110-storey towers, the Marriott Hotel, the US Customs House and three office buildings. Buildings five and seven also collapsed late on Tuesday.

For those who lived and worked there, life changed forever on Tuesday morning, as it did for the witnesses whose psyche will be scarred forever at the sight of falling bodies, among them children in three schools on Chambers Street.

Many financial workers escaped the holocaust, covered in blood and dust, but it was almost too much for them to bear to think of the people who would not be evacuated alive, the employees in 350 banks, insurance offices, law firms and investment houses trapped inside the towers.

Had a generation of financial workers, the best and brightest, those who occupied the prestigious top floors, been wiped out? Morgan Stanley Dean Witter was the largest tenant at the centre with 3,500 employees in one million square feet of office space.

Two thousand of them worked at mid level in No 2 Tower. Marsh & McLennan had 1,700 executives and secretaries on floors 93 to 100 of No 1 Tower. The Aon Corporation, the world's second-largest insurance brokerage, had 1,100 employees on floors 92 and 98 to 105. All the workers in Sidney, Austin, Brown & Wood escaped, and the 200 employees of Bridge Information Systems were able to walk down from the 58th floor of No 1 tower, but there was an ominous silence from other companies, like Cantor Fitzgerald, the leading brokerage company in Treasury bonds high in No 1 Tower, whose screens went blank at the moment the plane hit.

And what of all the workers in the sprawling malls beneath the buildings encountered walking across the busy pedestrian walkway, as wide as a street, over West Side Highway from the World Financial Centre — a smaller set of office blocks housing Merrill Lynch and the Winter Gardens?

The Financial Centre escaped damage but the glass-encased bridge, with a large banner advertising a Quebec circus act this weekend, lay crushed across the roadway, brought down by falling masses of concrete. The performance would have been held this Saturday on Tobin Plaza, the area between the towers where open-air concerts are held throughout the summer and visitors gaze in awe at the startling sight of two of the world's tallest man-made structures soaring above. It was closed in winter to protect people from falling ice which formed on the 1,350-ft-high towers.

Emerging from the pedestrian walkway people would also crowd onto escalators to go beneath the towers to get elevators to work or to post a letter in the marble-floored hallway, or shop in the malls, or take a subway uptown, or queue for last-minute theatre tickets at one of the only two such box offices in Manhattan, or to bring a visitor to the Windows on the World Restaurant at the top of Tower 2, in where *Irish America* magazine recently celebrated its annual Irish on Wall Street event.

It was also an air-conditioned short-cut in hot or rainy weather to Wall Street a few blocks on the south-eastern side or to the Amish Market store where Trade Centre workers liked to have wholesome buffet lunches, or to Borders Bookstore, where it was always impossible to get a seat in the popular coffee bar. How many of the people we encountered every day were doomed to die there on Tuesday, September 11th, a day which for all Americans will live in infamy, as Franklin D. Roosevelt described the day of the Japanese attack on Pearl Harbour 60 years ago?

How many of these tens of thousands of people will ever be able to resume normal life again? Many financial workers liked to end the day by going to Chelsea Piers sports complex on the Hudson to hit a few balls at the golf driving range.

Yesterday, Chelsea Piers was turned into a morgue and some were brought back there, in body bags.

A Pakistani Woman in New York

Humera Afridi

On Thompson Street where I live, blocks from the World Trade Center, I stepped out of my building on the morning the world changed to discover the street had turned into a space of communal mourning, a space from which to watch the horror unfold. I could make out the innards of the tower spilling out from where the airplane had dissected it. Amidst the quiet weeping, some semblance of daily life carried itself out as a vendor unloaded vegetables from a truck and delivered them to the restaurant across the road. And then I saw it fall, the tower, edges of airplane ensconced in it, watched it collapse as if it were made of flour, this edifice, this emblem of America's success, this essential limb of New York's skyline. Then the second tower crumpled. A bald sky met the eye where the twin towers had been.

I tried my phone again and again and again. I was weeping, even though I was new in this city, and the skyline meant nothing to me. A black man in his thirties staggered by. "My mama in that building. My mama in there," he repeated and then screamed, " I'll kill all you fuckin' terrorists if my mama hurt." Tears streaked his face; his repeated threat announced his despair.

I knew that my class tonight would be cancelled, but I decided to go to campus to check in on my department. In the lobby, the guard who has seen me numerous times pretended not to know me, refused access to the elevator, demanded to see my student ID card, refused to let me even use the phone to call upstairs, until a woman intervened. It struck me at that moment how I must look to the security guards. I am from Pakistan. I must look to them like I come from the sort of place that rears terrorists. I walked back to my apartment, picked up my ID, made my way back to campus. I waved my ID card at the guard as I headed towards the elevator. He pretended not to know me –again. He questioned me as to why I would need to be in this building, what possible association I could have with the Creative Writing Department. I sensed I was being mildly harassed. I finally got permission to go up but found the department deserted.

In a daze, I walked down to Little Italy and rang the buzzer at my friend Nada's building. We stood in front of Pizza Pomodoro and exchanged news. A woman passing by joined us, told us how lucky she was she hadn't gone to work today on Wall Street. And then she said: "These fucking Arabs, I just don't understand them. What do they think they are doing?" She suddenly looked at us as if seeing us for the first time. "You're not Arab, are you?" Her voice faltered. "I mean you're not *Palestinian*," she specified, realizing she had committed a faux pas. Nada, who is Moroccan, and I exchange glances. This is what we had dreaded, suspected, but not until this moment admitted in words even to each other: indiscriminate hatred directed at all those who may be related, somehow connected by skin tone, accent, religion, geographic affiliation, or dress to the unidentified but nevertheless palpable demon that has taken amorphous shape in the American psyche. Nada and I cut the conversation short and walked away, leaving the woman muttering about what a perfect opportunity to do laundry today.

I walked west on Spring Street towards my apartment but then decided to walk north across West Broadway to Houston Street. I wasn't ready to go back indoors. The broad length and width of Houston Street were deserted except for a bevy of navy blue National Guard trucks parked close to the intersection of Macdougal Street. Houston Street seemed to have become a base for security deployment, but on my way back home I learned that there had been a bomb threat at nearby St. Anthony's School.

The streets of SoHo were eerie. Hardly anyone was out, and not a single Yellow Cab in sight. Boutiques were shut, cafés shuttered. I could hear the hum and drip of air conditioners on streets where music, laughter, and polyglot chatter otherwise resound. At West Broadway, I turned my head out of habit towards the financial district and sucked in my breath at the amputated skyline. I walked towards Canal Street as the sun struck the bulbous clouds billowing from the rubble. Earlier, a friend had said how he had had a flashback of his childhood in Beirut. I stood among the few people who were still out, waiting and watching. And then, as if planted in a surreal drama, I heard the *azaan*. For the first time ever on the streets of America, I heard a muezzin's call to prayer, and it seemed so fitting in this moment that it took me a minute to register that I was in New York.

Later that night I unearthed a transistor radio from my closet, and now I had two radio stations playing at the same time to make up for the lack of a television. I was amazed to hear Pakistan mentioned over and over again, as callers and speakers tried to link the horrific events of the day to specific nations. I'd never heard Pakistan mentioned so frequently on US radio stations, with the exception of National Public Radio. On another radio station, a caller declared, "I am an American and I know what I have to do. I say drop me off in Palestine and I *will* strangle them. I will do what I have to do as an American." This caller was responding to the repeated television images of rejoicing Arab children.

I could not sleep. I was hyper conscious of the fact that my apartment was the very first apartment on the first floor, that if there were to be riots and break-ins I would be the first to be attacked. I realized that my name on the resident list at the entrance of the building stood out as foreign and Muslim. I felt exposed. I didn't have blinds on my windows. Since I faced the back of two buildings and a little patio, I had decided to forgo the expense. Now I wanted to board up my windows, hide under the covers. I felt like a child; my mind was full of my grandmother's stories of Partition. Was my South Asian predisposition to melodrama finally evincing itself? I don't know, but in my bones there was a visceral fear of the repercussions of the day's horrific event. I wished I didn't live alone, and yet curiously I did not want to be anywhere else in the world at this moment.

I slept fitfully and woke to the realization: the world *is* where we left it yesterday—destroyed, mangled, an ocean of splayed bodies and debris. Outside, smoke belched and curdled from the site. I could count the people on my street— three. I walked across Sullivan Street to the bakery. A note pasted on the door announced that the kitchen was only baking bread for rescue workers. Again, I counted the people on the street—one other dog walker, apart from me. I couldn't stomach the walk towards Canal Street, so I walked in the opposite direction. At the deli, I asked for a paper. No newspapers and no deliveries below 14th Street, I was told. The shelves were empty.

At Houston Street, the road had been barricaded. Police lined the street. No one was allowed to cross Houston to come into SoHo; no one was allowed to leave unless they had ID proving they lived on the street they exited from. I had an electricity bill in my bag and my student ID card. I hesitated before crossing the police line. And then, as I made my way across Houston to Bleeker Street—it felt as though I had left a country behind—I was beset by doubt. I turned back and looked at the people bereft of appropriate ID clustered on either side of the police line, some wanting to enter, others wanting to leave. I stopped at two kiosks. Neither had papers. No deliveries, they said. I decided to head back. At the police line, my ID was scrutinized before I was allowed back into the barricaded zone between Houston Street and Canal Street. I remained within this zone for the next few days, too fearful to leave, as I heard stories about racial profiling. What if they didn't let me back in?

Black clouds of smoke from the still-burning fire swept over SoHo; a haze of acrid, bitter dust settled on our tongues and skins. The few residents on the streets wore medical masks. My studio was murky with smoke. I buried my face in my sleeve and walked over to the deli to pick up a mask. No luck—they're all sold out. No deliveries ...

Was I imagining it, or were people squinting at me, looking closely at my face, trying to read my nationality from my features? This afternoon, the radio had reported hate crimes against Muslims; a mosque in Dallas had been shot at. The South Asian Journalists' Association list had notified us by e-mail that Sikhs had been attacked. My friends in Texas were scared to be seen in public places where they could be identified. They dared not go to their favorite Middle Eastern restaurant nor wear shalwar kameezes.

But hungry for company, I decided to eat dinner at Caffé Tina, one of only three places open in my neighborhood. The conversation was robust, but it was in Italian, and I couldn't understand what was being said until I heard Pakistan mentioned several times by a man at the bar. I swung around and looked at him, he saw me, continued to speak in rapid Italian and mentioned Pakistan again as he held my gaze. I was wearing a diamond stud in my nose, I suddenly remembered- a dead giveaway. I turned my face, slipped off the trinket and shoved it into my wallet. This was ridiculous, I thought, irritated at my own paranoia and yet aware that I couldn't be too careful. I paid and left. I was here alone, a foreigner, on streets that had overnight become primarily Caucasian. I too peered at faces now, looking for some affinity, suddenly aware of my minority status in this zoned-off area.

At West Broadway, an older man dressed in black leather pants and a bandanna talked to a neighbor, raised his voice, and pointed to a man yards away from him: "See that guy? He's a fucking Iranian. Do you see him? Unbelievable!" I hastened towards Canal Street, where a crowd had gathered by the military checkpoint. Trucks full of debris and wreckage passed by. We breathed in the dust and asbestos but despite the health hazard stayed and watched. This was the only way to understand what had happened. This was the only way to mourn the dead and the dying.

I walked to the edges of the frontiers set up on either side of me. I was stuck in a strange purgatory: south of me were the frothing clouds of smoke, the incessant fire, the smell of death, the particles strung in the air and subsumed in all this the dead and slowly dying. To my north life had superficially resumed normalcy. Shops and bars were open. There was laughter. Further uptown businesses were ticking and people had moved on with their lives, I heard on the radio. But framed between Houston and Canal, we were caught in an ontological dilemma, a time warp. Back in my apartment, I was further discombobulated. Pakistan had become so much more than a name tossed incriminatingly on the airwaves. According to a speaker on NPR, "Pakistan is the fulcrum of what the US is planning now." It is surreal to be caught so tight in this weave of politics. From the devastation of the World Trade Center in Manhattan, my new home, the focus of attention has swerved to Pakistan, my country.

Friday was declared a national day of prayer and mourning . The barricade at Houston Street had been removed. I am not a devout person, but I decided to go to a mosque, more for the sense of community. It was Friday, and it seemed fitting. I was not surprised to see journalists and photographers hovering around 11th Street and 1st Avenue. An eccentric old Caucasian man in a hard hat, waving a huge American flag in one hand and leading a fierce-looking hound in the other circled around, yelling incoherently. The police were there to ensure there were no incidents. Not a single Muslim woman was in sight when I got there. There were two white women journalists in denim skirts and bright stockings, and me. My dupatta was in my bag. I went up to a man in an orange kurta-pajama and asked where the women's entrance to the mosque was. He hesitated before he asked, "Why? Do you want to pray?" Did I imagine a sneer in his voice? Irritated, I went in through the general entrance. No women here, I was told by another man. So much for fraternity and community, I thought, thoroughly disillusioned.

Manhattan was like a palimpsest—a new city, an altered reality had layered the streets from which I'd been zoned for the past week. I stopped to read posters upon posters upon posters of missing people stuck to vans and phone booths and restaurant windows and windshields. Another day had passed, and there was no comfort. The president's insipid words fly over us like dust motes from the debris. I listened for news of Pakistan.

As I looked in the direction of the carnage it was hard to digest that the Brooks Brothers store in Liberty Plaza where I would wait for my sister on her lunch break when she worked at a law firm in the building had been turned into a morgue. From there smoke wafted into the charcoal night. I felt guilty as I thought this sky was like an etching, a piece of art. How could something so utterly gruesome create a night sky so beautiful?

The *Times* of Our Lives
Ellen Willis

"The newspaper is my morning prayer"
—G.W.F. Hegel

I was alerted to Tuesday's cataclysm by an e-mail message, saw the towers disintegrate on NY 1. In my apartment some two miles north of the epicenter, I sat riveted to the television as the day's grim events proceeded. I was awash in electronic information, in graphic images of destruction, and all day I kept thinking: I won't be able to make any sense of this until I read the newspapers.

On Wednesday I bolted awake about 7 a.m. and looked outside my door: a blank expanse of hallway. No papers had been delivered. I went out to my local newsstand, and then to a couple of others: no papers. Delayed by the disruption? But on such a day, wouldn't the press be all the more desperate to get through to readers? Finally I understood that my neighborhood had been cordoned off. Evidently newspaper trucks had not qualified as emergency vehicles; after all, it was not as if we needed them to find out what was happening. And yet I felt slightly panicky. I started walking uptown. I found the *Post* on 13th Street and by the time I got to midtown had gotten hold of the *News*, the *Wall Street Journal*, and the *NY Observer*. But the *Times*, it seemed, was everywhere sold out. The subway was working, so I rode up to 86th Street, hoping I wouldn't have a problem getting back home. *Mirabile*, a *Times* truck had just arrived and I stood in a long line, waiting for deliverance.

What was behind my obsession? Denial, focusing on a

small problem I could do something about? That was part of the story, no doubt, but not all. The rest has to do with the role of the written word in memory and history. The images I saw on TV will resonate forever in my brain and in the national life, but I can remember little of what was said—it all felt like filler, accompaniment. As a writer, I have a particular professional relationship with language; yet I am speaking also as a political person, needing to find my place in a public conversation about what to do. To be able to read and mull over the words on paper—the headlines, the various narratives as they are being pieced together by reporters, the eyewitness accounts, the early attempts at commentary (glimmers of insight and shafts of demagogy in a great cloud of anguish, confusion, bombast)—to be able to see it all side by side, compare different versions, keep it to refer to when I need it—this for me is the beginning of taking the measure of an outsized event and groping toward the understanding that makes intelligent action possible.

The stack of newspapers now cluttering my floor is a kind of fossil record of themes beginning to take shape and put down tracks: terrorism has burst its boundaries to become the face of 21st century warfare; things will never be the same; our security and intelligence are abysmal; we can't afford civil liberties now; we can't afford to abrogate civil liberties now; we know what we need to know and must retaliate massively and quickly; not so fast, it's a complex situation and we need to respond with reason, not hysteria; we must unite behind our commander-in-chief (large, ubiquitous footprints); the guy looks like a scared mouse and came to New York much too late (a few pointed quotes from rescue workers).

There are gaps, of course. Those first few days I could find no mention in the papers of our own role in the Taliban's coming to power. Nor did they remark on the discomfort some of us might feel about having Wednesday declared a national day of prayer (though now that Jerry Falwell has opened his big mouth and suggested that America is being punished by God for modernity and secularism, perhaps the question of religious fundamentalism at home will be open for discussion). For such subjects the internet and the radio were the media of choice. It's not big news, as they say, that there's much the mainstream papers won't and can't do: much of my own cultural criticism is an extended complaint about this. Yet I need my stack. I look at the front page of my morning-after Times and all the chaotic texture of those unbelieving moments and hours comes back, there to be recollected and deconstructed in (relative) tranquility as I decide what to do or write next. Electronic images are another matter entirely: the more I see that awful clip of the second plane slicing through its target, the more surreal and less intelligible it becomes.

A Priest's Diary, Day 2
September 12

Fr Julian Cassar

More people came to Mass this morning, and some even for confession, hurt, upset and angry.

The shock of the first day was now turning to anger in many people.

As I was writing to my family and friends and sending e-mails across the world, a man called me and asked me to pray for his son, who was presumed dead.

I left everything and went to visit Hans Klein, an Austrian immigrant who was alone at home after his wife had left to be with their daughter-in-law, now a young widow.

Their son Peter was thirty-six and worked on the 97th floor of the first building that was hit. Most probably the plane crashed right into his office. Peter was married a year ago, and was an altar-boy in our parish for many years. I spent an hour with Hans, and he shared with me special memories of his family and his son, as I did my best to comfort him.

I spent three hours waiting in line to donate blood, a process that normally takes half an hour.

Hundreds of Americans gave the gift of life by donating blood for the survivors. Many others turned to prayers.

I did a lot of counselling, even on the phone and through e-mail. People were trying to understand the meaning of this senseless act.

Others were quoting from Nostradamus and asked if the end of the world is nearing. I encouraged them to think positive, and as the motto of the Christophers suggests, "to try to light one candle instead of cursing the darkness," and to focus on praying, support, and unity, instead of vengeance or hate.

In Manhattan, September 12

Jay Rosen

I — "It traffics in symbols"

Terrorism, we all intuitively understand, is not about the explosion, or even the dead. It is an act of communication; it traffics in symbols. In the miserable cliche of the media age, the terrorist wants to "send a message." The medium is not the bomb, or the plane, or the television set. It's your own mind, which "conducts" the terror. It is impossible to overstate the psychological effect today's events will have on the people of New York, even beyond the immense loss of life, and utter chaos downtown.

The World Trade Center Towers were a symbol of the city, of course. But so is the humble bagel a "symbol" of New York. Far more than that, the Towers overawed us. Secular totems for a secular world, they were all about the might, power, richness and unlimited confidence of the civilization that gave rise to them. In other words, they were like religious sites. No matter how close you were to the Towers, even directly underneath them on the broad plaza at ground level, the buildings looked very far away, twin abstractions against the sky. They were almost ineffable in that way. They had no depth, like the blue in the sky has no depth. It was not possible to feel close to them. I'm not sure anyone ever loved them. But did we have confidence in them? We did, we did.

II — "Wanna live? Then let live"

An enormous act of hate slammed into my sky yesterday, and of all things big in this biggest event, it's hate that stands out for me today. New York is a great city because it is a liberal city, and also big, strong, powerful. Liberalism breeds the dynamism that holds people here—that, and the skyline. People know how to hate in New York, and they do. But they also know that they have not yet figured out how to live with hate. Besides, no one hates the skyline.

Here we understand in minute precision that to live is also to "let live." The density of our enviornment tells us to maintain that saving space between ourselves and the private demons of others. Two of us can be a quarter-inch apart, or touching, and we preserve each other's space. This happens on a packed subway car every morning, but the subways only work because our liberalism does.

Wanna live? Then let live. In New York, that's survival. We don't need posters or candidates to tell us about it. For we're aware of the power that one crazy has to wreck a thousand lives, and aware that he's only inches away, in those undisturbed demons. "Don't push me cuz I'm close to the edge." We remember that song.

If the fragility of the social peace is one, the fragility of the city systems is the other reason we're liberals. To live here, especially in Manhattan, is to live inches away from total urban crisis all the time. One transformer, one water tunnel, one gas main, or just one President visiting the UN and everything goes, all order is lost, the thing comes apart and Manhattan no longer "works." That's why it holds such a powerful place in the imagination of disaster, from *King Kong* to *Independence Day*. It's so easy to imagine New York's destruction. Trust me, we do that all the time.

When those airplanes slammed in, tearing a hole in the skyline, they were overturning the mental furniture of the cosmopolitan mind. Today, we have to begin the grim work of understanding that liberalism itself is hated. The city is closed for business, and so some of us have the time.

I can't agree with Martin Brown that the Towers were symbols of financial might, but not democracy, although everything else he told us about the present moment is powerful, urgent, vivid and real. Maybe across the ocean or in left-wing critique the World Trade Center meant commerce, capital, and markets triumphant. In New York we knew about all that, but here The Twins were democratic symbols too, simply because of where they stood. On ground we know to be fragile, over a delicate social peace we preserve because we're natural democrats: the subway car kind. My four-year-old daughter asked her mother if maybe they could be "fixed." My wife said she didn't think so.

Now our common sky is ripped and smoking from the crash of someone's public demons. The disaster we knew how to prevent ourselves fell upon us from above. We'd imagined it, a million times. But then everyone here agrees: we could never imagine this.

"The video store was closed"

Brian Pride

Tonight it all took a turn. It started earlier today when the winds changed. The acrid smoke filled the air around me. It burns deep down in the throat. I'm on the top floor and right in the middle of the path of smoke. The last time I went out to look, I couldn't see through the smoke and ran back in. I tried sleeping but only managed a couple of hours. I decided to go out to rent a video in the hopes it might relax me and put me back to sleep. Just as I was heading out the door, newscasters announced a bomb threat at the Empire State Building, which towers just outside my window. I decided to keep on going. Downstairs, crowds were gathered in the street looking up. They had been evacuated from nearby blocks. It was a strange but familiar scene. The strong industrial smoke hanging over the streets. The confused or lost people standing in the streets, with crews of police at every intersection. Just as lost and confused, different only in the detail of their uniform.

I checked with my night security to see if he needed anything before I headed out. I got a block and the familiar glow of klieg lights broke through the smoke as I realized I was headed into the armory just down the street, now the civil survivor center. The streets were full of a mix of relatives looking for lost loved ones. Dust-covered police units and fresh National Guard troops lined the sidewalks and doorways to the armory. Everyone eyeing me, and me them, with equal suspicion. It's a New York thing: the glance, just as much offense as it is defense, which says in an instant, "I am a New

Yorker," like dogs snarling in an alley. I rolled by on my roller blades, zipping around the emergency vehicles blocking the cross section.

The video store was closed, as were the one down the street and the one two blocks from that. At that point I would have bought a video; anything other than this same news, these same planes crashing, these same twin towers crumbling. Security had asked for a few burgers, so I took off for a Wendy's or the like. One after another passing places normally open, ominously closed. Passing one store after another of long lines and empty shelves.

Day two found me facing scenes much too familiar to me from years abroad and life in third world countries. Life in America, even here in New York City, the Capital of Capitalism, had been brought down to third world status in less than 24 hours, with just a few short blows to a few morally strategic targets. Trusting this will all change as soon as all the shops open and the streets are secure and safe to open, hoping my trust is not just vain or wishful thinking. It is then I look at myself and question what I will do now. What will I do for work? How will I build my tomorrow? Will I make it through this unscathed, have enough food? Is it ever going to be safe again? Was it ever? Or were we here in America living only an illusion? Was this the American dream? Did we all just wake from the dream with a start—a loud bang?

Perhaps one of the odder aspects of all this is its eerie silence. There was no enormously loud boom, no big bang, no loud scream of steel as the buildings collapsed. No thundering rumble. Yes, there was a roar. The roar of the jet planes flying low, the roar of the flames as they blew into blasts of smoke and flame, the roar of the crumbling walls of sheet rock and thud of cement floor into cement floor. The roar of fighter jets high overhead. The commonplace and often irritable roar of the city now silenced, with the silence broken now and again by the scream of sirens.

A Journalist Responds

Jade Walker

It was my first day back from vacation. I had worked a normal overnight shift at *The New York Times* Web site on Monday, covering international news and preparing for the upcoming mayoral primary.

In fact, I had just sent out my wrap-up e-mail to the day shift editors when the first jet plane hit the World Trade Center.

The rest of the office staff gathered in horror around the television screens; I returned to my desk and broke the biggest story I've ever produced. I wouldn't return home for 20 hours.

The editorial staff that lived in Manhattan raced to the office and joined me in my task. Advertising reps and marketing experts offered their services to the news room, tirelessly gathering facts and quotes from the phones. They compiled lists of blood donation centers and gave us transportation information. A team spirit permeated the 9th floor even as concern for friends and relatives in the attack zone settled just under our skin.

The news unfolded, but I did not cry. I did not get angry. I didn't even get scared. Instead, I remained calm and continued my working vigil in front of the computer screen. While I wrote, the carnage continued. A second plane was hijacked and aimed into the World Trade Center. A third plane hit the Pentagon. The twin towers collapsed. A fourth jet smashed into the Pennsylvania countryside.

People all over the world watched the events and were

filled with terror and worry. I stressed over the capabilities of our graphics server to handle the huge influx of traffic. What good were timely news stories when no one could access them?

For hours I was filled with the journalist's high. Adrenaline pumped through my veins. I forgot to eat, and a single can of diet Coke saw me through any caffeine urges.

I would still be sitting there jamming out stories if my bosses hadn't pried me away from the desk with strict orders to get some rest. "This is going to continue for weeks or months, Jade," they said. "Don't overdo it."

So I went home and restlessly paced in front of my television. Here I was helpless. At work I had a useful purpose, and I yearned to return.

On Wednesday night, I struggled to get back into Manhattan. The destruction had closed off access to all the bridges and tunnels near my home. Most of the subways were diverted in order to avoid heading into the city. But I was determined. I took three trains and walked two miles through the darkness to enter my office in midtown.

As I reached the 9th floor, I was accosted by a coworker who told me that a bomb threat had led to the evacuation of the Empire State Building and Penn Station, both mere blocks from our building. This event would only be the first in a series of such threats.

Later the next day, several other spots around the city would be evacuated, including Grand Central Station and 1 Penn Plaza. These scares led the police to shut down parts of Manhattan and cancel all subway service south of 42nd Street.

I was trapped in the city.

I didn't worry too much, though. An old mentor had taught me that the first rule of journalism is simple: If you're going to die, make sure you do it big enough to make the front page. I didn't have a death wish, but I had already accepted the possibility of dying at the hands of terrorists.

I was completely focused on doing my own small part in covering this news event. I had a job to do, and I was going to make a damn good effort. In times of great horror, the public is starving for information. I needed to feed that hunger with the truth.

This purpose kept me at work until Friday, when exhaustion (and the need to feed my cats) guided me home to my Brooklyn attic. Even as I entered the apartment, I yearned to be back on the job facing bomb threats and covering the president's visit to the crash site.

Though I was a bit weary and shell-shocked, I wasn't ready to stop. Rescue attempts needed to be acknowledged. The investigative process required examination. Family members needed the opportunity to publicly mourn the missing and dead. And heroes deserved recognition.

There were still so many stories to tell.

In Manhattan, September 13

Jay Rosen

Large candlelight vigil last night in Washington Square Park, possibly the gentlest event ever held there. I grab my wife and daughter and we take our candles to be with the other candles. Hoisting Sylvie on my shoulders, I slowly walk her and her four years around the great circular fountain in the middle. Normally filthy, the fountain tonight is shining, a big ring of light reflected in the faces. Many are NYU students, and as one of their professors I make a mental note of that.

Around the fountain father and daughter walk, stepping carefully by the faithful seated on the ground in circles, some singing, most talking quietly or just being there, with the candles. "This land is your land, this land is my land," say the soft voices. I notice more women singing than men, or does it just sound that way? "From California to the New York Island…" Sylvie is up high and can see everything. Or so I tell myself. Actually, I want everything to see her.

Two days ago, you could spot the Twin Towers from Washington Square Park, and that's where I stood Tuesday morning to watch them burn. "Why are there so many candles?" Sylvie asks. I tell her: many candles, just one light. People are laying flowers down, too. Not in any particular place, just around the Park. The fountain area fills up, and the more people there are the quieter it gets. Guess that's the vigil part.

We don't stay long because it's her bedtime. I'm not worried about what she will ask her mother tonight. Working silently over 24 hours, her mother has found a way to tell the truth of happened, one we can in good conscience share with a four-year-old. Last week Sylvie had stumped her parents and several doctors when she asked, "How does your heart know to beat?" Tonight my wife is ready. To the "why" question, she will say: "Sylvie, there are people who are makers, and there are people who are breakers."

"Children are pre-political," Hannah Arendt once wrote. Listening to the story of the makers and the breakers, I'm not sure Arendt was right. I do know this: I am so proud of my wife for thinking it up. We've completed one small act of repair by giving Sylvie a version of "America Under Attack." At least we're back in the same narrative universe with her, after TV's promiscuity with images had busted the trio up. A picture is worth a thousand words, people say, even this late in the media age. Well, it's true. It will take a thousand words to undo every picture Sylvie saw.

The winds had shifted, and the smoke from Ground Zero was blown out to sea. Last night was not just beautiful, but New York beautiful. And I feel good that we have a story for my daughter, that it can receive her complications at another time. "Hey, Sylvie," I say when we get back to our own building. "What if after they clean up the big pile of junk from the Twin Towers, they make a big park there? Wouldn't that be great?"

I wish I could tell you she smiled.

Traversing the Barriers

Grant Barrett

I've just traversed the barriers at Houston Street, heading south. The smoke and the acrid chemical smell of burning city grow thicker. As cars and cabs become rare, dump trucks and fire engines grow more common. A thousand kinds of municipal vehicles with flashing lights zoom and crawl, with the snaps and squeals from impatient sirens. Crowds mill about, with video and still cameras, American flags, face mask filters, and the normal baggage of daily life. Satellite trucks line the streets, and on Avenue of the Americas near West Fourth Street, a television crew from Philadelphia does a stand-up in front of strong lights. As always, the citizens crowd slowly behind the shot, some trying to see, some trying to get on television.

Many of the people carrying American flags are olive-skinned, some clearly Pakistani, Indian, Bangladeshi, Punjabi, Muslim, Middle Eastern. The flags are identification of loyalty. A friend told me a story of seeing a man in a turban being hauled out of a bar by a drunk man, kicking and beating. The turbaned man did not defend himself. I wonder if he was Sikh. Was he wearing the ritual blade? Did he consider using it? Why was he in a bar?

The barriers into the lockdown zone are the kind of challenge that New Yorkers appreciate. The goal is to get to the other side. You're only qualified if you have identification with the right information: a driver's license, a business card, someone who will come from the other side and vouch for you. All of Houston Street is Checkpoint Charlie.

Some try the same tactics they use at swank velvet-rope clubs. They find the widest space in the middle of the barriers and stride through, nonchalantly, as if they belong there, heads high. But this time they're stopped, always stopped, by the stiff arm of a tired cop.

A short squat white man, looking and sounding like a boatman on the Volga, tries everything to pass. It's clear he doesn't belong on the other side. He's not desperate enough. He tries slipping around the side. He wheedles, one at a time, with each cop, from the white-shirted lieutenant on down, rebuffed every time. A group of Puerto Ricans walk by, Boricuan and American flags intertwined, arms heavy with drinks and food. They flash ID. The Volga boatman slips in the group and meshes best he can. The cops pick him out, turn him around, and refuse him entry. He wanders to the back of the larger crowd, probably to wait until the shift changes and new cops that don't know him take their posts.

A rumor is going around: they're arresting reporters and photographers who have been dressing as medical personnel, firemen and rescuers, and then slipping into the danger zone where they take photographs of the carnage, of the slabs and scraps of flesh, of the snowdrifts of paper and ash, of the bent steel. Someone says they're shooting these interlopers, but nobody believes it.

The subways are closer to normal service than ever, but they are Tokyo-crowded. The patience of the three days is wearing thin, though the gallows humor and the camaraderie of "Ain't this just like the City?" have yet to be replaced by the "enough already" anger and the dragging impatience that are sure to follow.

In a nearly full subway car an old Jewish man, sporting a fur hat covered in pro-Israel pins, some in English, some in Hebrew, tries to hand out Zionist literature. The pages condemn anyone against Israel and promote a hard stance against "enemies." He is talkative and friendly, and a number of people take the pages. One young Latino man, with a thin Dutch beard that traces the line of his jaw, says, "Aw shit, this is not the time, man. Now is not the time. Now is not the time." He keeps repeating it. Now everyone else hands their pages back like children turning in homework. The old man looks a little abashed, but I don't doubt he tried again later.

At Columbia University, classes resumed yesterday, the 12th. Some people thought that was unacceptable, others commented on the need for structure: class schedules, deadlines, papers, exams. One professor tells the story of her babysitter who, after being trapped in the lockdown zone on the first day, walked four and a half hours to her home in Queens, with only pantyhose on her feet. High heels are not suitable. My roommate says the exodus across the bridge was like the New York City marathon, thronged with people of all ages, races, ethnicities, stopping to turn and look behind them, some jogging. Somebody else said it looked like Japanese running from Godzilla.

My heart is in this now, but my efforts are feeble. I am allergic to the chemical smoke, which when the wind blows seaward, I can taste on the bitter edges of my tongue even at home in Brooklyn. I cannot contribute financially to the relief. I have no belongings to give, except perhaps socks. So I sit at my computer for hours, reading personal stories, linking, writing, promoting, weaving a thin network of human beings and their stories. It's a small thing, but it is a record.

Faces and Names

Brian Pride

I'm not too sure when it was, but I had been rolling down the street and noticing the number of profile pages plastered on the walls of buildings. I saw a familiar face and stopped short. No, I thought, this has to be a joke. It was the face of a young fellow I had met who had just come to some interesting self-discoveries. He was having fun with his new life and thrilled with the prospect of everything this city had to offer. I just couldn't picture him working in the financial district. But I knew he wasn't the type to have done this as a ruse. Much to my chagrin there it was in black and white, the name that matched the face that matched the memory, and the confirmation that he had worked in the mailroom of one of the WTC offices. I couldn't believe it. He had been so full of life that ... that ... well, that is gone. I didn't know him well, but still, to have known someone enough to have shared in a conversation about their life, and then to see it all lost. I glanced down the wall, and there was another face staring at me from memory's store of perceptive resource. I could remember her complaining of how her shoes were just too uncomfortable, and how she just wished she could slip them off. Next to her another face with another name, and the fragment of memory to place her.

I stopped looking at pages and turned down the street. Coming back to the studio I passed the armory, and there on the side of a news truck were more profiles. I decided to test the theory. I would just look at the face and see if anything clicked from their image, and not read the profile until I got memory confirmation. After a few good clicks I could tell almost instantly the difference between those I actually recognized and other faces I did not. If the averages were correct, it was looking like I might have met at least a third, if not more, of the victims. I wasn't about to go down through each and every profile lining the walls of the armory. It would have killed me or worse.

The explanation was printed out in black and white on every profile page. I quite often work as a creative consultant. During the holidays, that means decorating. Most years I'll be solid in decorating from September through the New Year. Most of these people I had met while planning for their corporate affairs, holiday parties, and benefits they attended or sponsored. I quite often would be there helping them set up for their events. And in this you have to understand that many of these companies were like big families. They worked together with a family spirit and quite often enough played together. Though I wasn't part of that family when we were together, they quite often would come right up to me and talk to me as if I was. Though I cannot truly say that I knew these people, when your purpose for meeting someone is to be sure that they are happy, then it goes without saying that you are concerned with their happiness if not their general well-being. Also understand the circumstances in which we met. At times of celebration, relaxation, and merry making, people tend both to lighten up and to open up. So I would be there at many of these affairs, and many of them would come to me and start talking about some novel experience, or stand around in a group and share a joke or some fond remembrances. Several times throughout the years I would be standing at the door greeting them as they arrived and verifying their identification and checking their names off of a guest list. I had to stop looking at these pictures, because it was too much to bear. There were too many of them.

A Priest's Diary, Day 3
September 13

Fr. Julian Cassar

Many more people came to Mass today, and parents were wondering what to tell their children.

The stories of many of the survivors and victims were constantly being relayed on TV. Since I was on Long Island for 18 years, I knew many people who worked in the business district and in the World Trade Centre, and hoped and prayed that they had survived.

Another parishioner was on the 51st floor during the attack. She leads our congregation in singing every Sunday and is an active member of our choir.

Joanne Ernest told me the incredible story of her escape, having to walk down 51 floors into the streets.

These are her own words in an e-mail she sent me: "As I reached the street, I could see people jumping from the top floors. A sight I don't think I'll ever forget! I was two blocks away from the WTC when Tower Two started to collapse. As I ran, the debris cloud overtook me, and with several others I ducked into a store to get away from the debris.

"As I was waiting the first tower collapsed! During this time the police came in looking for eye goggles, and they told everyone they had to clear the area. I started heading north and just kept going and going! No subways... no taxis... so I ended up walking all the way to Grand Central Station, at least five miles."

As the rescue operations continued, I met a fireman friend of mine who was helping out in the recovery process.

He told me that all they're finding are body parts, and no one alive. I watched on TV the heart-breaking story of Howard Lutnick, CEO of Cantor Fitzgerald, who lost all 700 of his employees who were on the very top floors of one of the Twin Towers, including his brother.

He survived simply because he took his daughter to her first day of kindergarten and was heading towards work when the tragedy happened.

Indignant Patriots

Karen Houppert

A few blocks from the World Trade Center, two elderly couples sit in the deserted courtyard of their senior housing project. No one is being allowed into this southern tip of Manhattan, but these older New Yorkers didn't have to get past the multiple barricades staffed by cops and National Guard; they never left. In the eerie silence, the two men and two women have casually parked themselves around a card table. They are playing gin rummy, blue dust masks on each face.

Five blocks from Ground Zero sits the smashed and burned hulk of a car. Its color and make no longer distinguishable but oddly, its front windshield still intact. A half-inch layer of the chalky white ash that is everywhere here—on the streets, on the window ledges, on the rescue workers' clothes, in our lungs—coats the car. Someone has scrawled on the windshield, finger in ash, "FUCK THE ARABS."

Only three blocks from the barricades that surround the World Trade Center disaster site, financial documents blow lazily down the ash- and rubble-strewn streets like tumbleweed in a bad western. In the midst of this, a pair of Sanitation Workers methodically, ironically, make their rounds, emptying the mostly empty wire trash cans that sit on each street corner.

A surface peace. An undercurrent of violence. A reflexive desire for normalcy. The images butt up against each other as

New Yorkers move from shock to—what? No one seems quite sure how to proceed. At first we wanted to do something hands-on. Hundreds of volunteers were turned away from the World Trade Center site, the blood banks, the hospitals due to an abundance of help. Now, it seems that New Yorkers are following the rest of the nation, those who were quicker to move talk toward vengeance.

It's an interesting place for us New Yorkers to be.

And there is a kind of wisdom in the warped reasoning of these terrorists. After all, they didn't go after the Heartland, but attacked New York City. Yes, it was an attack on those twin towers of capitalism, but this city is also the bastion of liberalism, capital of the "cultural elite" and home base for much of the nation's liberal press corps, purveyors—and makers—of public opinion.

This is a city where yeah, we've got our gung-ho patriotic elements, but it's a place where you're more likely to run into a star-spangled gown on a Wig Stock contestant than a flag emblem on a veteran. In my Park Slope neighborhood, people have had to dig deep for their symbols. Not a lot of flags tucked away in the attics here. One hard-pressed household has taped a Fourth of July place mat to its wrought-iron fence. Another has cut out a Ralph Lauren ad. And everyone is walking around in the same Old Navy-Old Glory shirt they dropped five bucks for last Fourth.

And in the midst of such flag-waving, the idea of criticizing our government reads as nitpicking. And this, in the land of cranky columnists, pushy professionals and citizens who are notorious worldwide for their rudeness. Invasion of the body-politic snatchers; courtesy and consensus reign. Consider the way we've lauded Congress for suddenly dropping all partisanship as if agreement, not a healthy debate, were the hallmark of democracy. Or the way we've sat by in silence while talking heads refer to the "inevitable" sacrifice of civil rights for safety. Or the way we lapsed into polite silence after Bush's Oval Office speech on Tuesday instead of stating the obvious: It was devoid of passion, conviction, and empathy. It's not like we expected the likes of Lincoln. ("That we here highly resolve that these dead shall not have died in vain, that this nation under God shall have a new birth of freedom, and that government of the people, by the people, for the people shall not perish from the earth.") Or even the likes of Bill Clinton, who would at least have cried. In the aftermath of the USS Cole attack, Clinton remembered to speak of dead "people," not simply demolished "structures," and he remembered to acknowledge victims' families: "We are all mindful of the limits of our poor words to lift your spirits or warm your hearts." And Clinton paid tribute to the diversity of the victims—the way Bush might have acknowledged the diversity of both the victims and the tireless rescue workers— by rallying us. "It must surely confound the minds of the hate-filled terrorists who killed them," Clinton said in October last year.

But Bush never named the World Trade Center in that first speech. He referred to the 4,600 individuals who died as a tidy entity, simply the byproducts of "acts of mass murder." By way of comfort he gave us clunky propaganda: "Terrorist attacks can shake the foundations of our biggest buildings, but they cannot touch the foundation of America." And instead of solace, he offered only revenge: "[We'll] find those responsible and bring them to justice."

He speaks simply of "evil" (Arabs) and "good" (Americans), and if this were a run-of-the-mill political convention, eighty New York pundits would weigh in, sniping at this easy target. But this second day after the World Trade Center attack, we let it pass: This week no one's willing to point out that George Dub has no clothes.

Question is, will he be able to withstand the frenzy for

revenge that he has helped fuel? How will he respond to a plummet in public opinion polls during any prolonged, top-secret campaign to capture bin Laden et al? Will a formal international tribunal satisfy the appetite of those fervent patriots, like the old man standing out front the foreign legion club at the end of my street shouting to his friends: "Give me a fuckin' F-16, I'll go after those Arab motherfuckers." Will that constitute a flashy "war against terrorism?"

How do good governments work? You either have a wise and inspirational leader you trust, or you have a well-oiled system that functions to check the marginally competent leaders that sometimes slip by the populace. (Or at least the Supreme Court.) Sadly, we're lacking the former and in danger of losing the latter. Even here in New York, bastion of liberalism, a critical skepticism seems subsumed beneath a shrill patriotism. A kind of guilt-survivor's syndrome renders us New Yorkers incapable of resisting the lure of nationalism. Not so much because the rhetoric is compelling but because it seems, well, rude to point out that it's not.

Today, in the absence of an alternate narrative, we emerge from our silent state of shock to march lockstep with the indignant patriots across the country. Our buildings have been leveled. Out of the ashes, a message: "Fuck the Arabs!"

Stranded Airline Passengers
Count Their Blessings

Jaclyn O'Malley

Garden City, Kansas, September 13—One man flying on stand-by was looking forward to visit friends in Los Angeles. Another man needed to get there for a business conference. A woman and her mentally handicapped adult son were on their way to Canada for a family vacation.

Instead, they were caught in the middle of a national emergency and left to ponder their fate in Garden City—a place they never heard of.

Both Jeff Lockwood and Gabe Minton flew in on a United Airlines jet that left the same Washington airport (Dulles) as one of the planes that was hijacked and crashed into the Pentagon. The pair had just finished watching the in-flight movie, "A Knight's Tale," when their pilot told them they had to land for unknown reasons.

Their plane and two other commercial jets had to land in Garden City Municipal Airport after the Federal Aviation Administration ordered all U.S. flights grounded Tuesday. On those three planes were about 180 passengers, plus crew members.

"It was the same plane, carrying the same amount of people, having the same amount of fuel," Minton said of the plane used in the attack. "Only, we left an hour later. It was a couple gates down from us.

"That could have been me," he said. "I've been thinking about that a lot. I'm so thankful I'm alive. You know, there's a lot of close calls in life. Walking down the street you could get hit by a bus, or accidentally shot somewhere. But this was a really close call. It really makes you think twice about your life."

Minton said he lives in Washington, D.C., and was on his way to L.A. for a business trip. He said he flew out a day late because he worked Monday. Now, he said he's going to wait here for his co-workers to pick him up on their drive back home from the conference.

"We heard the bells go off and the flight attendants answered phones and rushed over to the cockpit," Lockwood said. "They came out with big smiles. The pilot said we had to land immediately in Garden City, Kansas. He didn't give a reason why. I figured there must be problems in L.A."

Then the men heard AM radio piped through the intercom, and learned of the tragedy.

"It was surreal," Lockwood said. "I was just sitting there trying to decide if we were under attack, our plane. I was nervous that our plane was getting hijacked right then."

Lockwood lives in West Virginia and was departing from Dulles on stand-by, a flying perk from dating a flight attendant. He said he got upgraded to first class and was looking forward to spending time with his buddies in L.A. Late Wednesday night, he took a train back to Virginia.

Linda Davis and her mentally handicapped son, Bryan, are from Houston and were flying to Canada.

"We realized as the plane cut back its engines and we could see land, we knew something was up," Davis said. "The pilot said we had to land, but he didn't know why. I just assumed there was a medical emergency on the plane, especially since we could see fire trucks and police outside our window."

Instead, they were in the middle of an American crisis.

"They said there were air traffic control problems, and it seemed that immediately after they said that, we landed,"

Minton said. "We were told the plane wasn't in danger, but when I saw how small the airport was, it was then I realized the severity. It really took a while for it to sink in. It almost felt like we were in a movie."

The three jets sat on the runway for more than an hour. Lockwood and Minton said passengers were calm and mainly were intent on listening to radio news reports.

Once they left the planes, they had to go through metal detectors and have their luggage cleared. The passengers said because the security measures took so long, many had to get out of line and use the restroom.

Because the airport isn't used to commercial passenger jets, the fire department's hook-and-ladder truck was used so the passengers could get out of the plane.

"That was a real adventure," Minton said and laughed.

After they were taken to Garden City High School's auditorium to give their names and information and to determine lodging plans, they were able to make telephone calls to family and friends.

Davis said she called her mother, who she said was hysterical with worry.

"They had phones for us, which was good because I needed to get ahold of some people and say, 'Hey, I'm alive,' " Lockwood said. "They knew I wasn't dead, but didn't know where I was ... Garden City, Kansas?"

The travelers said their eyes were glued to newscasts of the terrorist attacks while they waited at the school.

"We ate and watched CNN and saw the images of the atrocities," Minton said. "Together, we all realized what a close call this was."

During their two-day stay in Garden City, the passengers bowled, ate and went to local attractions. Wednesday, they were treated to dinner at Southwind Country Club and offered a chance to play golf. The Red Cross coordinated activities for the passengers while they were in town. Some passengers were taken to Dodge City.

Minton said he bowled for the first time since he was 8 years old. He deemed Garden City "in the middle of nowhere," but complimented the community on its hospitality and helpfulness.

"I'm glad we landed here instead of somewhere like Denver," Lockwood said. "Since there's only so many of us, it's a special event. In a bigger city, we would be like cattle."

Davis and her son were on their way to meet her husband in Canada for a vacation filled with fishing and nature walks. Now, she said they are going to fly to their destination and just go home.

"We're thankful to be here safely," she said. "But I'm terribly saddened by what occurred. There's this uneasy feeling about getting back in the air. I love to fly and take several trips, but I think we'll be staying home for awhile.

"You know, it's one thing to be at home watching all of this on television, but to be a part of it ... it really hits you more and makes us aware of just how fragile our safety is. I can't believe this happened in America."

A Ragged, Determined Army of Volunteers

Dawn Shurmaitis

Jersey City, New Jersey, September 12—We're packed shoulder to shoulder in a line hundreds of people long—students, teens, suburban women in good clothes and impractical shoes—lifting and passing 85-pound bags of fast-melting ice, 50-pound bags of Alpo for body-sniffing dogs, cases of steel-tipped construction boots, socks, aspirin, toothpaste, flashlights, bottled water and Gatorade. We're a ragged, determined army of volunteers feeding supplies to civilian soldiers waging war on "the amputation of our skyline."

We started a couple of hours after dawn, clothed in tee shirts and jeans soon gritty with soot from still-burning buildings at "Ground Zero." We know we are dusty with minute fragments of former lives of friends, family and colleagues who worked just a few days before at the World Trade Center. We wipe sweaty faces, stretch fatigued arms toward each other, load, twist and turn, load, twist and turn. A boat from Ken's Marine in Bayonne pulls up to the dock at Jersey City's Colgate Center, where just 24 hours ago a different kind of line formed to board ferries bound for Manhattan, a line of suits and ties, carrying briefcases, headed to another ordinary day on the job.

A Jersey City police officer directs 12 of us onto the boat, across a dock heaving from the waves of the constant flow of water traffic, tug boats and ferries making ceaseless, 10-minute trips across the Hudson to a surreal scene: the smoldering concrete carcasses of a long-familiar skyline. We introduce ourselves on the trip over. "Where you from?" "How long have you been here?" and the question everyone is now asking: "Where were you when the planes hit?" I work alongside Salman, a 24-year-old Pakistani computer technician who worked at World Trade. "I lost two," he tells me, as casually as if he's telling me he lost his two front teeth. The officer who's manning the crew says, "I lost four." He pauses, chokes up and wipes his eyes, making as if he's just tidying his dripping brow. "Don't give up hope," we tell him. "They're finding people

alive in there every day." He shrugs, sad and certain in his grief.

Everyone has a story. A retired cop whose wife is still on the force said she went into the flames with two captains and a lieutenant, after the planes hit and before the buildings fell. She was the only one who made it out. "She went into work this morning and saw the three empty desks. She's with the grief counselors now," he says. A man on the boat tells him: "Anybody with a turban, they should round them up and bang!—right between the eyes." Salman stands a few feet away, sharing coffee and a cigarette with another volunteer as the boat draws near the epicenter, which is cloaked in a choking debris cloud large enough to be seen from space. Salman is dark-skinned and speaks with a heavy accent—a fresh target for Americans' newfound hatred. He turns to me and points to the shattered city. "What people don't realize is that many, many Muslims were killed in there. They're Americans, too. Like me." Off to the side, another volunteer mutters: "We have to learn to hate as much as the Muslims do. From now on, it's the only way we'll be safe."

The trip over, the tugboat eases into a marina where 65-foot yachts—executive party boats—berthed just the day before. We dock below the Winter Garden atrium, a long-familiar glass entree for commuters bound for the twin towers. Miraculously, part of it still stands. But inside, under the now-blackened glass, the giant palm trees are near buried by rubble and shredded office paper—the stuff of former lives. Behind it, we see the twisted steel shards of what was once World Trade Center One. "It looks like Berlin," someone says.

We've watched the images on TV and from the Jersey shoreline for two days. But now, it is up close and horribly surreal, as if we'd stepped into a scene from a Jerry Bruckheimer film. We hear the whop-whop of the helicopter blades and the urgent whine of the cut-off saws slicing concrete and steel. We see a pair of German shepherds, tongues hanging, straining against their leashes. In the water, dead bloated rats bob in our wake. "Oh," a volunteer says, turning suddenly away. "I saw something back there. It was charred. And black. I looked to see if there was something—a ring, maybe a bracelet. But there was nothing."

The volunteers on the New York side line up as the boat comes to rest against the pilings. Their arms reach down as ours reach up to pass and pull crates of milk, orange juice, batteries and flashlights, hot burgers and fries, tarps for the coming rain, hand trucks, even cherry pies. The "hard hats" have worked around the clock since Tuesday, clearing rubble from what looks like a winter wonderland, a wonderland ghost town. "I found a spine. Just a spine. There were maybe some ligaments," Brian O'Neill tells me. Like many of the volunteers working the New York side he's a union man, from a New Jersey local. Plumbers. Crane operators. Welders. Forklift operators. They didn't even wait for the call. They just came. What they saw, they said, will stay with them the rest of their lives. "When you're over here, you don't feel like you're home," says Mike Smith, who's from Woodbridge, New Jersey. "You feel like you're in Bosnia."

New Jersey plumber Eddie Torres passed Tuesday into Wednesday digging, looking—hoping. "It's such a slow process," he says. "There's so much debris. But we gotta get rid of it and we gotta do it by hand. We're working in water up to our knees, we're breathing the dust, smelling the fire. Those firemen and those cops—they're exhausted. But nobody's complaining. This one comes from the heart. I saw those buildings go up," says Torres, who's 40. "I couldn't just watch from here after they came down."

The later the hour, the greater the number of fresh volunteers. "I'll step in for you. Go take a water break." Only a few break away. "Heads up! Boxes coming!" They come and they come and they come. Turn, twist, pass. Turn, twist, pass. New Jersey to New York and back again.

As firemen from New York, New Jersey, Pennsylvania and Connecticut pass the line, a woman reaches out to pat their shoulders. "Good luck and God bless," she says. From far down the line a cheer goes up. Like a wave, it moves down to the dock. "They found six people alive! Three of them were fire fighters!" someone with a radio yells. On the boat, two officers throw their arms around each other, tense faces finally broken by smiles.

At 2 p.m., all the police radios cackle with urgent news. "Everybody off the docks!" someone yells. We look across the river to read the smoke. When it's white, we know it's only dust from bulldozing debris. When it's black, we know there's a fresh fire, or another building fallen to the terrorists. This time, the smoke is billowing black. The police order everyone off the boats and far behind the yellow police tape lining the waterfront. "All the boats are going back empty. They're going to come back with casualties."

On the shoreline, the EMTs dive for bandages and IV lines, laying blankets on the only clear patch of shaded grass. "We got a cardiac arrest," an officer screams. Suddenly, the line splits open and the first stretcher comes through, carrying a soot-covered firefighter, face framed by an oxygen mask. "Call my family," he tells the nurses. "Let them know I'm all right." After he's revived and is lying in the shade pouring down water, a counselor cautiously approaches. "Do you need to talk about what you saw over there? I'm here for you."

At 7 p.m., the setting sun splashes the buildings across the Hudson with an eerie red light. From this side of the disaster, it looks like they are on fire. Again. We look at our forearms—they are covered by bruises from the bag or the box. "That's it for tonight, people," a cop calls out. "Come back for more tomorrow." As we prepare to leave, we're told: "Go see Lt. Brian McDonough. Tell him you earned a red-light courtesy card today." "Thank God," a volunteer says, "I run red lights all the time in Jersey City. Can he help me out with speeding tickets too?"

On the three-block walk back home I pass Jersey City Policeman Peter Midgley, who's on his way back to "Ground Zero" for another all-night shift. "We're getting a lot of support from the community. I can't tell you how many times people have passed by and given me food and coffee, told me to keep up the good work. It gives me hope."

Finally, I reach my front stoop. There's my door, and my pot of pink impatiens. I have mail. There's my newspaper. The comforting realities of daily life. I'm about to turn the key when my neighbor arrives. Until now, we've never even said hello. "How are you doing?" I ask. "Everyone all right?" "Ahh, we have trouble." It's his nephew. Tuesday, he was behind his desk on the 100th floor of World Trade. They've been to the Red Cross and all the hospitals. They've also been to the morgue. Nothing. MIA. "I was in the Mekong Delta," he says, "and I never wanted to experience anything like that again."

He heads off, to keep searching. I pull out my key. The impatiens need water, I think. Maybe tomorrow.

Humvees in D.C.

Steve Lanier

I work at 19th & L Streets NW in Washington, DC. I live near 25 & L Streets NW. On Wednesday, the day after, I awoke to find a humvee military vehicle with two military policemen at the corner of my street.

As I walked to work, I realized that there were humvees about every two blocks. It was an eerie feeling to pass three humvees on my normally uneventful walk to work. The MPs that first day were stone-faced and kept in or very close to their vehicles. I felt like saluting, but thought this might be inappropriate.

On Thursday, the MPs were still there but had loosened a bit. Today, I was almost used to the sight of the humvees. The MPs also seemed comfortable. They were interacting with us civilians (I almost had the courage to say hello) and directing traffic. The only problem being that they were obviously not experienced in traffic direction. It seemed that they were causing more jams than they were clearing. A co-worker confirmed this when she told me that she had been stuck at the corner of 19th & L Streets for half an hour last night as an MP directed the intersection into gridlock.

I'll look forward to seeing my neighborhood defense forces on the way home tonight. Funny how my perspective has changed quite quickly.

A Priest's Diary, Day 4
September 14

Fr. Julian Cassar

Today is the National Day of Mourning and Prayer, and the rest of the world joined the U.S. in prayer services and shows of solidarity and support.

I said an extra Mass at noon with another large number of people attending. I shared some encouraging reflections and even quoted the Pope's message in his Wednesday audience.

We sang together "Amazing Grace" and ended with "America the Beautiful."

In the afternoon, I visited again my friend Hans, after getting a pleading phone call from his daughter in New Orleans to kindly check on him, as he was by himself and emotionally distraught.

I spent two hours with him, and he was more calm and talked about his son.

His family will be getting together in a few days, after they've sent all the information and paperwork about his absence, including a toothbrush, an item requested by the police to check for DNA in case they cannot identify his body (or body parts).

At 7 p.m. I joined the thousands of Americans in lighting a candle and stayed in front of my church alone in silence.

Soon other parishioners joined. It was supposed to be a prayerful time, but it was impossible to control the patriotic exuberance of the many drivers going by and beeping their horns, while displaying and waving the American flag.

A New York Stroll, Three Days After

Robin O'Brien

I took a stroll this afternoon to buy some groceries. I've had this knot in my stomach ever since I found out earlier this morning that Monday I need to return to work on Wall Street. I figured that a trek to the grocery store might be therapeutic. It's nine blocks from our apartment to Fairway, the fabled, monumentally cranky grocery store that is our local. I threw on my bright yellow raincoat, grabbed the "old lady cart" (my apologies to any old ladies out there), and set off.

On the corner of 66th and Amsterdam, I passed by our local firehouse. The guys are missing eleven of their brethren. I paused and joined a small crowd scanning the walls covered in handcrafted cards and pictures, emblems of solidarity, love, and grief. Among them, a card of glitter and colored pencil, lovingly crafted by five of our girls. I imagine that the accompanying home-baked cookies have long since been devoured. Under a makeshift awning in front of the massive open doors, there's a table covered with flowers, teddy bears, and other offerings. Adjacent, small groups of friends, family members and neighbors. In the dozen times that I've been by over the past two days, the firemen have never been alone with their grief.

On Amsterdam Avenue between 66th and 67th stands the local headquarters of the American Red Cross. 66th heading toward West End is blocked off and clogged with vehicles and people of all shapes and sizes. The people in and around this makeshift staging area/parking lot/loading zone exude purpose; if only they could exude an equal measure of joy. I headed up the concrete steps and onto the plaza leading into the building. Yesterday, this area was abuzz with activity: rows of tables on either side of the revolving doors (volunteers to the right, blood donors to the left), greeters/recruiters patrolling the street in front, engaging with passersby. I swung by yesterday to sign up as a volunteer (I can't give blood because I lived in the UK for more than six months). I haven't heard anything yet, and want to help. But there was nobody outside on this dreary day, and through the fogged-up windows I could see that there was little room for a soggy guy and his rolly-cart. I retreated back down the stairs, moved on up the street, and resolved to stay close to my phone. Maybe they'll call me tomorrow.

A couple of blocks up, across from the McDonald's now overrun by a multiracial swarm of hyped-up schoolchildren, I lingered to read a flyer that caught my eye: "T.I.N.Y. (Teens In New York) bake sale for the American Red Cross. Broadway between 66th and 67th. If we're not there, please look around—we won't be far away." (I paraphrase, but that was the gist.) I wanted to go and find them, but then noticed the date: Thursday, Sept. 13. I hope they sold lots.

I continued up the road, across Broadway, onto Columbus and into Vinnie's (once proclaimed by my sublimely inebriated brother-in-law the home of "the world's greatest pizza"). I ordered a slice and Coke, stowed my cart between a rickety table and the wall, and prepared to sit down. The guy next to me looked up from his *New York Post*, moved over, and actually apologized. Not just under his breath, but while facing me and making eye contact. Astonishing. I acknowledged his apology, assuring him that it was not needed, sat down, and ate. The restaurant was silent, but for the voice of the president streaming from the radio.

I was now steeled for Fairway. One last deep breath

and in I went, alert as always for flailing elbows and Chanel handbags brandished in anger. Gotta get the last kumqat, you know. But it was quiet. When I took the elevator up to the organic section, a lady actually held the door open for me. We and another gentleman shared an "After you, no, after you" moment. On the way back down, an elevator companion agreed that the store felt different today. "It's nice," she said, "but isn't it sad that it takes a tragedy for people to act this way?" The swipy machines weren't working—"cash and check only" signs were scribbled on cardboard and taped onto the registers. I needed to jump hastily out of the line, squeeze by my fellow shoppers, plop my full carton on a corner, run across the street to an ATM, and line up all over again. I saw others doing the same. But nobody grumbled.

Over to 72nd for bagels. My wife has been working long hours comforting her kids and their parents, and I wanted to get her a treat for breakfast tomorrow morning. There was a bustle of activity on the corner of 72nd and Broadway. A guy wearing and selling cheap, hastily produced white t-shirts owned the corner by the subway station. He sold two designs, both featuring a sparkling, waving American flag: "America Under Attack" and "Evil Will Be Punished." Across the street, folks with colorful "Jammin' 105" hats and shirts collected for the Red Cross. I've seen them elsewhere as well—quite a presence for a mid-range radio station. Next door, an older gentleman sold flags from a makeshift stand next to a newspaper kiosk—flags on a stick and flags to hang out of your window. A twenty-something girl with black lipstick, ripped black clothes, and a lip ring walked by. Her hair was up, and a flag-on-a-stick flew from a secure anchor in her bun. Almost to the bagel place, I passed by a Citibank branch that has the ghostly faces of lost Citigroup employees taped in the window. One grabbed me: a young, handsome Latino man, well photographed, lovingly described. He worked on the 105th floor.

Bagels secure, I headed back down toward home. There was still a crowd down by the firehouse, but the faces were different. A young blond woman approached the table that separates the firemen from the well-wishers. One of the fireman recognized her, reached for her, and took her in his arms. They both broke down. I moved on, rounded the corner, and rode the three elevators that promised to take me home.

Safely inside, I hugged my cat, unloaded the cart, and put away the groceries. With the cabinets and fridge stocked, I felt a measure of peace, a measure of security. But the knot in my stomach was still there. I hope that it goes away by Monday.

Friday Night, Washington, D.C.

Alexandra Walker

Friends and I gathered for an impromptu candlelight vigil on the front stoop of my apartment in Washington, D.C., at around 7 p.m., as multiple e-mail messages forwarded throughout the day instructed us to do. We sought comfort with others, and convened on the stoop, as shabat started later, and the Friday night Christian jazz service was too far away. Within an hour or so police swooped in to the neighborhood and began blocking off streets—a ritual familiar to every Washingtonian and which signals the approaching motorcade of some government VIP.

But then, the unexpected happened: A procession of 200-400 people walked by, silently, holding candles and posters that read "No more violence" "No retaliation" "No discrimination against Arabs and Muslims." They handed out leaflets suggesting their loose association with the American Friends Service Committee, although questions soon revealed that most people did not know who had organized the march.

Their call for peace in the face of terrorism reminded me of a story I read here, about New Yorkers—wounds still smarting from Tuesday's attack—who grimaced at talk of revenge and air strikes. The article said they wanted no part of it, at least not now; they just wanted calm and peace. This reminds me of my work with victims of rape: In the aftermath, friends and family talk about ripping the perpetrator to pieces. In almost every case, the survivor pleas for no more violence— s/he just wants the violence to end.

I know many believe that violence committed against

the terrorists or governments that shield them is called for. Believe me, if I thought that military action would extinguish their movement(s), I would support it. But I, too, just want the violence to end. And tonight I was reminded that I am not alone.

The Coming of World War III:
An Open Letter to My Stepdaughter

Robert Manoff

Dear Kate,

As I stared into my television last night, straining desperately to make sense of Tuesday's Satanic act, Tom Friedman, who as *New York Times* correspondent in the Middle East became an expert on the meaning of death, appeared on camera, outlined against the black Jerusalem sky. "This is World War III," he declared of the Twin Towers and Pentagon attacks two days before. "*This is what World War III looks like.*"

That really shocked me. It immediately subverted the apparent normality of everyday life, which continues at this very moment for most of the world just as it did before. I'm reminded of the fact that grandmother went to work in her Navy uniform as a WAVE during World War II not far from where the World Trade Center once stood, and that life for her, as for most people in or out of uniform, continued to be normal, too. Life goes on in wartime. As it does today.

Friedman's declaration is all the more shocking since it could be true. It's certainly a self-fulfilling prophecy. I don't know whether you have had time to watch all the coverage, but it is already taken as a *fait accompli* that this country is heading off to war. The White House, the Congress, and the political class have all come to this conclusion. Warren Rudman, who recently co-chaired a blue-ribbon commission on national defense, said (on Jim Lehrer) that ground troops and many, many American casualties will be necessary. Former

Secretary of State Warren Christopher agreed. Talking heads speak knowledgeably about a war that will last for years. JFK's prophetic vision of a "long twilight struggle" against Communism was invoked by someone, and within 24 hours became a cliche. Joe Biden (on ABC) spoke about the World Trade Center attack having "inoculated the American people" against fearing the necessarily high casualties from this necessary war.

To someone of my generation, the specter of high casualties immediately raises questions such as, Will World War III lead us back to the draft? Could my 16-year-old son end up fighting in some jungle, desert, or mountaintop? Could this be another Hundred Years War, and if so will your young son grow up to serve, too? (Why am I only thinking about the boys? In a post-feminist world the draft would call up women: will my daughter go into combat shoulder-to-shoulder with yours?) Far-fetched? Perhaps. But, then, I remember the Vietnam War all too well.

One of the lessons we should have learned from the last few days is that what seemed inconceivable to most people 72 hours ago was actually inevitable all along (experts have been warning each other of such attacks for years). So here's the next thing that is "inconceivable," but actually inevitable: a biological, chemical, or nuclear attack by terrorists on the United States. The next time we are glued to our TV sets, it could be to watch some city glow in the dark.

The only question is: What do we do now in light of such inevitability? The only defense, such people as Friedman and Bush and our leaders and advisors and eminent journalists are arguing, is to fight and win World War III quickly, before Osama bin Laden can strike again. Fair enough. But here's something else that's inevitable: Because of what we as a country *do* around the world, and because of what we *are* — and what we represent — to the rest of the world, another bin

Laden will appear in place of this one. (No, I'm falling into a trap here. What is really inevitable is that we always fall into the trap of thinking that mass social movements are really the work of malevolent individuals, the proverbial "outside agitators" we invoke when our usual explanations fail us.) So here's what's actually inevitable: World War III may eliminate bin Laden, but what of the thousands, or millions, or even tens of millions who already see his struggle as their struggle, and who will prosecute it and carry it home (our home) with or without him?

They hate us. And to begin to understand why we need only recall that Jefferson, reflecting on the consequences of slavery for the future of his new nation, recognized that inequity breeds violence: "I tremble for my country when I reflect that God is just." He was right to do so. Lincoln concluded that a country half slave and half free could not long endure, but he did not do so until millions of men on both sides had signed up to fight a war also deemed inevitable, and not until we Americans had loosed upon ourselves a paroxysm of violence unmatched in human history.

There are many in the world today who now believe it to be half slave and half free, and the problem with thinking about responding to Tuesday's attack by means of World War III is that although we have just become familiar with *defeat,* no one has any idea of what *victory* could possibly look like. How do you "win" a war of the kind that is now being planned if you can't envisage the victory that would end it? Yes, we can say that we will have achieved victory when the U.S. is safe from terrorism, but do we seriously understand what we will have to do to other peoples, and possibly ourselves, to achieve this objective? Was it Tacitus who said of the Romans after their victory over Carthage, "They made a desert and called it peace"? Will we become the new Centurions, and what will we have to wreak on the world in order to declare it pacified?

Reading back into history, I have always been puzzled by the pages that spoke to me of the enthusiasm with which so many wars seem to have been greeted. The Civil War, World War I, World War II -- by the time the first shot was fired, there seemed to be a sense of inevitability about their coming, and a palpable relief that they had finally arrived.

Kate, this is what, finally, came back to me last night, when, late into the morning, I sat in the dark watching our American people sit around the "campfire" that Peter Jennings rightly remarked that the TV has become and discuss the coming of war. There in the dark, finding myself almost convinced by the sober arguments offered by men and women of evident experience, I suddenly realized that I had heard such words before, had encountered the inevitability with which wise men sat contemplating the immolation of themselves and their societies with equanimity, with reason, with justice, and even with care. These were the words I had puzzled over in my books, in accounts of how the Blue and the Grey, the "Frenchies" and the "Krauts," the "Yanks" and the "Nips," willingly, deliberately, rationally, brought down the temples of their own civilizations in the very same dust that now coats the streets of Manhattan.

I sat there in the dark, Kate, and trembled for us all.

Love,
Rob

Heading Downtown

Larry Hartsell

Thanks, Robin, for your interesting account. I'm delighted
to find that another Blue Ear member is my neighbor and also
shops at the loony Fairway Supermarket. My partner and I
also took a stroll in the same neighborhood on that very day,
and observed the firehouse and the Red Cross headquarters
(noting, incidentally, that gays like ourselves are still forbidden
to give blood).

I myself had a stroll today, Saturday the 15th, downtown,
on a bright, beautiful day. Most of the subway trains I normally
use were stopped at 14th St. or above because of the emergency
to the south, but after some false starts I figured out that the
N and R stopped at Canal Street station. Streets going below
Canal have been blocked by the police and the national guard,
and you must show proof you live or work south of there to
get further downtown. Canal Street is a crazy bazaar
street with cheap merchandise spilling out into the street, in
full operation despite the grim scene going on just to the
south. There was a run on $3 t-shirts showing the twin-tower
skyline. Computer-made posters tacked up along the street
showed photos of people last seen on the 86th, the 105th, the
impossibly high floors of the WTC.

I managed to evade the blockade by walking down Baxter
Street in Chinatown, toward the courthouse buildings, in a
corridor lined with yellow police tape, down the street with
virtually no traffic, patrolled by guards and police. I crept by
them, hoping they wouldn't ask for ID, and they didn't. At one
point an angry young guard barked at the crowd to "clear the

street," for no apparent reason, and his behavior reminded me that we ought never let teenagers with guns be in charge of anything.

At Reade Street I took a right, along with a number of other people, some holding flags or wearing American flag t-shirts, and before long found myself crossing Broadway, then Church Street, which borders on the WTC further south. I helped myself to a free face mask, which I put over my hat in case of need. Smoke and steam were still rising from the site, but it wasn't until Greenwich Street that I could look south and see, just as the smoke lifted for a moment, the wreckage of WTC 7 in front of a smoking mountain range, the compressed remains of the 110 stories of WTC 1 and 2.

I stood up on a police barricade to take some photos, looking past the blocked avenue, the parked ambulances, the amateur photographers, the Battery Park City residents trying to get past the barriers, the Channel 4 trucks filming the site from afar—until I heard a shouted order: "Don't stand on the barricades!" I reluctantly complied—unlike a couple of other intent watchers who pretended not to hear.

I almost didn't notice that several wrecked vehicles had been stored on the street in ordinary parking spaces. Two squashed cars occupied one space, a burnt-out carcass of a car on top of a flattened white Cadillac. A police van had been hit by falling debris, cab squashed.

A few stores were open to the street, and free health bars and bottled water were everywhere. A man carrying a box of bag lunches was yelling "Free food!" and I was so hungry that I took one of the brown bags, feeling guilty that I wasn't a rescuer, but he said that so much food has been donated that I should "eat, or it will just go to waste." The bag I chose contained a bagel with cream cheese, a hard-boiled egg, a crushed cookie, and a couple of "fun size" Snickers bars.

I returned past Bubby's, closed, but surrounded by dozens

of buckets of bottled water there for the taking, and then past the former home of JFK Jr. on N. Moore Street, through a few ghostly shuttered streets with graffiti-ridden metal doors, and then passed the barricades to return suddenly into the pandemonium of Canal Street, where people were craning their necks to get a glimpse of the smoking WTC site.

Some Measure of Stability

Shanty Nambiar

At 2:15 a.m. on September 15 the phone rang, jolting my husband and me from an uneasy sleep. "They have found my brother. He is dead," she said, her voice calm, belying the shock and grief of the past 72 hours. It took us several dazed seconds to realize who she was—one of the dozens of family members we had interviewed earlier in the day for stories about the victims of New York's World Trade Center attack.

Like many other correspondents who were dealing with families and friends looking for the missing, I felt powerless. The phone call was a turning point for me. The husbands, wives, parents and children were no longer just faceless strangers we called on a routine disaster assignment. They had become a part of me just as I had become a part of the larger story. Their tears became mine. Their fears became mine.

Until Tuesday, my life was that of the quintessential New Yorker. Until Tuesday, I was an international wire-service reporter, writing about debt defaults, currency crises, and the financial markets of emerging economies. That changed as I emerged from the No. 2 train into the clear blue sky of the financial district, beneath the towering shadows of the World Trade Center. I was late for work and cursing Manhattan's subway system, infamous for its delays, as I ran up the tunnel's stairs onto Park Place and Church Street, barely three blocks from the disaster site.

Police, firefighters and FBI agents wandered on the sidewalks. Herds of people had been corralled onto the streets across from me. I looked down Church Street and saw what

I could not then fathom: parts of a plane. My heart sank as I glanced up and saw balls of smoke and flames bellowing from the upper portions of the towers. I ran towards the BridgeNews headquarters in 3 World Financial Center on Vesey Street, a block from the World Trade Center. Grabbing my cell phone, I dialed my office and my editors. But the circuits were overloaded. I called my husband. A busy signal.

Fear and shock mounted as I crossed one police barrier after another, inching ever closer to the World Trade Center towers. The journalist in me needed to comprehend, needed some answers. Bits of news—hijacked jets crashing into the 100-plus stories of steel and glass, a fallen Pentagon, a plane spotted in a Pennsylvania field—started filtering towards me. Fact and rumor swirled into one incomprehensible story. "They have hijacked 6 planes," one hysterical woman shouted at no one in particular. Another said the White House had been bombed.

I was soon standing beneath 7 World Trade Center on Vesey Street, glancing at my building across the street in an attempt to locate other reporters from my work. That building would collapse later that afternoon. I found a pay phone and, with shaking hands, I fumbled with a quarter. Again, busy phone lines. Then someone shouted, "You guys shouldn't be in this area." Police officers ordered people to start fleeing the area, saying the towers were in danger of collapse. But many stayed put. I ducked under a police barricade and ran one block north. At that very moment emergency crews rushed past, headed for the burning buildings. Hundreds of them would not return.

Then the unthinkable happened. A deafening, ear-splitting thunder filled the air. The south tower shook and tilted, before crashing upon itself like a giant deck of cards. A dark plume of smoke rose upwards towards the sky before turning into a mushroom cloud that descended on the streets.

People ran screaming. Sirens wailed as police cars, fire trucks and ambulances raced out of the avalanche of glass, steel and fire. Office paper swirled into the air before settling calmly on the road.

I outran the smoke to a parking lot near Greenwich Avenue and tried to catch my breath and make some sense of what I had witnessed. My eyes stung, my lungs burned. But I was alive. I automatically punched away at numbers on my cell phone. It did not work. I could see the north tower, bellowing smoke and debris but still standing. I recall saying, "Please, please don't collapse," thinking there was still some hope. People around me cried; some hugged strangers; others froze in fear. But no one panicked.

Some twenty-five minutes later, the second tower began to sway. It rumbled and collapsed like a pancake, one floor sandwiching the other, trapping hundreds of people underneath. As I turned to run, another wall of dark black smoke, acrid burning smell, debris, sirens and screaming voices hurtled towards me. White ash rained on everyone as fire trucks and buses, windows blown out, appeared eerily out of the smoke. Police cars were scorched. People were falling on the sidewalks, coughing and gasping for breath. A man begged three firefighters, covered in ash, to rescue a friend trapped in one of the collapsed buildings. I gave him two quarters for a phone call, and as I moved away he stood there, tears rolling down his face.

I finally found my husband, also a journalist, at St. Vincent's Manhattan Hospital in Greenwich Village covering the disaster for his newspaper. Still in shock, I took on the role of the reporter, feeding him and other correspondents in the press area firsthand accounts of what I had witnessed. Television and radio channels interviewed me. I don't recall what I said. I interviewed the friends and families of the missing and scribbled notes, as New York City Mayor Rudolph

W. Giuliani gave an impromptu press conference.

We arrived home at 1:30 am to some grim realities. I was one of thousands of displaced workers, who had no office to return to and soon to join the temporary unemployment line. I had left my professional life behind in my office—source lists, rolodexes, business cards, reference books—all ingredients to validate one as a journalist. I still have my United Nations and New York City police press credentials, small reminders of life before the kamikaze attacks. I do not know when I will be able to retrieve my personal items from 3 WFC, now structurally damaged and part of a crime scene.

The situation is complicated by the fact that Bridge Information Systems, the parent company of BridgeNews, was in the process of disposing of its various divisions and affiliates. My employment with BridgeNews, the second largest international news service in the world, would come to an end shortly. Over the next few days, I learned that Bridge's approximately 500 employees at 2 WTC, 3 WFC and One State Street Plaza were unharmed, except for three employees who suffered minor injuries.

There is a vast emptiness where the World Trade Center and surrounding towers once loomed. The area and the WFC had been my second home for nearly four years. I recall the hallways I walked, the glass-enclosed overpass I crossed, the twists and turns that took me through an underground maze of stores, restaurants and the Winter Garden. A sales receipt from Cosi Sandwich Bar in the World Financial Center is tucked away in my wallet. The date reads September 10. I remember sources at U.S. brokerage Cantor Fitzgerald & Co., who perished on the upper floors of 1 World Trade Center.

In the days since, I have drawn some measure of stability by writing about the destruction of the World Trade Center, by foraying into what is called "Ground Zero" armed with masks, and by fielding calls from friends and family around the world. After all I had traveled the world, seen orphans with AIDS in Uganda and unmentionable poverty among Palestinian refugees in Israel, heard tales of terror during the massacres in East Timor. But nothing quite prepares one, even a journalist, for a disaster so close to home.

A Lone Sneaker

Dawn Shurmaitis

September 14 — Hard hat volunteer Eric Woelfel runs down the ramp to the ferry that will take him and dozens of other construction workers from Jersey City, New Jersey to Ground Zero. "My heart is in my throat," he says as the boat makes its way across a choppy Hudson to New York City. "But I couldn't just sit home and watch it on TV. I had to come. To help."

Help is all the volunteers want to give. But as soon as Woelfel's boat leaves the Colgate pier shortly after 7:30 a.m. word reaches the tent where dozens more union workers are lined up, ready to do their part for their country. "They just told everybody to go home. It's a money job now," says a disgusted union official who's been shuffling union volunteers from New Jersey, New York, Pennsylvania, Connecticut, Maryland and all points East to the site of the World Trade Center disaster. The union man, wet and weary from three days and nights of coordinating relief efforts from the Jersey City side, immediately gets on his cell phone. What he learns earns a collective groan from the crew. "The job's been contracted out, over in New York," he says. "They're telling me not to send anyone else over."

Woelfel, a construction manager from Bear Creek, Pennsylvania, made the first boat Friday morning. He'd driven in the night before and bunked with friends in Jersey City. When his boat docks at the marina where executive yachts parked until Tuesday morning, he and the rest of the crew get their first look at the devastation. "It's so eerie," he says. "It's the twilight zone."

Spackle bucket by spackle bucket, the volunteers who'd left behind jobs and family to lend their muscle to the relief effort carry rubble from what was once the World Trade Center. They call themselves "the bucket brigade." Crawling like ants up the rubble that is the epicenter of the disaster zone, the volunteers pass empty buckets up, fill them with bite-sized chunks of shattered concrete, and pass them down the line again. "We must have filled 400 buckets this morning alone," Woelfel says.

Bracing himself against a cold wind that's blown since daybreak, crane operator Louie Mari struggles to fit his rain gear over his tee shirt and jeans. He's already put in 60 hours manning his "clamshell," and his fingers just can't seem to work anymore. "This machine is supposed to be used for construction, for building things—not for this," he says. "We have to go piece by piece, careful like, because we're still looking for bodies. It takes time." In front of him a team of firefighters creep alongside the mountain of debris. "This is us right here," he says, gesturing to the remains of once-mighty twin towers. "Those towers, they represented unity. They can take the building down, but they can't take our hearts down."

Inside a building marked Dow Jones, wet and weary firefighters and police officers maneuver over snaking fire hoses to collapse into office chairs where World Trade employees sat just three days before. A lone, dust-covered palm tree still stands in the corner. John Dowden, a carpenter from New Jersey, has been working the line since 11 p.m. Thursday. What he saw, he says, will linger long after the last bucket is filled.

"I saw a hand sticking up out of the rubble. What caught my eye was his wedding ring," he says. "I'll never forget the smell." He says that his local alone has 60 men missing—they were remodeling floors at World Trade when the planes hit.

"This city has become one," he says, looking around at the men and women clad in the uniform of the volunteer: hard hats and rain gear, steel-toed boots and padded gloves, faces streaked with grit and determination. "No matter what color you are—and we got them all here today—it doesn't matter," he says, facing the Bell Atlantic building, which union ironworkers have topped with a huge American flag. "Today, I'm proud to be American."

Everywhere, the volunteers have left their mark, scrawling messages in dust caked on the walls, some alongside handprints: "The Lord Be With Us All. God Bless You." "It's Time Now for all Good Men to Come to the Aid of Their Country." "Wanted: Bin Laden. Dead" "We Are All One People." "Unite." "Remember." "Let Them Know We Were Here." "For the Victims: RIP."

Danger is everywhere. The men circumvent a 22-inch concrete column that shifted six inches from the impact. They leap over a small river of muddy gray water flowing past steel girders twisted like strands of fusilli. Ron Areres rests against an overturned Ford, its alarm system still sounding. Inside, a notebook sits on the seat. There are phone numbers for Bobby and Heather, phone calls that will probably never be made. Everyone has a reason for being there. "I helped build these buildings," Areres says. "I had to come." His partner in rubble is NYPD Det. Joe Sikorski. "I lost a fireman friend," he says. "We used to play ball together."

The men talk about the hatred that's blowing through the city like so much debris. "They fire-bombed a grocery store in my neighborhood in Brooklyn last night," says one. "The guy who ran it, he was the nicest guy. But I remember when I was growing up, just after World War II, there were some Russians who lived behind us and we hated them. At first. But then we started playing with them and it was all right."

Areres pulls on a facemask to guard against the acrid smell of burning plastic and prepares to rejoin the front line. "Let's go back to work, boys. What can we do?" he says to a line leader. "Just tell us what to do."

Inside 200 Liberty Street and up a grand staircase now slick with muck, a set of computers and security monitors at the guard desk still blink commands. There's an empty chair and a coffee mug with a chubby Santa printed on the side. A notebook is open to a page marked "Evacuation Drills." Under the desk a briefcase lies open. Inside, a hairbrush, calculator and unsharpened pencils. On the floor, an inter-office envelope with the name "Glen Braham" yet to be crossed out.

Outside, in the shadow of World Trade Two, there sits a lone sneaker. A calendar open to September 11. A checkbook and pocketbook. An Italian cookbook. A cell phone and a flower pot. Two baby strollers, side by side. A photo album filled with pictures of a smiling Japanese man, his arms around what look like his mom and dad. "That's what really hit home for me," Woelfel says. "That till Tuesday, that album was probably sitting on some guy's desk. Now, it's here. In this. I should probably take the pictures and give them to somebody. Maybe they'll make it back to that poor guy's family."

A fresh fire crew from Levittown, New York arrives on the scene. A fireman says: "We got one guy lost here. We gotta do something." Fire Chief David Fisk calls over: "We didn't lose anybody—not yet. Let's go."

Inside one of the few buildings still safe and standing, New Jersey resident Rob McGovern pulls on a fresh pair of dry socks, his hands shaking from the raw cold and steady drizzle that's permeated the fourth day of rescue and relief operations. "I guess I'm about soaked through and chilled to the bone," he says. "But it pales in comparison. This saved me," he says, gesturing to the warm clothes donated by stores and households across America. "Now I can go back to the front wave."

Stores and restaurants that once served the 50,000 or more who came to World Trade Center every workday ring Ground Zero, where police and military personnel now patrol, boarding up open doors and blown-out windows, guarding against the casual looting that's part of every disaster. Inside a mini mart half a block from World Trade One, batches of still-fresh flowers stand in buckets, the same kind of ordinary spackle buckets now used to carry concrete. The salad bar is stocked with oriental noodles, potato salad and greens— the spoons in mid-dig. A *Daily News* newspaper for Tuesday, September 11 waits by the door for a sale that will never come. The door to the ATM machine is open. Most of the stores' shelves remain stocked—but all of the cigarettes are gone. A firefighter taking a brief break to warm his hands points to the overhead security cameras. "I wonder what they recorded," he says. "I wonder if anyone will ever see it."

When a volunteer exits the store, two uniformed officers dash over. "What were you doing in that store?" they demand. "I was just getting out of the rain," the volunteer says. "Where's your ID?" they ask. "I don't have any. I just came over on the tugboat from Jersey City—I was bringing over a bag of burgers. I'm going back now. Honest." "You gotta come with us," they say, leading her off to a police van parked on the corner of South End Avenue, where a fallen sign pointing toward the downed towers reads "Dead End."

Bloom Off Rose for Struggling Florist

Wei Gu

New York, September 15—Even though Heart to Heart Floral Decorators on Beaver Street was open on Saturday, the store was empty. Hundreds of flowers were in the shop, half on the shelf, half in the trash.

The store was one of the first to open in the Wall Street area after September 11. Although the attack twisted and destroyed tons of steel, the store's delicate and perishable flowers survived.

The morning of the attack, $5,000 worth of flowers, including white and pink orchid lilies from Holland, yellow roses from South America, and purple spidersmom from Hawaii, were delivered to Heart and Heart. They would normally be sold out within a few days, bringing in $8,000 to $10,000. That shipment would be a total loss, said the store's owner.

"I don't care about those flowers, but I am really worried about the future business and the economy," said George, who declined to disclose his last name. "I hope that we can all survive somehow."

Most of George's customers work on Wall Street. He has delivered flowers to all three of the buildings that collapsed—No.1, No.2 and No.7 of the World Trade Center complex. Although he doesn't know how many of his customers he will meet again, he was most concerned about a woman on the 35th floor of the first tower, to whom he delivered a bunch of birthday flowers on Monday. A man in Britain called in the $50 order last week; he phoned the store on Tuesday afternoon and was relieved to be told that the flowers had been delivered before the crash.

Heart to Heart helped a number of people after the attack. Following the collapse of the twin towers, people were screaming and running aimlessly on the street, blinded by the dust. George invited them in, gave them water and shelter, and let them use his phone. After a while some people moved on toward the north, new people came in, bringing in more dust and rubble, and George continued to provide supplies. "I tried to calm them down, but we were shaking ourselves," said George, while sweeping an inch of ash from a shelf. He didn't close the store until 2 p.m., when the police came in and said that he and others should leave.

Although the attacks cut off most of the electricity in the World Trade Center area, Heart to Heart's refrigerator is still working. Flowers have been preserved at 40 degrees, and most are still in good condition. But George insists on throwing away at least half of them. "We are not like a liquor store—the longer they put goods on the shelf, the better they will be," George said. "If I still want to have my customers again, I need to throw out all the old flowers." He has lost at least $3,000 worth of flowers, which would have been sold for up to $6,000.

But the surviving flowers may still go into the trash soon. Last Saturday morning it was quiet in the store, and he didn't sell a single flower. Every now and then the phone rang, but the calls were from relatives or friends of the staff.

George hopes that when the New York Stock Exchange opens on Monday, the traffic and customers will be back. But streets below Canal Street are still closed for cars, and the whole Wall Street area reportedly may not ever allow cars again. Cleaning up will take at least three months, so there won't even be many pedestrians. At least 6,000 potential customers in the World Trade Center are gone now. What's more, many of those who survived may move away, taking away Heart to Heart's business with them.

Above all, the mood has changed after the tragedy, a blow to Heart to Heart. "When people are happy, they order more flowers," said George. "I don't think anybody is in the mood for shopping now." Having worked for four years in the financial district, he knows that a growing economy brings good sentiment and good business. Last year when the stock market boomed, his business also hit a record. This year the market tanked, and his business suffered, too.

However, George is still upbeat about his business, ordering another $5,000 worth of flowers, which will arrive this Tuesday. He expects an increase in demand for memorial and funeral services and promises a 30 percent discount for those orders. "Flowers will bring us a little hope when New York recovers," he said.

A Priest's Diary, Day 5
September 15

Fr. Julian Cassar

All sports events were cancelled for this weekend, and we expect many more people attending church as well as for confessions.

We make ourselves available for counselling services, as many still incredulous people are seeking emotional support, and the first place they look for is church.

Today the first moving funeral took place, of Father Mychal Judge OFM, the NYC Fire Department Chaplain, who died while administering the last rites to another fallen fireman.

After he was killed, four fellow firemen carried his body to a nearby church and laid his body in front of the altar.

They then joined hands and recited the prayer of St Francis while covering his body with a sheet and placing his stole and badge on his lifeless body.

This was the first of thousands of funerals that will be taking place in the coming weeks. Soon I will prepare to bury Peter Klein, comfort his family, and probably concelebrate in many other funeral Masses.

One final point to ponder. Next to the World Trade Centre is Holy Trinity Church, surrounded by a graveyard.

While all nearby skyscrapers were also badly damaged, the cemetery is littered with rubble and debris, but the church remained intact, with the spire still standing.

The metal and concrete of the Twin Towers collapsed, but the spirit of faith and the presence of God survives.

Let us remember and pray for the New York martyrs, whose feast day should be celebrated annually on September 11.

In Manhattan, September 16

Jay Rosen

Shrines to the dead at bus shelters, hospitals, parks. Vigils nightly. Along the West Side Highway and 34th Street, streets lined with big boxes of food and supplies for the rescue workers — far more than will be needed. Ambulances moving in formation, seven, eight at a time. Subway lines that just stop, discouraging further movement downtown. Police motorcades tearing about. Nervous glances when aircraft appear overhead: "... commercial jet?" All over the city, desperate notices asking about the vanished, which many people stop to read. At night the floodlights from ground zero make the southern sky glow. And the smoke keeps rising from fires that burn underground, as if destruction itself could sink roots into New York.

"Collapsed" is not the right word for what happened to the Towers; they were somehow turned to dust. Steel beams, glass window panes, cement and gypsum board made those dark surging clouds you've seen on television replays. Engineers are starting to explain how, but what engineer can explain dust that was steel and must now have in it human DNA?

Do you want to know what we think about? That is what I think about. Last night I made a friend show me how he downloads video from the Web. I felt ready to watch the Towers go down again and again. Hannah Arendt says somewhere in her writings: "The struggle to believe the evidence of our senses is at the root of all moral life." Show me how to download so I can begin.

I think about ecstasy. The ecstasy of that half-trained

pilot as he approached the moment of impact and his instant transport to heaven. What time means for me, time did not mean for him. This much I know: there's a deep rupture there. We call him a suicide. They call him a martyr. There is too much optimism in this language, which relies on our power to name things and thus define their sense. The struggle to believe the evidence of our senses is a struggle with the lie of language, which cannot hold Tuesday's evidence or make it available to the human mind. When I reflect on that I would sooner have poets bring me the news.

Think about this, because as a professor of journalism I have: There were more people killed in one hour this week than in all the news stories from all those years of trouble in Northern Ireland. The time scale of one is incommensurate with the time scale of the other, although both are held to be "news." You can have funerals with bodies in Belfast and Gaza. We will have our funerals in New York, but most of the bodies are somewhere in that surging cloud I'll watch again and again on video.

Television reporters do what they can within the word games they've mastered, but their subject exceeds their sense. You cannot report on a rupture in time, you can only stand near the scene and report right into it. There is a reason candlelight vigils are silent vigils. And there is a good moral sense in the three minutes of silence the people of the Netherlands observed this week. They "said it all," and when I think about thanking them tears cloud my sight.

Soon workers will be sweeping up the dust in lower Manhattan. The traffic will eventually return. Pedestrians will walk the streets again. And the struggle to believe our senses will enter a new phase. So when tomorrow's news from New York tells of the city getting back to normal, hold onto your doubts and imagine a poet with a microphone reporting live from a rupture.

The View from the Frozen Zone

Andrew Ross

For several days last week, in the wake of the attacks, downtown New Yorkers lived in what the authorities termed a "frozen zone." Troops in urban camouflage (lately a fashion world favorite) policed the traditional boundary of Fourteenth Street that divides Downtown from the rest of New York, and—many of its denizens like to believe—from the rest of the country. Additional checkpoints on Houston, Canal, and Chambers streets heightened the feel of an occupied, semi-militarized zone. Outsiders with no claim on residency were barred from entry. Even in the age of the three-thousand-dollar rental, downtowners had still imagined themselves in that "other country" which wry nineteenth-century cartographers had depicted as *le pays de boheme*. Suddenly, now, this was the least urbane of urban quarters, and on our most civil of streets and avenues a freakish assortment of paramilitary vehicles held sway, bearing unfamiliar acronyms.

Of course, our mute sector was not the real center of attention; it was serving as a buffer—a temporary urban sacrifice zone—for the precinct to the south, where the hapless thousands who worked in the nerve center of global capitalism had tragically fallen. Living in such close proximity to the citadel of finance has always provoked unease and ambivalence. In the 1960s, the Downtown Lower Manhattan Association, spearheaded by the Rockefellers, spawned a plan that incorporated Robert Moses's dream of a Cross-Manhattan Expressway on Broome Street. Everything to the south was to be the preserve of the business community. Soho artists, among other community activists, fought the plan, and prevailed. Over time, the northern border of the business quadrant was fixed at Chambers Street, and now this was where the National Guard had established its final no-go line.

When I first took up residence in Tribeca, at the exit to the Holland Tunnel, I often joked that if something went catastrophically wrong in the neighborhood, I could always run to New Jersey. The joke soured a little after the 1993 bombing, and is now drained of its potential humor. Yet, the twin towers had always been a catastrophic site. After 1993, I researched the buildings' history for a book chapter titled "Bombing the Big Apple" (in *The Chicago Gangster Theory of Life*), and learned of its own role in the devastation of a downtown neighborhood. The project plan had displaced over 30,000 small merchants and their employees, and the new buildings were viewed from the first as unsafe, even by the city's Fire Department. After the first of many fires, in 1970, an Assistant Attorney General commented on the city department's bleak assessment: "We chose not to further alarm our people ... In the case of a real fire like *The Towering Inferno*, we knew there was no escape."

The WTC had been the last of the postwar urban renewal projects, and it was the first of the new office complexes to embody the city's transformation from the nation's largest manufacturing town into a center for financial services. The development of the towers razed a neighborhood that was especially rich in the kind of diversity that characterized business and trade before global finance took over. *The WPA Guide to New York*, published in 1939, describes the area as the Lower West Side, an appellation that has disappeared entirely: "Though this district has a few modern skyscrapers with impressive marble facades, the character of the neighborhood is derived from produce sheds, crates, smells of fruit and fish of Washington Market, and the amazing variety of retail shops selling radios, pets, garden seeds, fireworks, sporting goods, shoes, textiles, and church supplies." The Washington Market at the neighborhood's core overflowed with the produce of world trade: "Caviar from Siberia, Gorgonzola cheese from Italy, hams from Flanders, sardines from Norway, English partridge, native quail, squabs, wild ducks, and pheasant." Its residential center was the Syrian Quarter, composed of "Turks, Armenians, Arabs, and Greeks." The guide's authors note that "although the fez has given way to the snap-brim, and the narghile has been abandoned for cigarettes, the coffee houses and the tobacco and confectionery shops of the Levantines still remain." Shish kebabs, knafie, baclawa, and other Middle Eastern specialities were widely available in neighborhood restaurants, and stores sold "graceful earthen water jars," "tables inlaid with mother of pearl," and "Syrian silks of rainbow hues."

All of these commercial goods and practices, dating back to the storied Levantine trade of the Ancient World, were cleared away to make room for a physical structure that, for thirty years, was called the World Trade Center. Now, all that may be left is a lavish memorial to the accidental victims of an economic system that tried to impose new rules of global trade, at its own peril. Yet long before September 11th, the victims in other countries had numbered in the tens of millions, starved and crushed over the years by the impact of the financialization of the world economy.

By chance, I had recently done a word search for Osama bin Laden in the digital files of my research for that book chapter. The files, culled from the thousands of pages of media coverage of the 1993 bombings, bore no mention of his name. In 1994, at least, bin Laden was simply not on the radar screen as a potential enemy of the state. Indeed, he had only recently been a CIA asset, a vital U.S. ally in the last of the official Cold War conflicts in Afghanistan. Today he, and others on the suspect list, are America's chickens coming home to roost, to cite a dictum of Malcolm X that is currently doing the rounds. Though every corporate TV channel and newspaper in the country will deny it, many Americans know we are reaping some of the vast carnage that Washington has sown in the decades since it began to oversee the petroleum concessions of the Gulf states.

The day after, since I have neighborhood ID, the authorities allow me to go downtown as far as Chambers Street. Past the checkpoint on Canal Street I find some bizarre sights, like the crushed cars piled on top of one another that have been dumped outside one of Tribeca's fanciest restaurants. The local bourgeoisie is nowhere to be seen, and the folks on the streets are artsy, indie types—the kind of folks who used to live here. In my building on Laight Street, it's the older residents who have stayed, and the newer ones who decamped. I run into some people I haven't seen in ten years. The throaty white dust thickens as I approach Chambers Street, buzzing now with new kinds of traffic. All of the marks of authority—city, county, state, and federal—merge here, alongside fringe, paramilitary organizations like the Salvation Army and the Guardian Angels (New York City's version of vigilanteism, circa 1980). A machine gunner atop a jeep stands guard outside a shuttered bank.

Four blocks to the south, when the smoke and fumes momentarily clear, I can see the mangled wreck of the towers, and every so often, the sunlight catches what looks like a flame. I manage to get access to the bridge over the highway that links the Borough of Manhattan Community College to Stuyvesant High School. For as far as I can see north, the West Side Highway is crammed full of heavy trucks of all shapes and sizes, waiting to cart off the shrapnel. The yachts off the piers are bobbing merrily. The trees in Washington Market Park are snow-white with dust. Someone has traced out graffiti in the dust on the bridge: "Fuck Woodstock! Time to Fight!" A sentiment to which the decent New Yorker can only say, Oy!

I am guessing that the graffitist was not a visceral, flag-waving warmonger of the sort that is easily caricatured or, sad to say, easily found in the present climate. Something in the phrasing of the message suggested that he or she had some knowledge or experience of the discarded option, and, at one time or another, may even have embraced the pacifist spirit that Woodstock embodied. Let us give the benefit of the doubt and assume this was indeed the handiwork of a peacenik who had decided, under the force of circumstance, to trade a ploughshare for a sword. If so, the implications are all the more doleful. Now, more than ever, we need to remember how and why the peace movement blossomed into mass acceptance thirty years ago. Two full generations have grown up since Woodstock and Vietnam in a world laboriously excavated and worked over in order to reconstruct, on behalf of our gilded youth, the myths of American innocence and noblesse oblige. How many times is it possible for American innocence to be shattered? In my estimation, this has been happening with some regularity, at least every two generations, since the Mexican War of the 1840s.

Perhaps, this time, things will be different. Perhaps these really are extraordinary circumstances, which will prompt truly inventive responses. Perhaps we will astonish the world with solutions that will not inter tens of thousands more civilians. As for the perpetrators, let the U.S. pursue them through the channels of international justice, at the Hague and elsewhere. Demystify the would-be martyrs by putting them on trial. Nothing reduces the all-powerful to banality more effectively than a court proceeding in full public view.

But don't hold your breath. No one in high office is capable of surprises and, besides, Bush and his circle need a war to bolster their approval ratings. As always, we must now fall back on our own resources—education, public debate, and movement mobilization—to supplant the grisly drumbeats of war with the tempo and cadence of justice.

Homeless Man Loses Home

Carol Lee

The twin towers had been the roof over Richard Morelli's head, the walls of his bedroom, and the neighborhood he made his home since the early 1980s. "They call me the mayor of Greenwich Street," he says, referring to downtown New Yorkers, like Ted, the owner of Barry's Pizza, the guys at Firehouse No. 10, and Alicia, who lives in a nearby apartment with her husband, two kids, and a golden retriever.

Morelli governed only between Rector and Liberty Streets. He rarely left the World Trade Center area. Sometimes he'd find a warm nook in Bowling Green Park behind Wall Street's infamous bull. On nicer days he might ride the ferry to Staten Island, but he's an old man now, with a gnarled, gray beard and a bad back. Besides, he's been making friends around the Financial District since he worked at the New York Stock Exchange. The young Morelli traded on the floor before working at Lazard Freres for 17 years. He remembers when those towers went up, too. His wife had just left him, his boss let him go, and he could get a bottle of vodka for under $5.

Rather than trek to the parking garage, Morelli put on his sweatshirt and settled in at a small park just three blocks south of the World Trade Center. It was a Monday night. He figured he'd meet up with the others in the morning after saying hello to the guys at No. 10. The next morning was Tuesday, September 11, and he's yet to find all his constituents.

What seemed to him only minutes after the piercing of each tower, Morelli's home crumbled to the ground and chased him to the river. He tried to run, but his aching back idled him. Eventually he made his way to South Ferry. The left sleeve and the right shoulder of his blue jacket ripped during his escape. But every stitch of the name "Mike" remained intact on the jacket's left breast. "It was coming at me. I never seen anything like it in my life," he recalls. "I was covered in dust, debris; I don't even know what I was covered in."

But he thinks he knows who's responsible. "They" displaced him from the places he calls home—the WTC parking garage and the "dugout" near Pussycat Lounge, a strip club on the corner of Greenwich and Rector Streets. There are two things Morelli doesn't go through the day without: a bottle of vodka and his hand-held radio. "I get my news every morning, " he says, patting the radio in his pants pocket. "They say Osama bin Laden did it. He's the only mastermind that could do something like this. Bush said he'll prove it to the American people that bin Laden did it."

And George W. Bush, Morelli says, is the man for the job. "Once he gets all the countries on his side, forget it. Just look at his record with the death penalty in Texas: Guilty," Morelli says, jolting his hand above his head the way he imagines the no-nonsense governor would have done, then he thrashes it down sternly adding: "Execute him!"

Puffy hands, jaundiced yellow eyes, and thick skin give the impression that Morelli is older than his 57 years. His life has been a series of disruptions, mainly stirred by alcohol. After losing his job and his wife, Morelli says he moved into an apartment at 161st St. and Flushing in Queens. That's the last apartment he's ever had. He says he gave it up for Queens House of Detention, where he served eight months during 1978 and 1979 for robbing a bank. He has a son in Florida with whom he says he lived after his release from jail. But Morelli's tenderness for the city that reared him, especially its southern tip, brought him home a couple years later. "I love my New York," he says, bearing a toothless smile. "I always return down here. The streets of New York keep pulling me down here."

Back in New York with nowhere to go, Morelli started sleeping in the subway stations. He'd just settled in at the Port Authority of New Jersey and New York when he heard from his pal Bandanna Joe, the Cisco-drinking nut. According to Bandanna Joe, life under the towers beat the hell out of the Port Authority's grimy digs. Never one to pass up an opportunity to tip back with a friend, Morelli made New York City's most ill-fated structures his home.

Wednesday morning, September 12, Morelli tried to go back to the WTC—he wanted to say hello to the guys at No. 10, check on the others, and look for Alicia. He was rebuffed by police officers guarding his home in every direction. On his way back Morelli ran into Pete, Joe, and Jack. He joined them in their search for an open liquor store. They found none.

"I lost my clothes, my home, everything. If I could do something about it I would, but I'm too old," he says. Morelli is homeless again. He tries going back to the World Trade Center every day. There's a fence around it now, and the military and police officers keep turning him away. Sometimes he sleeps at the Catholic Church at 17 State Street, but most nights he sits on the southeast corner of Greenwich and Morris Streets. The building there blows warm air onto the sidewalk.

Although it's difficult to see with one glass eye, Morelli spends most nights watching flatbeds loaded with pieces of his home disappear inside the Battery Tunnel. "It's two towers; 110 stories each," he sighs. "Sit here and watch and you're gonna cry too. All the twisted iron and the debris. Oh my Lord have mercy it's so bad."

So Morelli waits. "After they clean it all up, they'll give me my house back. It'll take time, but I know they will," he says of the police officers who worked the WTC. "But it's gonna take a lot of time. So I'll live with it. I got nowhere to go. They took my home."

Suburban Fallout

Mary Quigley

First the number was 4,000 missing, then it climbed to 6,000. How does one comprehend that abstraction in terms of individual lives? The impact of 6,000 missing hits hardest in the suburbs. City residents witnessed the attack and the fallout, but it's the families of the fire fighters and police officers and stockbrokers and executives whose lives have forever been radically changed.

The 5 p.m. Saturday evening mass in my suburban Long Island church usually brims with energy as people hurry in from soccer games, a day of errands and chores, or an afternoon jog. But Saturday, September 15 there were no soccer games, the stores were strangely empty, and people took long walks instead of jogs. The 1,000 congregants who filled St. Agnes Cathedral in Rockville Centre were somber, seeking solace in the familiar ritual.

For his sermon the pastor left the pulpit and stood directly in front of the parishioners. He talked briefly about the horror and sadness of the terrorist attack, all the while fingering a white piece of paper. Then he stopped, unfolded the paper, and slowly read the names of 30 men and women missing from our town. Each name was like a blow to the chest. Heads bowed, tears flowed, adults held hands, and children clung to their parents. Everyone, it seemed, knew at least a few names on the list. Many were familiar from my children's schools and sports activities; two were particularly painful to hear.

Eddie was a New York City firefighter who had just won

a promotion to battalion chief. He had gone to work at his New York City firehouse on Monday night for a 24-hour shift, leaving his wife and three young sons in their safe, snug home. He lived a few blocks away, next to my elderly in-laws, and was a good neighbor, shoveling snow and helping when my mother-in-law had medical emergencies. My father-in-law, a retired New York City police officer, loved to talk to Eddie and recounted how city firefighters are a special breed. They never hold back, never wait for a fire to subside before they run into a burning building. Indeed, many of the fire fighters who died were high-ranking officers who did not have to go into the burning towers. My father-in-law imagines that Eddie and his comrades where charging up the stairs of the World Trade tower when it collapsed. That's what they did, unquestioningly; that's why they lived together in fire "houses," so they would back up each other no matter how dangerous the situation.

Eddie's wife was in her driveway when I first saw her on the morning of September 12, sitting in a white plastic chair with a phone in her hand, waiting for some word, any word. A cadre of friends and relatives formed a protective semi-circle around her. She grabbed my arm. "I know he will come home," she said, explaining that she was sitting outside because she couldn't go inside her house and face her children. "I haven't told the boys yet that Eddie is missing. They think he's just working."

I stopped by again a few days later. While relatives maintained a vigil outside on the driveway, Eddie's wife was now inside, too distraught to face the neighbors. An American flag with a yellow ribbon hung on the front porch, a sign of hope for a miracle, that he might be found, alive somehow, in the rubble.

John Sr. is not hoping for a miracle for his son. John Jr. is dead, perishing when tower two crumbled.

John Sr. is a longtime friend, the father of three daughters and a son, all in their 30s. His children, like many in our town, had moved away for college and careers and the early years of married life. And, like so many others, they moved back to Rockville Centre when they started families. They wanted the Little League, the good public schools, the ocean 20 minutes away, and the city an easy 35-minute commute on the Long Island Rail Road. John Jr. had bought a house not far from his sisters and was the father of three children, aged four, two and one month—and infant son, also named John.

A bond trader, John Jr. was on the 102nd floor of 2 WTC when the first terrorist plane struck. He called both his mother and his father to tell them he was okay, that there had been some freak airplane accident in the first tower. A few minutes later, he was talking to a friend on the phone when an alarm rang and he told the friend he'd better go, according to his father.

In his office at 42nd and Lexington, John Sr. turned on the radio. When he heard that a second plane had hit, he ran out of his office and ran over to Fifth Avenue, where he could see the towers as he ran downtown, trying futilely to get closer to his son. Just as he reached 34th Street, the tower collapsed. John Sr. collapsed too. "I knew he was dead. Vaporized," he said, choking on his words.

Two weeks to the day after the terrorist attack, I attended John Jr.'s memorial service in St. Agnes, his family formally acknowledging that he will never return home. Instead of a coffin, there was a collage of smiling photographs of a son, father, husband and brother. After the service I stopped at my in-laws'. Eddie's wife still has the yellow ribbon around the flag, still hoping.

On a warm Sunday a little more than two weeks ago, two young men both stood on local soccer fields watching games with their children. Now they are gone, changing forever the lives of their wives, their parents, their sisters and brothers, their children and their children's children. More than 6,000 other lives are also forever altered, a statistic that is inconceivable except one Eddie, one John at a time.

Don't Understand America Too Quickly

Todd Gitlin

Of all I have seen and heard in the last days, the story I most want to tell is this:

Thursday afternoon, around five, my wife and I went down to the perimeter of the ruins along the West Side of lower Manhattan and fell in with a crowd that was greeting and applauding rescue workers—police, firemen, phone and gas company people, iron workers and welders, most driving slowly northward out of the smoking WTC area as other trucks drove south, heading in. Some came trudging out of the zone, their boots caked in gray ash. Some faces were gray. Mainly the firefighters on foot had grey faces. The calls from the crowd were mainly: Thank you! Some people passed out cookies, bottles of water, soft drinks, cups of soup. There were some American flags. Some people came around handing out pictures of loved, lost ones.

We ran into a friend and walked a bit eastward along Canal Street, where the scene repeated itself. At one, an off-duty New Jersey cop with a Central Casting tough-guy demeanor said he'd been working on-site for more than a day, taking time out to go back home, get a haircut, and come back with a truckload of supplies. He impressed a young woman to get into the back of a pick-up truck with her, all the while casting aspersions on the masculinity of George W. Bush, who had just arrived to visit the remains of the WTC. This is the week of working-class heroes.

Out of the zone of ruins walked a man and woman in their early thirties, handsome, clear-eyed, wearing yellow slickers and boots. They were trying to figure out how to get to the subway. We advised on directions and fell in with them. Mary and Dean, friends or lovers, had driven down from the small city of Syracuse — 250 miles northwest — to volunteer, and had just spent some 36 hours in the belt of destruction, digging in rubble, dispersing whenever horns went off to signal that buildings near the WTC were in danger of collapsing themselves. They'd been directing themselves, more or less. Now the Federal managers were coming in to take over.

They said it hadn't been easy to get into the damage zone: in fact, they'd had to trick their way in. They had reported to the main volunteer depot at the Javits Convention Center a mile and a half north. Mary, an image consultant at a cosmetics company, had some therapeutic experience and wanted to work with children. They found 300 people lined up in front of them.

So they attached themselves to an upstate fire company, got their yellow slickers, boots, and smoke-protection masks, and made their way to ground zero. They didn't know George W. Bush had made his appearance that afternoon (or that he'd been given a far less vigorous reception than Mayor Giuliani), nor were they impressed. At the time, they'd been catching a couple of hours' sleep. Soaked by the first rain in days, they'd gone first to the shell of a nearby hotel, but there was a stench, and someone came up and told them not to sleep there, there were bodies. Looking for some other structure that looked as though it wouldn't collapse on them, they followed some firefighters into another building. There too, Dean had seen human remains under the rubble.

I asked him what he thought the U. S. ought to do now.

"We have to do something," he said, "but it's not easy. We have to be careful about retaliating. We need diplomatic pressure. We can't go bomb a lot of innocent people. *Then we've done what they've done.*"

You will hear a lot in the days and weeks to come about jingo Americans who want to bomb someone, obliterate anyplace. There will be talk—there is already some—about bombing Afghanistan back to the Stone Age, as if it is not already close to that. The talk shows batten on bravado-laden would-be cowboy bombers, eyeballs saturated with endlessly recycled TV images of the explosions. There are probably more of these reckless talkers living out in the vastness of the republic beyond New York City—in what Mr. Bush is pleased to call "the heartland"—although on second thought Syracuse ought to qualify as a piece of that.

If and when military power lashes out in the days to come, Washington will claim that all Americans agree on what the government is doing. But there are an awful lot of Americans like Dean who feel spasms of anger and vengefulness and have not succumbed to them. Those who plan indiscriminate war may well roll over their doubt and dissent. But they are here. They have not been stampeded. They are heartland. These patriots are not going away.

There's more than one America. During the painful days ahead, let our allies and critics remember that we are not all mad bombers, racist or authoritarian bullies—far from it. The White House may claim that the American public demands all-out war, but there's little sign of that. Even in high places in Washington there are counsels of restraint and focus—starting with Colin Powell. Don't understand America too quickly. Don't box us in.

On Getting Close

Mitchell Stephens

I just returned from a trip around the world, which I found, during this eight-month circumnavigation, to be big but not particularly bad. However—and here is my own tiny irony to go along with all the terrible ironies exploding around here—something very big and very bad has happened in the world, not in the Sahara, the Amazon or any of the other exotic places I have been visiting, but near my home.

I keep getting pulled toward the place where it happened.

Home is a suburb of New York City. After the planes hit, as the towers crumble, I'm watching TV like everyone else. Outside my window is a perfect, blue day. On television are the most awful, the most chilling, the most dramatic images I have seen in my life. Yes, it does feel unreal. The two biggest buildings around are just gone? I sit there and watch the plane slicing into the tower over and over.

I don't go into Manhattan in the next few days. Nevertheless, various back-home responsibilities have me looping around it. I see the amputation off in the distance—from the Jersey Turnpike, from the George Washington Bridge, from an apartment building in Queens. I watch smoke pouring from the wound. It is difficult to turn my eyes away.

Sunday, five days later, is yet another day of the sort New York is adept at producing at this time of year—a day when you can wear a T-shirt but not sweat into it, when the skyline stands clear. I ride my bicycle over the bridge. I follow the new bike path along the Hudson. I'm headed downtown—as far south as it is possible to go. People on roller blades, tourists with small cameras, rescue workers, FBI agents. It isn't feeling any more real. The barricades stop you at Canal Street. From there I catch a glimpse, between buildings, of the smoldering pile. What's in that pile? The remains of two 110-story buildings. The remains of six thousand lives. Riding back home over the bridge, I stop to stare at the skyline; I'm trying to see what is no longer there.

The TV networks have mostly stopped showing those shots of the planes burying themselves in the towers. Too upsetting, apparently. But I think I need to see them some more.

On Monday there's a "teach-in" sponsored by New York University's Journalism Department. A colleague, standing off to the side, tells me a story about her friend, whom I know a bit. On the morning of September 11, she says, he heard that tower number two had been hit, and immediately left his office and began running south. His son worked near the top of tower number two. While he was running, my colleague's friend watched that giant building being replaced, in a matter of seconds, by a violent column of smoke.

Tuesday—exactly a week after the attack—I take a small class of journalism students and start walking downtown. This time—by following a narrow open corridor that leads past City Hall to Wall Street—it is possible to walk almost all the way to the bottom of the island. We can see, from some blocks to the east, that pile from another angle. We can see some of the cranes that have been pulling out the twisted steel girders that have been lifting out the crushed fire trucks. We can see the blackened skeleton of one of the buildings in the complex.

Some of the students are nervous about breathing in the dust and the smoke. Some of them are wondering what we're doing here. I say, or at least want to say, that journalists must see things, that they must get close. Close is where a kind of truth resides.

On my round-the-world trip, I have wandered—via bush taxi, alongside a camel—into the desert. I have slept in a nomad tent; I have dipped my hand in a communal bowl of couscous and goat meat. Travelers are also committed to seeing things and getting close. We, too, believe that kinds of truth are at stake.

There's so much talk of war in this country now. America hadn't been handed a lot of bad fortune. We've now been presented with a large dose. We're dealing with it with no more maturity than others tend to display. We're raising our fists. Dinner guests arrive at my house on Saturday evening bringing red, white and blue napkins.

I, too, am outraged. I do believe those who committed this atrocity need to be brought to justice. But war, as I understand it, is a sure-fire way for more sons to die. Vengeance, as I understand it, inevitably leads to more vengeance, to more very bad things. And I can't say that on my travels I have noticed a great need for additional American patriotism. Indeed, the kind of world I've allowed myself to believe I was finding—a place where a man from the New York suburbs can be warmly received by Muslim nomads in the Sahara—will not benefit from the waving of flags, of any design.

We're drinking, this evening in the suburbs, single-malt scotch. Battlefields seem very far away. At some point I find myself raising my voice.

Sunday the weather is once again showing off, with its characteristic insensitivity, and I'm once again on my bicycle. This time you can pedal within a few blocks of the rubble. You can see, from this angle, that the pile is many stories tall. It looms. Is the point to get near enough so that the tragedy, in some physical sense, looms?

I personally have not been handed a lot of bad fortune.

It seems odd to talk of my own small feelings at a time when others have been forced to feel so much more. But sometimes, lately, I feel—I have had the luxury of feeling— like an astronaut too long without gravity. This also helps explain my urge to travel, my hankering after adventure. I've wanted the world, in some physical sense, to loom—as if a sense of the earth's weight and girth would orient me, would make it and that which takes place on it seem more real.

The site of what may be the most devastating terrorist attack in history pulls me toward it. But in the end, I must confess, it wasn't the rubble that really got to me on these September days in Manhattan. I wasn't near anything that was smoldering when the tears finally came to my eyes. That happened when my colleague told me that story about that father running toward the towers, towards his son.

The real power, the true horror, of course, resides in that to which you get close emotionally, that which, in some psychological sense, looms.

I read in the newspaper that they've hung tarps near certain street corners downtown to stop people—weightless tragedy tourists like me—from gawking at the ruins. Seeing may not be the most powerful way of knowing, but it's a start. I think they're making a mistake.

A Moroccan Driver and the Great Experiment

David T. Z. Mindich

Last week, I flew from Burlington, Vermont, my adopted home, to New York City, where I spent my first thirty-five years. Although a bit scared to fly, especially with my wife and two small children, I never miss spending the Jewish New Year with my parents and extended family and did not want to give terror even a small victory.

On the way to the city from Kennedy, I started talking with the driver, a Moroccan Muslim. He took pains to show his sorrow at the terror. I took pains to express my abhorrence of the attacks on Muslims and Sikhs in the United States. He told stories of Moroccan Jews; I of being a Jew visiting Morocco. I asked him if he felt worried about being an Arab in America. Not in New York City, he said. His brother, in Seattle was worried, but New York is used to diversity. At the end of the ride, I said goodbye to the driver, feeling fortunate to be in a city in which diversity trumps terror, even fresh, immediate terror.

New York has always had to balance fear and accommodation. In the 1970s, when many families fled the city's violence and escaped to the suburbs, mine and others didn't. Those who stayed behind were faced with a city that was impossibly violent but had an unexplainable hope as well. Those who stayed were driven by a stubborn optimism, sometimes misplaced, that we could all somehow live together. New York was, and continues to be the world's greatest experiment in communal living. My New York was a city in which my black karate teacher would chat in Mandarin to

Chinese delivery men. It was a city in which my best friend, a black Jamaican, and I could watch a pick-up basketball game on West 4th Street involving nine blacks and one Orthodox Jew. It was a city in which everyone mingled together: artists, Brazilians, bankers, Italians, doctors, Puerto Ricans, engineers, Madonna, Indians, construction workers. One of my greatest loves has always been walking down New York streets, wrapped in a throng of people from all over the world.

It would be poetic to say that everyone lived together under the shadow of the World Trade Center, but this is not true. The city is so vast that the Twin Towers were never more than a tiny part of it. The terrorists, in destroying them, did far less and far more than they imagined. Far less because those big dour buildings were shells and will be rebuilt, either there or elsewhere; far more because of the six thousand killed, but also because the terrorists have attacked New York's dream of living together in peace.

During my trip to the city, I lost my wallet. Was it on the street? Was I the victim of a pickpocket? If I left it in the taxi, I told my wife, the driver would return it. The wallet really wasn't a big deal anyway, especially in the face of a city grieving for six thousand. I went to the local precinct to report the lost wallet and saw police officers hunched over desks, reading newspapers. They all looked tired. While filing my report, a policewoman spoke matter-of-factly about her twelve-hour days. She lost two cousins in the Trade Center. Later that night as a subway we were taking into Brooklyn crossed the Manhattan bridge, we peered into the bombsite. Illuminated by rescue lights, the black smoke still pluming out of the rubble looked an iridescent and ghostly gray. Against the normally twinkling New York skyline, the buildings around the rubble were black silhouettes. And under it all were more than 6000 lost. Lost from America, but also lost from Britain and Germany, Israel and Egypt, India and Pakistan, Iran and

Iraq. The scene said something terrible and special about
New York itself.

The essence of New York is an experiment in getting along
with others, regardless of race, creed, or color. True, people
haven't always been kind to each other, terrible inequities
exist, and the city's civility is often fragile and tenuous. At
times the tribalism seems to crowd out everything good in
the city: the black mobs in Crown Heights, the white mobs in
Howard Beach. But, increasingly, New Yorkers were beginning
to recoil from such events and the city's tempests had begun
to subside. By the end of the 1990s, the city had become
much safer and had cut its murder rate by two thirds. Every
day, New Yorkers hurl through the subway tunnels along with
representatives of more than a hundred countries; the vast
majority get to their destinations unscathed.

What the terrorists will never know is how beautiful it is
to rise above tribalism. To be a Czech in a Turkish restaurant.
To be a Korean who dates an Irishman. To be a black who
loves yoga. To be an Arab who loves bagels and Kafka. To look
out from the World Trade Center's observation deck and see
in one of the greatest cities in the world, an army of people
trying their best to see each other for who they are, not where
they're from.

Not that where we're from is unimportant. New Yorkers
have all escaped from somewhere. One of my grandfathers
escaped from the Cossacks. Another escaped from a Polish
shtetl, and then from the Nazis. Whether it's the African
American who fled the South in the 1920s, or the Haitian
fleeing poverty in the 1980s, they came and they continue
to come. They come from Russia for the extra Glasnost of
Brooklyn. They come from Oklahoma to be gay in Chelsea.
They come as outcasts from ten thousand small towns around
the world to reinvent themselves in the Big Town.

Can the terrorists blast away New York's fragile trust and

humanism? Will we be a society of roadblocks and security checks and preconceived notions? I don't know.

What I do know is that the cab driver showed up at my parents' building with my wallet. Unclear about my address, he had combed the neighborhood asking doormen if they recognized me. The Muslim Moroccan had found a Christian Dominican who recognized the Jewish American. But that night we were just plain New Yorkers.

Watching and Waiting

Monica Haim

Once the ultimate paradise for New York's youth culture, downtown now is a montage of forlorn expressions and shattered illusions. The tragedy was a swift kick in the ass to a generation that grew up spoiled and, yes, naïve. On the bluest, clearest, crispest fall morning, Manhattan in 2001 felt like what I imagine much of Eastern Europe felt like on fall days in the thirties and forties. There we were, mingling over coffee and cigarettes; envying someone's new fall boot; finding a sunny spot to sit over a leisurely bagel and cream cheese, when the faceless mask of evil reared itself.

We all joined the mass exodus uptown. The thick black cloud hovered over us, pungent with the smells of loss and impending doom. We scurried like rodents, and some of us cried, hopelessly trying to make some sense of the indelible mark that was being branded on us, on our freedom.

Now we wait in paranoia for The Next Big Thing, our once-meaningful lives suspended indefinitely in a global tangle of bullshit. We cry because the word "missing" has taken on a whole new meaning. You see a photo, and wonder if the gentleman featured there was sitting beside you on the F train last week, or if that young lady wasn't the one who held the door for you at Bloomingdale's the other day. We guiltily watch the families, the firemen, the mayor—the void—and we feel like sinners for getting up just one week later and moving forward.

Bombing Us

Anna Arutunyan

When I saw the smoking hole in the first tower of the World Trade Center, I had been walking through Washington Square Park, on my way to class. I had been thinking about my new American passport, reflecting that this was my second class of my second year at NYU, and how, whether I liked it or not, an American education and an American passport were two things crucial to my personal and professional stability.

I had emigrated from Russia with my family when I was seven. By now both of my parents were citizens, and even though I kept returning to Moscow, where my husband lived, my footing was really in the United States, where I had been educated. Every time I took a long trip to Russia, my parents urged me not to give up a pending passport and a pending education. America, for them, was a safe harbor, and every time we heard new reports about deaths in Russia's war with Chechnya—whether in battle or as a result of terrorist attacks on Moscow and other cities—we would collectively wince.

Terrorism is a touchy issue for Russians, who have struggled for years in the conflict with Chechnya while the West relentlessly criticized them for human rights violations because they were cracking down on the Islamic fundamentalist sect of the Wahhabists. Chechnya's Russian federal leader Akhmed Kadyrov wanted to ban the Wahhabist sect in 1999, in response to allegations that Chechen terrorist leader Hattab—the same one considered to be linked to bin Laden—was a Wahhabist.

Wahhabism, founded in the early 18th century by the

Arab Muhammed ibn Wahhab and considered heresy by the majority of Islamic leaders, holds almost official status in Saudi Arabia, and is an almost overused word in the Russian media. The name bin Laden has been familiar to us for years, long before his face began appearing on Wanted posters all over New York. So perhaps Russians know more than they should about Wahhabism, and at the same time not enough. But they have also been living in an area where these kinds of struggles have reached back for centuries. Leo Tolstoy's account of real-life Chechen militant Shamil, in his novel Hadji Murat, differs little from recent news accounts of terrorist leader Shamil Basaev. And though the word "terrorism" didn't exist in the 13th century during the Tartar-Mongolian raids, Russia is still recovering from the damage.

So while most immigrants to America are striving blindly to convince themselves that this country is still a "safe harbor," Russians in Russia are having strange reactions. The initial one was of horror and sympathy. Even though hundreds of people flocked to the U.S. embassy in Moscow in 1999 to splatter it with paint, in protest against the U.S. attack on Belgrade, now people flocked to bring flowers and candles to a building many Russians, especially those who had tried to get visas, cringed at while passing. One group of youths came with a poster saying, "Remember Belgrade." But the general reaction was that America the safe harbor no longer existed. My husband summed it up pretty well when he said that America had suddenly "acquired a human face" for those parts of the world still struggling with history.

My father, a programmer, has lived in New York for thirteen years. He worked at Deutsche Bank, on the fifth floor of tower two. Since he immigrated, he has been back to Russia twice—each time realizing that America was the only nation he could live in.

He was on the first floor when the second plane hit, and

he ran. He walked home, and didn't want to talk about it when I finally reached him by phone. Later that day, all he said to me was, "Didn't think we'd live to see that."

Later he said something else: "Can you believe how we ever ended up here, in this city? Can you believe that that was us they were bombing, us?"

Whether in Manhattan or in the Congo

Nuno Andrade

I was born in Angola four years into a civil war that has yet to end. Immediately after the country gained its independence from Portugal in 1975, Angola became one of the many staging grounds for battles of the Cold War. In a country with more land mines than people, the effects of the struggles for world domination between the United States and the Soviet Union are still being felt. This is the environment in which I was born, and this is the context with which I experienced the terrorist attacks of September 11, 2001.

I left Angola at the age of six and have never returned. As a child living in the capital city, one of the only areas of the country not ravaged by war, my six-year-old mind was not yet sophisticated enough to understand why there was a bullet hole in my parents' closet; it was not sophisticated enough to understand why my father had loaded weapons in the house; nor was it sophisticated enough to understand why we housed a man in army fatigues. Even so, my existence was a privileged one.

I have called the United States my home for the past 13 years, the last three of which I have spent living in and around New York City. My past experiences have not desensitized me to the suffering of others.

My immediate feeling on seeing the World Trade Center towers collapse was that of every other resident of this city, one of utter amazement. How could this be happening? This isn't possible. I shared in the sadness for those who had perished, and for so many families who would have to cope with so many losses. That sadness quickly turned to anger. But my anger was not directed at those responsible for these heinous acts of terrorism. I was angry at the United States.

To explain fully just how much the course of Angolan history was altered by external influences, one would have to write a book. I won't attempt to do that, but let me say this: in the sixties and seventies, the U.S. government covertly aided Jonas Savimbi, the leader of one of the factions fighting for dominance in the Angolan Civil War. In the eighties, Savimbi had his own lobby in Washington, which he used to fund that war. When the Cold War ended, and the threat of communism was defeated, Savimbi was dropped—as were the Angolan people. Savimbi, now discredited and lacking financial support, has nevertheless been able to continue the war with the surplus weapons that had been provided to him by the American government.

I was saddened by the deaths of so many people on September 11. But I am also saddened by the millions of people who have died or been displaced in Angola as a result of over a quarter century of civil war; as I am saddened by the 2.5 million people who have died in only three years in the neighboring Democratic Republic of Congo. And my anger is not directed at Americans for any responsibility their country may have in the situation in those two countries; it is solely directed at the U.S. government. I am angry that the United States helped to install and support a dictator in the Democratic Republic of Congo, then called Zaire, over three decades for the sake of American interests. I am angry that the United States attempted to do the same in Angola with would-be dictator Savimbi.

This has been United States policy towards Third World countries during the Cold War, and it continues to be so today. This foreign policy is visible not only in African countries, but also in South American countries, and for that matter, Middle

Eastern countries.

According to Khaled Fahmy, a professor of Middle Eastern social history at New York University, there is no shortage of U.S.-supported anti-democratic regimes in the Middle East. "The U.S. is supporting tyrannical regimes, as a matter of policy, because these are deemed to be more stable," he says. According to Professor Fahmy, this has been the source of a lot of feelings of hatred towards the United States. "[Some of] those allies of the U.S. have a miserable record of human rights, and the U.S. has consistently been turning a blind eye to their abuses. This is felt in the region very strongly."

When I think of the 6,000 people buried under the rubble in downtown Manhattan, I can fault nothing and no one but the government of the United States. I would never condone the actions of those responsible for the deaths of innocent people—regardless of whether those responsible are so-called Muslim extremists or agents of the U.S. government, or whether those innocent lives are lost in Manhattan or in the Congo. In order for there to be no chance of a repeat of the attacks of September 11, there needs to be a radical change in U.S. foreign policy. What has happened has a direct correlation to the imperialist actions of the United States government in foreign countries. To paraphrase Malcolm X's statements on the assassination of John F. Kennedy, sadly, the chickens have once again come home to roost.

Something Chilling

Natalie Stevens

Only this morning, exactly a week later, I became teary-eyed at the sound of the children swinging in Washington Square Park. There was something chilling about the metal squeal that screamed from the chains. The children seemed so happy. Yet it was haunting in a way that it had never been before. Their innocence is tarnished now, much like my own.

I'm twenty-two years old and have lived in New York City for just two weeks. The first week I was here, I felt so grown up, living on my own and knowing no one. Everyone kept telling me how brave I was for moving here by myself. Than that idea crashed down on top of me.

The second week I denied events. I no longer felt daring; I felt lonely. I spent most days walking uptown, away from the smoke and the surgical masks on the Village streets. At night I sat with my cat watching the news, and calling every friend and relative I could get on the phone. I wanted to be with someone.

A few days later I realized I could no longer stay strong alone. So I took a weekend trip to Boston with my boyfriend. After two nights there, at a friend's, I'd received the emotional support I needed. But I realized that only people in New York had shared my experience. We don't ask each other what we feel or what we saw; we accept that it has affected us all. Selfishly, I liked to think I was even more affected, down here in lower Manhattan. That thought gives me some comfort as I return to my little studio on Eighth Street.

Comfort

Bonnie Zimmer

I cannot comfort you, my friend. We sit here together, unquenchable tears silently, relentlessly tracing our faces. And I do not know how to comfort you.

In those first few minutes and hours of shock and disbelief and anger, it was somehow easier than now. Like you, I raced to the phone to make sure that all of those I love most deeply were still OK. Slowly, over that first day, my fear turned to sorrow leavened by relief and then wrath, as the stories of miracles and near-misses filtered in.

Emily overslept, awakened by the noise of the first blast, then rushed to the street, camera in hand. Greg missed his usual train. Buses going through the Holland Tunnel were delayed, and Maria stepped off the bus just as the second plane hit the tower. Sarah stayed home with a sick baby. Joel heard the news, got off his train, and boarded a northbound train toward home. Davis stayed over at his girlfriend's house. So many stories of barely averted tragedy.

The trains stopped running. At 6:15 the first morning after, the parking lot, usually filled to overflowing, was empty—except for the cars scattered here and there that were not claimed the night before. I suppose they were an omen of news to come.

Gradually, house by house and street by street, the black crepe bands spread like a grim contagion, overshadowing hundreds of flags. These new stories, whispered in the aisles of the grocery store and over the backyard fence, were not sighs of relief. Tears replaced the initial fury.

Michael was on one of the planes. Josh is missing. Steven had a job interview. Jenny went in early, shopping for a wedding dress. Yesterday, her mother took her hairbrush, in hopes that someday they may find enough to bury.

Fighter planes appear over the beach, and from my window I can barely see warships on the horizon. The constant reminders color the texture of each day.

I can no longer tolerate the grim photographs. I fear that the bits and pieces of bodies belong to those who helped to define the fabric of my life. Or perhaps I fear that there will never be a trace, never be a way to truly say goodbye, that generic memorials will replace the funeral mass.

But this grief goes beyond these losses, horrific as they seem today. It is the grief for children robbed of parents and thus in some measure of childhood itself. It is the grief of a band of young African boys walking for years to find a home, any home. It is the grief of Afghan children, bellies swollen by starvation. It is the grief of men long ago returned from Vietnamese jungles who can still not sleep inside, who still awaken every night in terror. I cannot stand against the enormity.

And yes, dear friend, it is also at last the grief of this disease that inexorably steals my life one small bit at a time. Tears come unbidden, streaming down my face until only the immense sorrow remains.

I cannot comfort you, my friend. I can only sit with you, cry with you, until I learn at last to comfort myself.

In Manhattan, September 19

Jay Rosen

Normally I am a political writer, or let's say I try. But things are not normal, and neither am I. You cannot declare that nothing will ever be the same again and then exempt your own mind. If those Towers could collapse, why not the categories where we try to make sense of politics?

I stopped making sense of things through left and right the moment I saw for myself that New York City's skyline was burning from the top, the moment (which took only minutes) that I realized why. Before, it was at least conceivable in public imagination that a fire could consume a skyscraper. But not the fall of the World Trade Center from an airborne attack by hidden enemies of your people. There were no categories for that, no public and political space where it stood imagined by some that United States Air Force fighter jets, ready to kill, would soon be flying over Times Square if we don't wake up and ... Ask anyone who was there and looked up: this came out of the blue.

Down went the twin pillars of the skyline, and all my public categories fell. I'm not thinking about politics proper yet. I am thinking about saving other cities from the terrible thing that happened to mine. Whichever party in politics can do that—left, right, middle, or parties undreamed, coalitions uncounted—that is the politics I am prepared to believe in now. For the moment. And I suspect many others feel this way too.

Intuitively we know that a great city is not just an urban landscape, an exterior thing like its buildings seem to be. The important landscape is interior. Half the reason people come to New York is to experience the soaring height of Manhattan inside themselves, in their personal ambitions, their chances in life.

There is no point in moving here unless you seek an enlargement of some inner sense of self. Walk across the Brooklyn Bridge toward Manhattan and be able to say, "I live here now." You'll know instantly what I mean. Millions of us did that, got bigger. Now we don't know what that enlargement means. We know the bridge walk has changed forever and become a darker thing. Once, the Twin Towers dominated that view.

Hopes impossibly high but real enough are the very essence of what it means to live amid very tall buildings, especially for those who came to the Big City from provinces beyond. We knew we were lucky. We knew we had this big thing inside, replacing the smaller one our hometowns were. We knew we could fail, go back defeated, but it would only be a personal failure: can't make it there. We never thought the high canyons above would get hit and crash into rubble and dust. But it happened. Now we are to dream the Big City dream all over again, with new information.

Early on in this crisis, and by reading Blue Ear, I became aware that people writing from certain cities had a special feel for the destruction in New York. Call it a civic emotion, globally shared. Europe's international cities, like London, Paris, and Berlin, are the most obvious examples in my compass, but maybe Hong Kong and Tokyo are too.

The one I know the most about, because I have visited recently, is Amsterdam. Like New York, an international city, with an amazing interracial poly-cultural mix. Like New York, an irreplaceable cultural capital. People on the streets of one fit perfectly on the streets of the other. Both known for tolerance, for vice. And of course there's the mysterious bond with a city that was New Amsterdam long before it was New York.

Because we have the Internet, I know people there are having a hard time since September 11, like everyone else but in their own anguished way. Perhaps they feel the inner collapse that would follow from an equivalent attack. Dam Square and the nearby Palace are rubble, but there's still the life you wanted in Amsterdam to be lived. The Eiffel Tower is taken down, but there's still Paris the great capital, and after all it is your home. The British Parliament and Buckingham Palace are blown apart, but traders in the City of London have to go to work and trade. In Rome, the ancient Coloseum really is in ruins. In San Francisco the Golden Gate is gone from view. Fill in the rest for me, because I know you can.

What shall we call the politics that will save us from any of that? Do you think it can be found somewhere in your prior categories? Take every monumental city you know around the globe, and see it as a collection of targets. Now tell me your aim is still steady after that.

Sailing School's Fortunes Ebb

Caleb Frazier

New York, September 21—Winter came early to the Manhattan Sailing School this year.

Located in the North Cove Yacht Harbor, just a few blocks from where the two World Trade Center buildings once stood, the school is usually bustling with activity at this time of year, with each of the school's small sailboats carrying four or five students at a time into New York's harbor. But now the school's 17 sailboats, each covered in a thick layer of ash from the recent explosions, float idly in the abandoned cove.

"Right now we have no cash coming in, but we still have general operating costs," said Michael Fortenbaugh, the school's owner. "We have a cushion, but we're burning through it at a very fast rate."

Like many small businesses in the area, the Manhattan Sailing School has been hit hard by the recent terrorist attacks on the World Trade Center. While the school didn't lose much in the way of capital — except for a small amount of damage to the school's computers, Fortenbaugh believes that many of its assets are okay — it may still lose out in the long run.

"The World Trade Center was the major economic hub of downtown," Fortenbaugh said. "We're going to get a lot less students going forward."

An offshoot of the Manhattan Yacht Club, the Manhattan Sailing School was founded in 1993 in order to provide sailing instruction to New Yorkers who otherwise wouldn't get the opportunity.

"The sailing school isn't a leisure business, it's a quality of life business," Fortenbaugh said. "It was begun as a way to make life more enjoyable in the city."

Fortenbaugh established the Manhattan Yacht Club in 1987 with $60,000 he had raised from investors right after graduating from college. He had previously spent his summers working on Wall Street and, like many other sailors, had given up the recreation entirely when he moved to Manhattan. The club began at Manhattan's Southstreet Seaport but has been in its present location in North Cove since 1994.

Now, however, Fortenbaugh operates the club from his house in New Jersey.

While slower than the summer season, autumn is usually a busy time of year for the sailing school. Each week 21 students usually sign up to attend sailing classes at the school. But instead of the usual activity, plans are being made to store the boats for the winter.

Fortenbaugh estimates the school will lose $97,000 in revenue this quarter and is preparing to scale back its operations.

"We're going to begin pulling boats out of the water, not renting as much dock space, and liquidating assets," Fortenbaugh said. "Right now, we're just doing everything we can to conserve cash."

Other than paying his six full-time employees, Fortenbaugh said he has stopped writing checks altogether. He has put off payment for the computers the sailing school leases, sending a note of explanation instead. He's also trying to sell one of the school's boats at a bargain basement price. The boat, named "Magic", is worth $15,000, but he is asking only $8,000 in order to unload it quickly, said Fortenbaugh.

Like other small-business owners in the area, Fortenbaugh is counting on loans from the United States Small Business Administration to help him get through this difficult time. The

SBA, in association with the Federal Emergency Management Agency, has pledged loans of up to $1.5 million to small businesses for physical damages. That, however, is unlikely to be of much help to the Manhattan Sailing School which sustained few losses resulting from physical damage.

"If the boats are fine, then we're out of luck," Fortenbaugh said.

The SBA has also pledged loans of up to $1.5 million for working capital, for which the school is likely to qualify.

"We're going to try to get as much of that as possible," Fortenbaugh said.

But despite any help it is likely to get in the short term, the Manhattan Sailing School is likely to feel the effects of the attacks on the World Trade Center long after such funding dries up.

"Our students used to ride the subway down after work and get off at the World Trade Center," Fortenbaugh said. "Now there is no World Trade Center."

In Manhattan, September 25

Jay Rosen

My colleagues and I held a teach-in last week for journalism students at NYU. An intellectual vigil, if you will. For the first time since I became a professor, I saw in the faces of students how much they needed us. Events had made them vulnerable to knowledge they hoped we had. Of course we needed them too. Their hoping most of all.

Too young, I never went to a campus teach-in during the 60s. But I read of them, and why they happened. When events got too big, you couldn't teach about anything else. Here was that event again. So we got a room, collected the faculty, printed our posters, and went forward into cultural memory. "Sixties, don't fail me," I remember thinking, yet only for a moment.

In one of the first comments, a young woman said she wondered if she has what it takes to be a reporter. All she wanted to do on September 11th was stay in bed and hide. Because she couldn't bring herself to head for Ground Zero, she began to ask: Could I ever be a real journalist?

Of all forms of courage a good journalist needs, the willingness to place yourself in danger has a small part. I'm grateful there will always be reporters and photographers who do that; and when a correspondent is hurt or killed trying to cover the news, the story is of heroic sacrifice. Most of the time, for most in the press, intellectual courage is most demanded.

Look, I wanted to say, you are present and vulnerable today, which can take even more guts. Your career begins now;

there's no waiting. Here you sit, eyes open, pencil drawn. And outside the auditorium that massive thing: the reality of the event. Now is when you'll need your bravery and poise, in achieving an education when there's too much reality landing. "Firemen Rule," reads a sign hung outside an NYU dorm on 14th Street. And I can see why for students it is so.

I wanted to tell her there's time to grow the tough hide of a "real" journalist—if that is what you want. I hope you want better than tough. So often a hard-bitten pose conceals a soft and sentimental core, but in tense times to come we cannot afford that. Better to be tough, determined and democratic in your core. Then you can be bruise-able, teachable, impressionable on the outside. As someone said at the teach-in, "I wouldn't trust a journalist who didn't break down last week."

When my daughter got her first bicycle, I had to teach her about courage, especially after she tipped over in Washington Square Park on one of her early rides. She asked me what the word meant. "When you do something that's hard and scary, but you keep going, that's courage." Soon she was reporting to me, "I had two courages today, Daddy." I am not prepared to tell her that it may take more than two per day just to live where we live.

Nor am I able to know how many courages were demanded of her in the days after the attack, with adults reeling, TV blazing, and sirens in the streets. My child is brave, I have no doubt. But where she is brave is a place I am forbidden to go. In the majestic privacy of a four-year-old's inner life ,there is all the stoicism any watchful adult requires. Come Saturday, Sylvie and I have a city to build.

It started a few weeks before the crash, on lazy weekend mornings. While her mother slept late, we would use blocks and books to make a building, a little apartment house suitable for her population of "homeless frogs," as she called them.

The next week it was two buildings: mine and hers. Then we decided on a whole city. The table was cleared and from it rose Froggietown, and right next door Fishtown, a school, a hospital, office building, police station, ice cream store, a park with benches, walkways.

The buildings rose a bit higher each week, and kept rising after the attack. With Legos holding up kids' books and two frogs per floor, the contractors could build eight, nine, ten stories. Not once did Sylvie knock down what she created. If was as if she knew the tenderness in her own act of repair. Last week we added a train set and rebuilt Gotham around it.

Begun in all innocence, the making of this metropolis is parent and child communicating across the expanse of age and terror. In our tabletop city this week, there will be housing again for homeless frogs. Thus do we teach the unteachable of the countless ways they cannot win.

In the Bull's Eye, 2

Scott McLemee

It is good to remind yourself from time to time that every television program you watch is a piece of your own death. But after September 11, for a little while there, anyway, watching the screen meant facing your own mortality, rather than drowning it out.

For several days, I came home from work each afternoon and turned on the box. (During the day, I would hear back from friends in New York; they were all okay, but I wept even so.) Then, while absorbing the news, I would fight the overwhelming desire to sleep. There did not seem to be anything else to do. Nothing in the world was interesting or important except for this reality. Which was unbearable.

Going to bed at seven in the evening seemed like a bad idea, though. Everybody at work or on the street looked like a zombie. An entire city of people either getting no sleep, or getting way too much.

In the middle of the night, we would hear the sound of helicopters overhead. There were men in uniform on the streets. I never did see the humvees, but I heard about them. Each siren in the distance turned my insides into ice. You also knew there could be somebody with a small thermonuclear device in his backpack. In the street outside. This very minute.

It could have happened yesterday. It might well happen tomorrow. And nobody is at all sure about right-this-second. That's the way it is. It is going to stay that way forever. If things remain perfectly uneventful for the next decade or two, they could still change on the day after that.

The following Saturday, Rita told me she had been crying but hadn't wanted to tell me. This hurt, in a number of ways. But at the same time, it was understandable. Each of us was mourning. The misery of the families on television could be unbearable. At the same time, we knew that, in slightly different circumstances, either of us might be dead. A part of you already was. So it was time to mourn.

Love involves, not the possibility of grief, but its certainty. That knowledge can be, in its way, profoundly humiliating. There is a hidden part of the self where the idols are kept, a dimension of the personality that believes, blindly and stupidly, in its own sufficiency and invulnerability. It believes it will live forever, and that all of its dreams come true. (You don't want that part to get an unsecured line of credit. Much worse is when an entire nation lets that aspect take over.) Love smashes the idols. It does not seem likely that anything else can.

"Everything has changed," the people on television said, repeatedly, that day. As though the legacy of a low, dishonest decade were that easy to liquidate. As though this were a chance for profound self-renewal, or something, instead of a reminder that the self will be extinguished, in due time, and that you don't know when.

So you donate blood or money. You do ordinary things with some sense of determination, of mindfulness. I mean, what was I thinking, that day, paying so much attention to our laundry? Well, not much, at the time. But it also seems, now, after the fact, like an effect to keep faith with ordinary life. There didn't seem much else to do.

We are married. We grieve some, for the dead and, in a different way, for each other. We do not plan to move. Our home is right here: henceforth (as, in fact, it always was) a target. We must become the kind of ghosts who try to help the living.

To Bring New Life Forward

Hali Weiss

On September 11, when The World Trade Center fell, the center fell out of my world too. What had constituted my own structural core, my sense of home, tumbled down.

I have lived in New York for twenty years. New York's reputation as a dangerous city didn't frighten me. I built a sense of physical security from the familiarity of the skyline, faith in the permanence of our well-built American infrastructure, intimate knowledge of my neighborhood, and practical street smarts. Before September 11, I experienced the chaos of New York as a predictable system. New York is still my home but, suddenly, I don't quite recognize it.

Loss is always disorienting. In loss, what was powerfully present is suddenly and permanently absent. The void created by any loss is at first impossible to gaze at, and then painful to gaze through. When someone we love dies, we who knew the deceased gather. Often we are known to the deceased but strangers to each other, now connected through a shared absence. When an individual dies, the center falls out of one small shared world.

When the World Trade Center fell, and more than 6,300 people died in an instant, an enormous shared center fell out of our collective world. Now, a city is in mourning, the nation shaken and saddened. We look to each other across an enormous void—the loss has affected every one of us. Crying in front of strangers is suddenly comfortable, discussing depression is common, and insomnia typical. None feels pressure to pretend she is fine. When we ask, "How are you?"

to friends, colleagues and strangers, we are braced to hear of pain and loss. No one makes small talk, because small talk assumes a stable world. Instead, a different set of relationships has begun to emerge. They seem more substantial, even if things are more unstable.

We feel more American. Somehow, through this loss, we have become fellow citizens with a shared depth of concern. We feel grateful to firemen, rescue workers, and governmental leaders. I guess it is clear that a single family is too frail to fend off violence at this scale. The everyday "us" is, in general, a much larger group, the boundaries of which are still in flux. We are all rebuilding our sense of meaning and self-identity, discarding assumptions and shifting priorities. We're not sure what really matters.

But what we do know is that we feel pressed to have more meaning and purpose in the here and now, in this world, in this time and this place. Tony Walter has written of "the eclipse of eternity"—the gradual evolution away from notions of the afterlife. Whether secular or religious, Americans today believe that our present world is shaped by our actions. (We are entirely disoriented by the suicide bomber's far stronger belief in promise of the world to come.) It is in this context of here and now that we will rebuild our broken insides and our broken city.

My office is on Union Square, largest site of candlelight vigils and mass mourning. On Monday, the candles, signs, flowers and tributes were cleared away. Yesterday, a city employee was washing off the spray painted word "LOVE" from a light post. We know now that the "missing" are dead. Time, though shattered, moves on.

I am 38 weeks pregnant—carrying new life and due to give birth in two weeks. I feel frightened for this infant's vulnerability, sad for the anxiety that will be part of all he learns of the world. But I also feel honored to bring new life forward now. While it is true there is a hole in our hearts, and a hole in our skyline, I expect that through millions of small acts of birth and re-birth, we will begin to fill it.

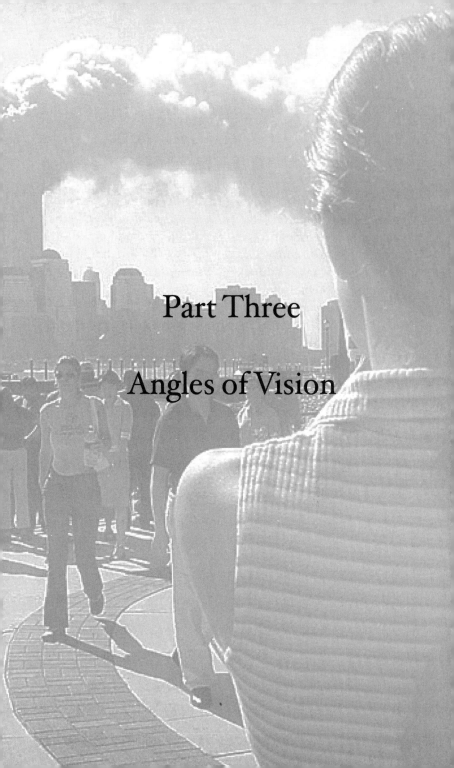

Part Three

Angles of Vision

Quiet in America

J.R. Lankford

September 11—I have never felt such quiet in America. You can almost hear it. Like our hearts have stopped together. We are keeping silent for the people in the buildings, on the planes, who died today. Did the pilot in the Pittsburgh crash fight his hijacker? Did he give his life, sacrifice his plane to save a more precious target? Is that why his flight went down? I have never heard such quiet in America.

Has this happened before? In some other country, at some other time? Were they quiet when their own people died? Did they retaliate so we would feel it too?

Will this awful silence spread? When we strike back and they strike back again? Will it be so quiet we can't hear each other's words, get so dark we can't see each other's tears?

Stranded: A Pilot's Story

Leonard T. Miller

On September 10, 2001, I prepared to fly a routine trip from Dulles International Airport outside Washington to San Francisco, making one stop in Denver.

At home I packed my bag, laid out my uniform, gathered plenty of reading material for the layovers, and made sure any bills and family concerns were satisfied. I was going to be away for four days. I kissed my wife Renee and our ten-month-old daughter Lauren goodbye, grabbed my bag, and drove the forty minutes to the employee parking lot at the airport. Rain was coming down in buckets when I left, but by the time I parked my SUV at the airport it had stopped.

At about 4:00 p.m., I arrived at United Airlines operations to meet the captain to review the weather, aircraft status, and flight plans for Denver and San Francisco. I checked my personal mailbox, read a few bulletins on the wall, and chatted with two of my colleagues whom I hadn't seen for several weeks. Then I grabbed my flight bag, hooked it onto my overnight bag, and joined the captain for our walk to the gate about one hour before our 5:30 departure time.

Even though the summer peak season had passed, people of all walks of life were bustling through the airport waiting to board their flights, buying items in the stores, waiting in line at McDonald's, Starbucks, and Burger King, exchanging currency, stopping in the music store, running, walking and talking. Arriving at our plane, the captain and I performed our standard operating procedures, introduced ourselves to the flight attendants and were in position to depart on time as the passengers boarded.

The gate agent checked with us ten minutes before departure, made the last announcement to the passengers and closed the door. Minutes later, the plane was being pushed backwards by the mechanic steering the tug on the tarmac in position for our taxi. The radios chattered as we configured the plane for takeoff on runway 30.

After twenty minutes taxiing out, we were in the air heading west. In three hours, give or take ten minutes, we would be in Denver. There was talking on the radios as we penetrated various air traffic control sectors. Between radio calls, the captain and I ate our crew meals and talked. The weather was good all the way to Denver and was forecast to be decent in San Francisco.

We arrived at Denver on schedule, and the passengers deplaned. Glad to be home, the flight attendants collected their belongings and said goodbye to us. Several minutes later, a new group of flight attendants boarded to perform their routine safety checks. The captain and I introduced ourselves, and he briefed them on the leg to San Francisco. I walked outside to do the external checks. As I returned from outside, passengers of all shapes and sizes were flowing down the jetway, boarding the flight.

The captain and I performed our routine safety checks in the cockpit, and a flight attendant brought us two bottles of water and two cups with ice. The gate agent asked if we were ready and made the last announcement to the passengers, reaffirming that they were on an airplane headed for San Francisco. The mechanic steered the tug, placing our airplane in position for taxi, and we proceeded to the departure runway. We took off in darkness over the Rocky Mountains, heading west. The flight time was a little over two hours. Our body clocks were on Eastern Time, so for us it was after 10:00 p.m.

Our scheduled arrival time was 9:45 p.m. Pacific Time.

Time went by quickly. The weather was clear, and several towns and cities stood out in the darkness. I remember the lights of Modesto, California and seeing the glow of lights from San Jose and San Francisco on the horizon. It was a nice, routine night. We started the approach that eventually took us over the brightly lit San Mateo Bridge and landed on runway 28R. Seven minutes later, we were parked at the gate. The passengers deplaned swiftly, and the flight attendants lost no time grabbing their bags and heading for the jetway after the last passenger was through the door. The captain and I secured the airplane, walked through the terminal, which was winding down for the night, and caught our hotel transportation.

Downtown, the city was in its late-night mode. A few people were walking around, but things were getting quiet. The lobby was sparse, which made the check-in expedient. The captain and I noted each other's room numbers, which is routine in case any emergency or personal concern surfaces that would affect our operation. These situations are rare, although I did experience the life-threatening October 1989 earthquake in San Francisco, and on that occasion knowing what rooms the crew were in was helpful.

I didn't waste too much time preparing for bed. I was exhausted. I glanced at my watch, which I keep on Eastern Time, and it was 2:00 a.m. I turned on the television for a brief moment and scanned the channels. Then I turned off the TV and the lamp. The room was pitch black, and I easily fell asleep. Luckily, we didn't have to leave the hotel until about 2:50 the next afternoon. I was looking forward to the rest, and the next day would be easy, just one leg back to Denver for a short layover near the airport.

When my eyes opened about seven hours later, the room was still pitch black. I glanced at the hotel clock and noticed

that the bright red time display read almost 6:00 a.m. I had
to use the bathroom and felt like I needed another hour. I
felt around for the remote on the nightstand and managed to
identify the "on" button by feel. I thought the television light
would be less blinding than the bright lamp right next to me
on the nightstand.

I got out of bed while the television came alive, set on
CNN. I watch a lot of CNN, especially on international
layovers, because sometimes it's the only station in English. I
used the bathroom quickly and returned to bed.

I started to focus on the news and heard anchor Leon
Harris talk about an airplane hitting one of the World Trade
Center buildings in New York City. But there was a lot of
uncertainty in the broadcast; the information was sketchy.
Harris was talking to an eyewitness who was confirming the
accident. I thought a small private airplane might have hit the
building. I've flown south down the Hudson River myself in
a Beechcraft Sundowner, enjoying the majestic skyline, and I
knew that it's very common for small airplanes to fly visually
up the Hudson.

Then video clips that looked distorted started to unfold
before my eyes. There was no doubt that an airplane had hit
one of the World Trade Center buildings, but the clips CNN
initially aired were confusing. The silhouette on the initial
clips looked like a smaller twin-engine airplane, possibly a
turbo-prop commuter plane. The discussions on what actually
happened were speculative. I was glued to the television.
There was talk about navigational error but, from the pictures
that were showing a clear day in New York City, I was certain
that it was almost impossible for any pilot to hit a skyscraper
by mistake. They would have to be suicidal or incapacitated.
The video clip was disturbing, to say the least.

When I heard the news report that the airplanes were
Boeings from United and American Airlines, I was shell-

shocked. The news on the television became addictive, and speculative information hastily became fact. Two skyscrapers collapsed before my eyes, and I watched thousands of lives perish. Then words such as "hijack" and "commandeer" became sound bytes.

I had been in the World Trade Center a few times in the 1990s, having lunch with college friends employed in New York's financial district. I had ridden the PATH train from Newark a few times with my father, who was a consultant for a firm headquartered in the World Trade Center and frequented one of the towers several times a month in the 1990s.

When I heard that the Pentagon had been hit by another American flight and that a second United flight had crashed in a cornfield in western Pennsylvania, I was overwhelmed. I called the captain to see if he had heard the news. It was immediately apparent that he had. We predicted that our flight to Denver would be cancelled.

The maid knocked on my door to ask if I wanted my room serviced. She could barely speak. I told her I didn't need service, and she told me that the entire hotel might be stranded for a while. I remained glued to the television, not even realizing that I was hungry. Lunchtime on the West Coast came and went. I ordered room service when dinnertime arrived. I couldn't leave the room.

Announcements started to surface of crew members on all the hijacked flights. I looked at the United lists several times to see if I knew anyone personally. I didn't recognize any of the names, but that was irrelevant. Several of my co-workers had fallen.

My wife called me; she had heard the news on the car radio. When she picked our daughter up at the day care center, she had been greeted by a manager and two security guards, who checked her identification before she was allowed on the property.

All through that evening and the next day, my room phone kept ringing. Friends were tracking me down in San Francisco through my wife in Virginia and my parents in Pennsylvania. I watched the video clips of the attacks several times through the next day, still in disbelief.

On the morning of September 12, I ordered room service for breakfast. I wasn't in the mood to leave the room. I was glued to the television. I skipped lunch again. Letters from United were being slipped under the door with contact numbers and guidance for crew members. Airports were shut down across America. I figured it would be days before I made it home to my wife and daughter.

The captain called me around 4:30 p.m. to ask if I wanted to go to an Interfaith Service of National Mourning at Grace Cathedral. I told him I would meet him in the lobby at 5:30. We walked about five blocks, up the steep sidewalks of San Francisco, to the cathedral. Hundreds of people were approaching the cathedral from all directions. Candles were being distributed just inside the front door. It was the first time I had even been outdoors in nearly thirty-six hours. The standing-room-only service started promptly at 6:00 p.m.

After the service, the captain and I ate dinner a few blocks from the hotel then retired for the evening, mentally exhausted. I could not help but turn on the television and watch CNN until I was fighting sleep.

The next day was more of the same. The captain and I checked in with each other at least twice a day. We still didn't have any idea when we would get back to Dulles. I decided to go downstairs and get a shoeshine. The shoeshine man, mentally exhausted and dumbfounded like everyone else, told me that the hotel had received a bomb scare the previous evening. Some guests were trying to rent cars or take trains and buses out of town. Everyone was frustrated about the attack and the predicament it had put them in.

On the 14th America's air transport system was projected to become active on a limited basis, but the captain and I had not yet received an official assignment from the United crew schedulers. We could not get through to the shedulers on the phone, so we decided to leave the hotel on our own at 5:30 a.m. and proceed to United's San Francisco flight operations to try to find out our status. We were willing to volunteer in the office if necessary, but when we arrived, the office was fully staffed. We hung around for seven hours, watching CNN the entire time in the pilots' lounge. At 9:00 a.m., a staff member summoned us to join everyone for a moment of silence. A group of thirty or so bowed our heads and were silent for exactly one minute. Then a United pilot read off the names of the crew members who had died in both United flights on September 11th, and the semi-circle solemnly dispersed.

Around 2:00 p.m., the captain finally got through to the crew schedulers in Chicago. They informed him that we would deadhead home the next day and told us to go back to the hotel.

Finally, on Saturday the 15th, we were on our way home to Dulles. The San Francisco airport had a much different appearance. Hundreds of passengers were in line at the ticket counter. Know one was allowed to go through security unless they had a ticket. The security was much more stringent, and it took a lot longer to get through. Once we passed through security into the gate area, the terminal looked almost abandoned. The few flights operating were full of stranded passengers. Heading home, I had an empty feeling. You could sense that the airline world was going to change forever.

When I got back to Dulles and retrieved my car, I felt as if I had been separated from my family for a month. I started the drive home that usually felt routine, but this drive felt completely different. The future felt uncertain, but I had fared better than the victims of the September 11 attack and really didn't have any problems. On the way down my rural road, I saw my neighbors Rob and Melonie in the driveway with their two sons. They had called me at the hotel in San Francisco. After about ten minutes of sharing stories and concerns with them, I drove down the road and parked my SUV. My wife and daughter were happy to see me back.

I tried to wind down, but we were all glued to CNN. About 7:00 p.m., the phone rang. My wife answered it, spoke very briefly, and hung up. It was our neighbors, she informed me, advising us that if we heard some noise, it was just them testing their guns.

Mourning in Amsterdam

Alex M. Dunne

Jo, a former boss of mine from when I worked on Wall Street years ago, called me this afternoon.

Yesterday morning, she was working from her home across the water from lower Manhattan when her building shook. Thinking it was the concrete pilings beneath her, which routinely settle into the Hudson River, she went back to work. Moments later, a man from her Wall Street office called "to verify that I was alive." "Why?" she asked. "Look out your window," he said.

She looked east out her window at the burning North Tower of the World Trade Center. A moment later, she saw the second commercial airliner strike the South Tower. Shaky and crying, she reported, "I saw several people jump from the Towers, I think from the fireballs inside." Many of those who jumped, she later found out, landed on firemen and rescue workers, killing them. "After the South Tower collapsed, a priest went in to deliver the last rites. But he was killed in the collapse of the North Tower."

She informed me a mutual friend of ours, now safe, had been caught in the debris shower from the Towers' collapse. From her vantage point across the river, Jo reported on the view of the new New York skyline, with the gaping hole now opened up in it. "It doesn't look like New York City anymore. It just looks like Pittsburgh. Or any other city."

Afterwards, I left CNN and my home to find solace at a cafe. As we scanned the photo spreads of the tragedy in *Het Parool*, the silence at our table was eerie and observed.

Within minutes, the friendly Dutch chatter at surrounding tables turned to sideways glances and quiet English language discussions of the tragedy and "the Americans."

On the ride home, we stopped at the U.S. Consulate, across the street from our house. From a distance, the Consulate looks open for "business as usual." The steel shutters on the windows are up, but the American flag is down, lufting in the breeze at half mast. Closer up, one sees an officer of the Dutch Politie stationed in a mobile kiosk on the corner. Two private guards from the Consulate patrol outside the perimeter fence, asking people not to linger too long. There is much to linger over. Over a hundred bouquets of roses, tulips, carnations and sunflowers, a Dutch favorite, have been passed through the steel bars of the fence and dropped onto the lawn. Many bear cards with inscriptions. "We'd like to wish the people of the U.S.A. strength in this time of terror," says one. "God bless all of you," says another. Many cards are individually signed.

Three television satellite trucks are parked nearby. A reporter from a Dutch radio station stopped me to ask a few questions. "How do you feel about the flowers?" he asked. "It's clear the impact of this tragedy is felt by more than just Americans. We're grateful for that," I replied. While his tape machine wound up my words, a dozen more people arrived on foot and by bicycle to drop off flowers.

One well-meaning soul carefully placed small white candles on the ground ringing the perimeter fence. Each candle was equidistant from its neighbors. Shortly after being lit, all of them blew out in the constant Dutch breeze.

An Immigrant's Thoughts

Derrick N. Ashong

My name is Derrick N. Ashong; I'm Harvard Class of '97. I'm writing this more to clear my own heart and mind than to share a cogent thought, so please bear with me if I lose focus.

I have an uncle who worked at the World Trade Center. He is one of my closest family members. His name is Japhet Aryee. He and his wife are the only people my mom would leave my sister and me with when we were little. He is my dad's best friend. As of 9 a.m. today, 9/13 he is unaccounted for. ...

I feel very hurt by what has happened this week on a number of different levels. First, my heart goes out to all of the families who have lost loved ones and who fear for the safety of those who are missing. I also pray for all who have friends, co-workers, acquaintances et al. who are today stricken with fear, foreboding, uncertainty or loss regarding the status and whereabouts of those for whom they care. To call this a tragedy would be to say too little when words cannot say enough. Perhaps it's better not to call it anything at all. Then again, sometimes sorrow needs a name in order to be drawn from the hearts of a people.

I want to share with you my feelings about our current situation. My perspective is a bit peculiar, so I hope it will offer others cause for thought. I was born in Accra, Ghana and grew up in Brooklyn and the Middle East. I spent my formative years (8-16) in Saudi Arabia and Qatar, a small peninsula in the Arabian Gulf. My family returned to the U.S. in the summer of '91, and I have not been back to the region since.

In the summer of 1990, when Iraq invaded Kuwait, my family was vacationing in New Jersey. At the time we received word of the Iraqi incursion my father, who is a physician, had returned to work in Qatar, while my mom, sister and I hung out in South Jersey. Hearing of what was happening back "home," as I would have referred to Qatar then, we were all very frightened. In weighing the choices available to us, my parents decided that the most important thing was for our family to remain together. And so, during Desert Shield we flew home to be with my dad and face whatever the future held in store for us, together.

When most Americans think of Desert Storm, I imagine they must envision a "video-game" conflict. We went in there with computer-guided weaponry, laid waste to the incompetent Iraqi military, achieved our stated goals, and got out from under the shadow of Vietnam-era humiliation. It was a bang-up job with relatively few casualties, and it proved the might and technological superiority of American military power. I won't get into the validity or degrees of verity of these previous statements, because it is not my present intention to argue about the Gulf War. I would, however, like to state that for many, Desert Storm was far from a video game.

When we returned to Qatar in the summer of 1990, the desert air was rife with speculation. Why did this happen? Whose fault is it? What's going to happen next? Questions we are all currently quite familiar with. I remember hosting American soldiers who were barely older than myself at the time. I remember their courage, I remember the fear beneath it, I remember their youth. I remember the primary concern at the time being the potential use of chemical or biological agents by the Iraqi military. Various nations were evacuating their citizens from a country populated primarily by expatriates. Many of those who stayed were being issued gas masks by their respective governments. I remember thinking: "There's no way the Ghanaian government is going to send the four of us some gas masks." Fortunately, there turned out to be more than four of us in the country and, as members of the British Commonwealth, we got the hookup anyway. Unfortunately, this was not the case for everyone.

At the instruction of authorities, we turned one room in my parents' house into a "safe" haven in case of chemical or biological attack. We sealed all of the doors, windows and vents with electrical tape. Once the conflict began, my family would sleep in that supposedly secure room. My father would carefully seal the main door and check the tape on each window and vent before settling down next to me on the air mattress we shared. The four of us would put our gas masks by our pillows, gather by the bedside, and pray together before turning in for the night.

As the imminence of U.S./international intervention grew, I saw many of my friends evacuated by their respective governments. I wondered if I would see them again. The halls of my high school did not pulse with the same vigor, nor bubble with the ready laughter I had grown accustomed to. I recall one day in particular, sitting in my biology class when we heard a loud BANG. Immediately I reached beneath the broad wooden table at which I sat and grabbed the plastic bag housing my gas mask. In moments I had removed it, and as practiced countless times before, secured it to my face, being careful to ensure that it was properly sealed.

I believe it was then that I got my first glimpse at the alien face of war. As I sat there behind a mask of thin security, praying for clean air, I saw it reflected in the eyes of my classmates whose governments had not been able to provide them with even that modicum of protection. Many of them were Palestinian. For a moment we sat in silence, lips sealed by fear, hearts rent by epiphany. If at that moment the gas hit the fan, some of us would watch our friends die.

This past weekend, I went to my college roommate's wedding in Montvale, New Jersey. I helped herd folk from Boston down to New Jersey, then shuttle them around the villages of North Jersey and in and out of the city, all the while referencing, yet taking for granted, the awesome New York City skyline. Upon returning to our hotel after one such excursion, my car was hailed in front of the hotel lobby by a group of orthodox Jews. They wanted to know if I could sing. I told them I do it for a living. They asked me to join them. I told them I had to park my car. They said screw the car, it will be there when we're done.

It's about 1:30 a.m., and I have been approached by a group of guys I don't know in a town I'm unfamiliar with. But they want to sing, and I'm a musician. Besides, other than Palestinians, who's afraid of a conservative Jew? I hopped out of the ride and walked over to them. They wanted me to teach them a tune. I taught them a traditional West African song, which translated means "peace, be still, all is well." They taught me a traditional Hebrew song about friendship. We traded tunes, and they marveled at my pronunciation. I told them I had grown up in the Middle East and used to speak a little Arabic. We sang and danced and made a lot of noise. Eventually, two of my roommates came down to the lobby to look for me and saw me outside laughing with a group of strangers. They joined us, and within minutes we were again singing, dancing and making even more noise. Imagine the scene: three Blacks (an African, an African-American, and a Trinidadian) raising hell at three in the morning with a gang of Orthodox Jews. I remember thinking, "This is what I love about America."

That night as we parted ways, I was visited by a growing sadness. How would I feel if I was to learn that Abraham, Gershi and the others had been blown up by a terrorist bomb while dancing at a party? Could I imagine the joy they had shared with me, stifled by a political vendetta? Then I thought, how would I feel if Hesham or Rami or Nadia or any of the other kids I grew up with were cut down by Israeli bullets while protesting for their freedom? Freedom. What is more American than that?

There is so much more I could say. My high school sweetheart is half-Palestinian. My freshman roommate is half-crazy but all Jewish. I love them both, and before I see their ethnicity I see their humanity. But in my life I also see the pain of people who have been near mortally wounded. People who have been stripped of their dignity, their livelihoods, indeed their very lives by forces with great power but little value for "the other." These people are Black, they are Jewish, they are Palestinian, they are Irish, Croatian, Rwandan, Indonesian, South African, Nigerian, Chinese, Japanese, they are the world. Today my heart bleeds with fear for my own family, and my eyes burn with tears of acrimony, vengeance and sorrow. But as I look beyond my own grief, I wonder how many others also grieve. Around the world, how many have known the never-ending twilight of suffering? How many have looked into the eyes of those they love and seen their own shame? How many have cried to the same God for retribution?

It is time for us as a nation to wake up. The struggles of human beings around the world are indeed our own. We are not exempt from the asphyxiating roots of hatred and intolerance; indeed we sit in the highest branches of the tree they built. And today we see that though we live above the clouds, we cannot ignore the turmoil that threatens to uproot the foundations of our global society.

At a time like this, I can feel myself moving into "Patriotic Mode." I think "God Bless America," I pray for all those who may risk their lives in defense of our nation, I ponder the ways in which I can contribute, and I even pay attention when

Dubya speaks. I believe we must stand together as a people.
But I also believe we must look at where we're standing, and
be sure that we are truly grounded in what we say we believe
in. Liberty and Justice for ALL. Not just for some Americans,
not even all Americans, not just for our allies but for ALL. I
pledge allegiance to the World.

I wasn't born an American. I chose to become one, and
I thought long and hard before doing so. I made the choice
I did because despite her faults, I believe in what America
STANDS for. And so I stand prepared to defend the nation
to whom I am promised. Still I pray that she recognize that
the only way to truly fight "evil" is with truth. If we stand
for Justice, we must hear the cries of all her people, even if
they don't speak English. My mother taught me as a child
that "charity begins at home." I pray for my family. I pray for
yours. I pray for our nation, our leaders and those around the
world. I pray for peace. God bless us all.

"Maybe we should go to war"

William Davis

September 13—I spent part of my day today with a class of 11th-grade honors history students in Jacksonville, North Carolina. A day before the class, in one of those small pieces of irony that litter our lives, the students were studying how and why the U.S. has gone to war—a list of eleven dates marking the country's major conflicts remained on the blackboard.

Despite the fact that Jacksonville is a military town—its borders include Camp Lejeune, one of the country's largest Marine Corps bases—most of the students spoke out against war, wondering how it could ever be justified. War, to them, was evil and inexplicable.

Two days later, everything has changed. One boy told the class that he always thought he would never go to war for his country. Now, he said, he would sign up to fight today because "I don't want my kids to grow up in this."

Not everyone beats the drums for war, it must be said. But those who did not seemed lost, confused. As the discussion began, one girl in the back raised her hand and shyly said she didn't want any innocent people to be hurt in other countries; that she didn't want people she knew to go to war.

As the class came to a close, she raised her hand again.

"I don't know what we should do. We can't let this happen again. We have to do something. Maybe we should go to war," she said.

Far from Home

Challiss McDonough

As an American living abroad (South Africa), I have felt incredibly cut off from my friends, family and indeed my whole nation. I feel this way despite my access to satellite television and the Internet—access that most in this country do not have. Your dispatches (and e-mails from my family in D.C.) helped me feel more connected.

The weather here in Johannesburg is bleak enough to match my mood—raining and unseasonably cold. I write for a living. I am not accustomed to having words fail me. But I have written and re-written this note over the last 36 hours, and I just can't describe what I am feeling: the emptiness, the sadness, the anger, the sadness, the fear, the sadness, the isolation, the sadness.

I am a journalist. In the past, I have been in traumatic situations and managed to set my emotions aside for long enough to do my job. But I had no job to do on this one, no task to focus on; I just sit there numb in front of the TV and computer screen, a spectator. I feel helpless. This far away, I cannot even donate blood.

Yesterday, I cried. All day. A South African TV station asked to interview me. I had to turn them down; I did not want to break down in tears on national television. Today, it is starting all over again. The tears just do not stop.

The reports from home help, but also reinforce how far away I am. My 16-year-old niece can't sleep, she has nightmares, she will not watch TV news anymore. One of my sisters is sleeping in her guest bedroom, away from the outside windows. She lives in Capitol Hill; she hears military aircraft buzzing overhead. She was supposed to go to San Francisco on business this week, but she says she won't go even if the airports are open. She is afraid to fly.

I cannot comfort them from the other side of the planet. I cannot seek comfort from them, either. My expat friends are going through the same thing, and we have turned to each other for strength.

Everyone has friends and/or family who work in the Pentagon or lower Manhattan; we are poring over e-mails, running up massive phone bills trying to track them down. Many of us have somebody we have not heard from. They might be fine. We feel so far away.

Lunch yesterday turned into a group therapy session: five of us, all women, from four nations, all trying to wrap our brains around what has happened. We share news, we send SMS messages, we remind each other we are not alone. And we still feel so far away.

Tonight, we are going bowling together. Our informal "therapy group" has grown to more than a dozen. On the surface, it seems like an odd thing to do, but it seems more productive than sitting around in a bar, drinking, or than sitting in front of the TV at home, crying.

Surreal

Laurel Sheppard

Although I was miles away from all the death and destruction, the events of September 11 have obviously changed me and the rest of the world forever. I no longer feel safe and secure and am very worried about the future. I am skeptical about making it to retirement, some 20 years away, and am waiting anxiously to see what happens next. My emotions have been on a roller coaster—one day I hate the terrorists, another day I hate the television media for showing the images over and over again.

Surreal has become the word for this event. Those who have seen the wreckage firsthand say it is surreal, and those who have only seen it on their television screens feel the same way. A week later, everything still seems surreal: the continuing search and rescue operation, the talk of war, the faces of the victims and their families, and those awful images of the plane crashes and building collapses.

On that day I was in my home office and just had turned on the small television on my desk. It was a few minutes after the first crash and I saw the two towers behind the commentators, one on fire. I immediately called my friend at her office to relay the news. She told me to keep her informed on what was happening. Some minutes later I was on the phone to a colleague of hers to ask a question, and suddenly saw the second plane hit. I screamed into the phone about what had happened and continued to tell him what was happening as I watched. Next thing I knew they said the Pentagon had been hit. I finally hung up the phone and e-mailed a friend who worked near the Pentagon to see if he was okay. Don't ask me why I didn't call him. Around noon he called me to say he was safe.

The rest of the day was a blur. I called my parents near Cleveland and found out my sister, who works in the tallest buildings downtown, was evacuated. I tried to send work-related e-mails but finally gave up trying to concentrate and watched CNN the rest of the day. I found out my conference in California for later that week was canceled. I was supposed to fly to LA on Wednesday morning. It was hard to accept the fact that that was the same destination of three of the doomed flights. Will I ever want to fly to that city again?

My suitcase was almost packed and ready to go. I had started packing on Monday and, looking back, was it my imagination that I was not looking forward to the trip? Or were these uneasy feelings because I had just gotten back from Cleveland and did not want to be away again so soon? If this wasn't a premonition, perhaps my friend's dream was. On Monday night she dreamed that I crashed a small green plane onto the roof of her home (but no injuries). I say it was a prediction that my flight was canceled, not the other alternative.

The following e-mails describe some of my emotions during September 11 and the days that followed.

September 11, 10 a.m., e-mail to my friend who works near the Pentagon:

> What the hell is going on? How close are you to the pentagon? Are you evacuated?
>
> This is horrible and I am supposed to fly out tomorrow.

September 11, 10:08 a.m., e-mail to my sister in California:

> Who knows if I will make it out to Cal. tomorrow due to the terrorist attacks. I actually saw the second plane fly into the trade center live...

> I am sick to my stomach right now. If the Palestinians did it we should blow up their entire country! [this was in reaction to early reports a Palestinian terrorist group claimed they did it]

> they just said part of one of the towers collapsed onto the street and people were running from the falling debris

September 11, 2:54 p.m., e-mail to my friend who works near the Pentagon:

> I hope none of your coworkers were over there, just heard there is probably casualties. Did you hear the eyewitness who was the pilot who saw the crash? Pretty scary.

> Keep in touch.

September 11, 5:56 p.m., e-mail to a local friend who was concerned about my flying on Wednesday:

> no surprise but my conference got canceled and luckily I got a full refund on my tickets.
> I am relieved.

Just saw a third building collapse.

Remember my friend Bill? He works near the Pentagon and is safe though some of his coworkers might not be since they have to go to meetings there all the time.

I still can't believe it.

September 12, 10:35 a.m., e-mail to friends in Japan:

Yesterday morning I went into my office and turned on my computer to start working and also turned on the small TV on my desk, my normal routine. I was shocked to see the first report of the first tower being hit. Then I watched in horror as I saw the second plane hit the other tower live. I kept the TV on as I tried to check my e-mail and do some work but it was impossible not to continue watching. Next I learned about the Pentagon and finally saw one of the towers collapse live on TV. I still can't believe this has happened.

I believe there were Japanese working in the trade center and I hope they all got out safely though know that is probably impossible. Hope no one knows anyone that was affected.

A friend of mine that works near the Pentagon is safe but haven't heard about some of his colleagues who could have been attending meetings there.

I hope nothing like this ever happens in Japan. Earthquakes are bad enough.

It will obviously be difficult to fly in the future. I was supposed to fly to LA today for a conference, obviously both were canceled!

The civilized nations must join together and wipe out terrorism.

Yesterday was a day of tragedy for both the U.S. and the world, since many of the people that died were from other countries. And it was also an attack on democracy, not just the U.S.

September 12, 2:09 p.m., e-mail to my friend near the Pentagon:

Today the power went off at home, which freaked me out. Looked in the backyard and saw 2 AEP [American Electric Power] guys working on the box.

Told them I thought the terrorists had come back.

September 12, 11:20 p.m., e-mail to my sister in California:

Are you still coming in October, I heard 3 aviation experts today who all agreed the safety measures FAA have proposed are worthless. I don't want to alarm you but it sure scared me.

September 14, 2:23 p.m., e-mail to the O'Reilly show on Fox TV:

Any person, terrorist or otherwise, that has no respect for life whatsoever, I do not consider a true human being. To me such a person is more like a rabid dog that cannot be cured and must be destroyed to prevent spreading the disease. I do not consider this murder since they are not my definition of human beings. True human beings have compassion and a conscience; obviously the terrorists of 9/11 did not.

September 17, 7:38 p.m., e-mail to Fox TV:

In the television public service announcement for the Red Cross, Dr. Healey provides suggestions on how to help and deal with the tragedy. She says "avoid repetitive viewing of the images" or something similar.

However, how can people follow this suggestion if they are watching 24-hr news channels like yours, where the plane crashes and building collapses are shown over and over again? (I cannot provide a specific count because I can no longer watch them to do so.) Do you have no compassion for the victims and their families? I am sure they want to keep updated on the search but I can only imagine what they feel when they see those images over and over again. (I am fortunate to have no relatives or friends directly involved but still cannot bear to watch those images any more.)

September 18, 1:58 p.m., e-mail to friend in California:

What is the world coming to!? Humans (especially the war mongers) are the most stupid species on earth. Maybe an asteroid should destroy earth before we do. If it is not

pollution it will be war and perhaps nuclear/
biological/chemical weapons. I sure hope I am
wrong.

September 19, 1:49 p.m., e-mail to a friend in Maryland:

I have mixed feelings about all this war talk.
I hope they are working on peaceful solutions
as well and there was more publicity about
that. I feel that the cycle of violence will
just continue as we seek retaliation, then the
terrorists will attack again, etc etc.

Old Glory, New Pride

Paula Porter

Two of my co-workers were on Flight 11, and though I have dealt with death before, I could not believe how profoundly this has affected me nearly every day.

I didn't have an American flag. And with the events of the last week, I felt guilty about it. I couldn't find one anywhere. Stores were sold out. And then I remembered the one flag I had sitting at the top of a bookcase in my home office.

That U.S. flag had flown briefly over our nation's capital. Its last official act before being ensconced in the plastic zippered case was to cover my husband's casket before we buried him in the rich, black Iowa soil four days after his death on Christmas Day 1987.

That U.S. flag, its white stars on blue, then sat on a chair next to my bed. For weeks I touched its plastic case in reverence as the last closest object to touch a piece of my husband. I used it on my lap as I poured out my grief in a journal, as I wrote bitter poems toward the country I once believed had killed one of its sons through the cancer colored orange that fouled his veins. Some nights I held it in my arms as a physical sleeping pill.

That U.S. flag was the last thing I packed when I moved to Massachusetts and the first thing I unpacked as I settled into my new home.

Yet that U.S. flag, as the years passed, became forgotten.

I realized today that I did have a flag. Then I fought with myself. It needed to be preserved and saved because of what it once meant to me. Yet, something in the back of my heart kept pushing.

Fly me.

Release me.

Let yourself remember me.

And it suddenly became vital.

I took it down off the dusty bookcase and wiped the plastic clean.

I held my breath as I unzipped it and held it for the first time in nearly 14 years.

I brushed my fingers over the embroidered stars as I remember the four Vietnam veterans — their white-gloved hands as vivid in my memory as the red against the white — as they folded then handed me its tight triangular form.

I unfolded it, laying it gently on the bed, and smoothed the creases of the past away.

I watch it now out my window as I write, flying as it once did.

And I remember.

Who Are the Terrorists?

Helga Ahmed

Islamabad, Pakistan—This absolute devastation and the heartbreaking human tragedies are difficult to face, and the whole world mourns. Christianity, though, does emphasise the need for reflection and also imposes penance on those who cause harm to others. But this has been forgotten long ago, just like the true teachings of Islam are nowhere visible today. It is all just dirty politics by a small group of people who manipulate us all. I belong to the Second World War generation and have now lived 45 adult years in a Muslim country: Pakistan. When I left Germany I was given up as lost forever.

Perhaps I am, because my heart today also bleeds for all the Muslims killed, maimed, orphaned and widowed in the battle initiated by the superpowers. Those powers that were to free Afghanistan from a puny group of communists—an era I was deeply involved in, as we moved to Kabul after the '78 coup and left after the Russian invasion in 1980. Soon after that, by a quirk of fate—which always made me wonder if God intended me to give up my part of the world, just to work for the cause of the poor in this region—there I was, working in a voluntary capacity in some of the Afghan refugee camps in Baluchistan [province], Pakistan.

Just a few days back, when recounting some of my memories, I was asked to open a website, so that others also could learn/gain from my experiences. Although not taking it seriously, it nevertheless made me open that box which held 16 years of my association with Afghans and then them as refugees. It was on the 11.9.2001.

That agony, which has been part of me for so many years now, I have to share with you all, as there was no global outcry at the cruelties committed by the so-called freedom fighters, trained and fully supported by the western world, and now their offshoots are known as the Taliban.

It was 1982 when I came to know that the FREEDOM FIGHTERS had thrown acid into the faces of young female students who insisted on continuing to wear their school uniforms, female teachers and government servants who refused to give up their jobs and become refugees in Pakistan. I was told by an Afghan girl who worked with me that these were her former students and colleagues/friends. Her brother too, who refused to give up his job in Kandahar, died of a broken heart; the heavy beatings crippled him. There were thousands of similar stories.

I was keen to get these stories published and willingly shared them with western journalists. I'm sure you all would be able to guess what their reply was. But for those of you who perhaps are too young to know about the complicities of western politics in the third world, the reply was: Oh no, this goes against our present-day political interests.

Before me, too, I have a newspaper clipping brought out of that box. An article by Martin Walker: 27th June ... THE GUARDIAN. "CLINTON 'BLEW IRAQ COUP'"— approximately six years old. "A CIA veteran emerges from retirement to tell the *Washington Post* how he helped run the CIA's successful campaign against the Soviet Occupation in Afghanistan," etc. I remember him well, but he had left months before the Soviets occupied Kabul. He will probably go down in history as having contributed to creating a situation which resulted in that "planned" Russian invasion.

Here another incident comes to mind. The Pakistan government was hated by the people of Afghanistan. One day, when walking towards the Pakistan embassy with my daughter, and wearing traditional Pakistani clothes (otherwise we could have been mistaken for Russians), we could hear shouts from a distance: "Death to Zia-ul-Haq", etc. Aware that this would be one of those many state-organized demonstrations walking past the embassy, I was double-minded about continuing on that same road. However, Bavarian stubbornness persisted and, holding my teenage daughter's hand tightly, I faced the oncoming, well-organized demonstrators. Suddenly, a group from amongst them approached us. I put my arm around my daughter, ready for the worst. And what happened? "We love you, God bless you, people from Pakistan." I sat right down at the curb and cried. Just could not stop that flow of tears, as I was aware how our government had sold them out.

But what effect do my stream of tears and all our tears today have, when we, as caring and loving citizens of this world, cannot influence our governments, who seem to be bent on revenge?

Is it not time that all of us joined hands and started sowing that seed that will ensure that our younger generations too have a future to look forward to?

I have to add here that today my teenage granddaughters are faced with insults and abuse in that Democratic State of America, although born American. Compare it with my Afghan experience.

The World Wide Web

Betsy de Lotbinière

Running towards silence clutching roses.

White with red tips,
stripes
burning, blasting, blood,
roses held together by blue ribbon
good weather skies choked by black smoke,
Stars catching flying souls while
business-suited bodies jumped in their ballet of death,
the white tissue blanket
around green thorns
in the crook
of my arm, I was
running down bustling Oxford Street
past international shop signs
an hour before noon.

There were other runners
Dashing down every side-street
I passed,
men and women running,
cradling bouquets that would never touch
water.
Jogging in high heels,
trying to catch
the silence
at 11.

Gather in the circle
of Hanover Square beneath
a bronze of Roosevelt standing with
a stick and his cape, concealing his crippled state.

For a long time I've been
estranged from my homeland
learning subtle Euro-truths and hiding
the puff-breasted earnestness that marks
a home-grown American,
slowly downgrading the
volume of a native New Yorker. . .

I stand and weep with hundreds too dazed to appreciate
we are standing in silence in the middle of what is
a busy London artery.
A plane flew through our hearts
A jumbo jet through our minds
As giant twins curtsied
in plumes of umbrella smoke
ash was snow
skyscrapers were headless witnesses
their shoulders seeming to shudder
in silent tears.
The old world stood to
deliver their bouquets and bow their heads
We filed, some four-abreast at first and then singly through
Security.

Chinese to my left,
Croatian couple in front,
a German in a brown suit
A huge, stately Sikh in black turban, giant buds bunched

in black arm beneath the golden eagle
of the embassy.

Where I come from you could all be one of us.

Every flag in England set at half mast.
Who are you?
What is this? The old questions slowly returning
when yesterday it was only
Are you all right? Are you okay? Or the worst question of all,
Acrid and stinging in the throat:
Where is _____?

Friends call relations from Mississippi to Mesopotamia
because Manhattan's tip was exploding.
From Wiltshire to Wisconsin electronic mail was
sent because the protectors of a Williamsburg dream
working in the Pentagon were hit,
If you were in Paris you needed to fax Peking
because in Pennsylvania a plane —
well, I love you.

They rang from mobile phones
through fire, smoke and tears and

certain oblivion

in every language they called out
I love you
I love you
the best and only words.

© 2001 Betsy de Lotbinière

"I did not join them"

Roger Tatoud

September 15—Yesterday, millions of people of the "civilised world" paid their respect to the victims of the World Trade Centre attack with 3 minutes of silence.

I did not join them.

Not that I am not feeling compassionate for the victims and their families or that I have anti-American feelings. I feel for the victims and their families, but I cannot associate myself with such hypocrisy. A few months ago, Channel 4 (UK) aired a report on the situation of women in Afghanistan. I was shocked and disturbed by this report. The next day, I tried to get my friends and colleagues at work to get involved, to sign an on-line petition and write to their MP to question them (it wasn't a one-off action). Only a few got involved. So I'd like to ask: where were you mourners when the people of Kosovo, Chechnya, Rwanda, Sierra Leone were wiped out, killed, tortured and raped? Did you grieve for the Palestinian child killed by the Israeli soldiers this summer?

Death, like Life, does not seem to have the same value everywhere, but that is far from new.

People who can mourn the death of strangers puzzle me. Here in Britain, it was the biggest outpouring of public grief since the death of Diana, Princess of Wales. Could it be that, in the present situation, the victims were from this side of the world? Will they grieve for the innocent victims of a now probable military retaliation against Kabul? Will they stop their daily shopping in Oxford Street and think about the innocent victims of a U.S. missile sent to "smoke [them]

out of their holes" as G.W. Bush announced today?
No, I cannot join them.

War Party

John Bebow

Ann Arbor, Michigan, September 16—We gathered Saturday night on Sunset Street, a farewell party for a departing friend.

Liz, a lawyer with a striking resemblance to Jackie Kennedy, is moving back East. We drove up in our SUVs and imports. Jews, Catholics, and Protestants, dressed in casual mall-bought clothes, all walked through the front door of the $300,000 home. The crowd of couples fueled at the bar with Labatt's, Dos Equis, Beringer Cabernet, Asti, Pimms.

The sprawling backyard had tall hardwoods, rows of vegetables at the end of the season, and flower-covered tables. Our smiles showed strength, industry, intellect and budding wealth. Each new arrival heard "Hey!" "Hi!" "Howyadoin?" Not the new American social custom: "So, where were you?" Halfway through the first drink, though, the real questioning commenced.

Tuesday was the worst of it, right? What could possibly be worse than the torching of New York's skyline and the breaching of the castle of the most powerful military force in history? Why weren't we ready? What about the economy?

Do we have enough ice?

I kept another question to myself. Were we really saying goodbye tonight to more than one friend? Our Jackie Kennedy lookalike and the American elegance and strength that doomed first lady embodied?

Steadily, we shared where we'd been Tuesday morning. I think the digital clock on my office phone said 8:54 when I picked up the receiver. It was my lifelong hometown buddy, a flight dispatcher at O'Hare Airport for a major airline. "Good morning!" I shouted into the phone, expecting, as always, a new madcap tale from a guy who once worked on a halibut boat in Alaska, rewired a nuclear plant near New Orleans, and makes more bar friends than Budweiser.

"Maybe for somebody, somewhere," he said. "A plane just hit the World Trade Center. It's a hijacking." I don't think anybody in the newsroom I run heard me hours later when I muttered to the television, "Did it feel this bad in 1963?"

The calendar said it was still summer Saturday, but it was chilly. It was warmer inside the Sunset Street kitchen. Anna, our hostess, showed the ceramic tile and sleek wood cabinets they had installed. A liberal lawyer for the Michigan State Bar cited something from a recent issue of a foreign policy magazine about America's "World Cop" role. The rest of the kitchen clique didn't offer follow-up quotes. How could we? We don't know the source material. The 34-year-old Republican marketing whiz reads Archie comics when he's in the john. Five fresh golf magazines were in the mailbox when I returned from vacation last month. The very social roots of Saturday night's party grew from a women's book club. Fiction mostly. They've met sporadically this year. No one has the time.

Foreign policy? Does anyone remember a single foreign policy snippet from last year's presidential debates? How many of us asked one into the television?

Bin Laden kept warning us. He finally figured out just how loudly you must scream to break through America's arrogance and attention deficit disorder. Sure, the '93 World Trade Center bombing killed a half-dozen people and backed up traffic for a while, but, hey, that's New York City. The embassy bombings in '98 were pretty ghastly, but, as our departing friend Liz mocked, "It was only Africa. You think we were going to wage a war over that?" Six months ago bin Laden distributed a bellicose training video, repeating previous promises of American bloodshed—civilian and military bloodshed.

"America is much weaker than it appears," he said.

We didn't hear him. Now, we can't refute him.

In the adrenaline of Tuesday afternoon, I interviewed 79-year-old Suzanne Auperle, who lives in western Michigan. Pearl Harbor forced her sailor husband to cancel a New Year's date 60 years ago.

"Our generation understands this better than anyone else," she said. "The Pearl Harbor Survivors motto is, 'Remember Pearl Harbor. Keep America Alert.' I'm not sure that was today. They weren't too alert."

It took no time at all for journalists to document Mrs. Auperle's assertion and incite some citizen ire. The airport security holes are laughable. The FBI had been hunting two of the hijackers, but didn't find them in time. The military couldn't get fighters in the air fast enough to stop the attacks. Most galling, the villains use our own modern conveniences— postal services, online ticketing, rental cars—to our own spectacular demise. And they'll do it again.

What right did we have to expect better preparation? We don't exactly demand good government when only half of us go to the polls to pick a president. And many of us who do fatalistically wonder whether the lines and inconvenience are worth it. No excuse in November 2004. The airport lines will have steeled us by then.

Our collective "fix-it" mentality quickly steeled Americans for war. None of us have any idea what we're talking about, but so many of us have theories on how to gain vengeance. Andy Heller, a humor columnist for the *Flint Journal*, was dead serious in suggesting we're already too late in invading Afghanistan. He wants terrorism havens "turned to glass," too. One friend suggested ten divisions of killer Navy Seals in the Middle East, paid assassins to hunt down terrorism everywhere over the next ten years or more. A neighbor and I took five minutes to cook up a scheme of beneficent conquest. We could take out Gadhafi, Saddam and bin Laden in one glory campaign. Flatten their militaries and governments. Loot them and use their treasures to create a new Marshall Plan for the inhabitants of their regimes. I don't think either one of us has ever so much as fired a gun.

We raise amateur cautions, too. The Russians lost a land war in Afghanistan. Will we follow them there the way we followed the failed French into Vietnam? None of us have answers to the most important questions. How do we ever declare victory in this war? What will it take to regain "peace in our time"?

I had one peaceful thought this week. It was almost dark when I left the office Wednesday night. The sky was perfect, completely unstreaked by airplanes. I remembered a couple we'd sent off into matrimony last Saturday. The honeymooners planned to sail for the week in northern Lake Huron. Was it possible they didn't yet know our nightmare? I tried my own escape with HBO when I got home. But HBO spit more warfare back in my face—the first rerun of the new World War II tribute, "Band of Brothers."

Oh, how we rightfully honor that "Greatest Generation." Must we now out-do them?

For a while there, we thought we'd mastered out-performance. Our businesses routinely out-performed themselves quarter after quarter in the go-go '90s. But the brakes were on for months before Tuesday's invasion. At the very moment the first team of hijackers followed the Hudson River to apocalypse, my managing editor and I chatted about the future of our business. One hundred thousand journalists have been laid off nationwide this year. In the pre-Tuesday lexicon, we all thought that's what "carnage" meant. No layoffs at our place. We felt sheltered.

Sheltered? We had no idea.

On Sunset Street, I cited fresh news of massive layoffs at Continental Airlines. The CEO had summed up his industry: "We'll all be bankrupt by the end of the year." Somebody else at the party asked something about terrorism clauses in insurance policies.

"Will we all be in the same jobs in six months?" I asked.

Mark, an American Culture professor, figured that this, like most wars, will be good for the economy. "Think how many jobs will be created by ridding the world of evil," he said, citing the president's televised assurance to do just that. Well, I had to agree that ridding the world of evil was certainly a more ambitious campaign pledge than the Bush family legacy of "No New Taxes."

And e-commerce seemed alive and well. The spam email continued to pour in Tuesday afternoon and the rest of the week. "Marlboro cigarettes—50 percent off!" "Bigger Breasts—Guaranteed!" "How would you spend $500,000?" A telemarketer called the house a couple nights after the tragedy just to make sure we were getting our *TV Guide*.

On Sunset Street, after a dinner of grilled salmon and fresh vegetables, commerce was a sensitive topic back in the kitchen. A doctoral student shook her head at the Wednesday political discourse she heard at the hairdresser: "We should have never let *them* in the country. *They* own all our party stores. The price of gas is going to go sky high." On Friday, Michigan's attorney general announced she'd go after nine gas station owners who'd gouged as much as five bucks a gallon out of drivers in Tuesday's panic. In detailing the suspects, a news story quoted good American names like "Wilcox" and "Fleming Brothers."

I heard a wholesome sound on Thursday night when I

called a college pal in Denver. His 21-month-old daughter, Aria, happily blabbered in the background. "I can't believe real-life has out horrified Hollywood," he said. His wife is seven months pregnant with their second child.

"So, are you ever gonna have kids?" he asked.

I evaded the question, feeling only slightly less resolute than two nights before. Then, in the horror of that day, I'd asked my grandchild-craving mother, "Why would you want me to bring kids into the world right now?" It's a cowardly copout that would likely incense all the people trying to figure out how to parent in this situation. My neighbor, Dan, ran past the house on Saturday afternoon, pushing his three-year-old son, Andrew, in their three-wheeled jogging buggy. It was an odd time for a run. Four o'clock in the afternoon. They usually watch Michigan Wolverines football at four o'clock on Saturday afternoons. The stadium's empty this week. We're not yet ready to have 110,000 people all in one place again.

While Andrew frolicked, Dan said he was just thankful the boy and his five-year-old sister, Ruthie, are too young to comprehend anything but the fringes of the new reality.

"They know there was a plane crash and a lot of people were hurt," Dan said.

Andrew had thought about that for a while before posing a question. "Dad, are all people bad?"

"No, son," Dan had responded. "Only a few are. Very, very few."

On Friday, the spectacle had taken on a sense of fantasy for Andrew. Dan had to discourage him from rebuilding the World Trade Center and re-enacting the "plane crash" in the family room.

For at least this week, even the entertainment industry discouraged itself. A couple months ago, a group of misguided would-be rap artists produced an album cover featuring what turned out to be a chillingly accurate picture of an exploding

World Trade Center. The record company quickly pulled the trash from distribution. The makers of the new *Spiderman* movie pulled scenes showing a giant web between the World Trade Center towers. Television producers tried to airbrush the twin towers from shows' skylines, as if that might somehow erase the collective memory of America's couch-bound, microwave-popcorn-popping crowd. Hopefully, no one rented a copy of *The Towering Inferno*.

On Sunset Street, the debate briefly centered on another cultural spectacle—the Winter Olympics just months away in Salt Lake City.

"It must go on," insisted Matt, the conservative marketing whiz. "We can't give the terrorists the gratification of the symbolism of shutting down the Olympics. There will be a parade of humvees and tanks, but it must go on."

The liberal State Bar attorney wryly implored us to remember the economic damage of cancellation. "Think of all the wasted bribes in Salt Lake City alone," he joked.

And there's symbolism there, too. America's boundless fortune and industry have always insured that scandal and greed are mainly filed away as sources of cultural entertainment themselves. In that twisted sense, the jihad's maniacal case against America has quite a few evidentiary exhibits. One of the many shots in an unbelievable parade of photos over the Associated Press wires this week featured a rally in Pakistan. Two demonstrators gave a resolute, icy stare. A sign in the background read, "Americans, THINK! Why are you hated all over the world?"

We are thinking. Finally. We don't have any answers yet, but we are thinking.

Someone on the radio called it America's "cold fury." We're talking. We're debating. We're questioning. We're reading. We're donating—time, money and energy. The stores sold out of Old Glory. College students are carrying newspapers under their arms.

By dessert time on Sunset Street, we'd bottled up the week. We laughed at memories of old wardrobes while eating Haagen Dazs and chocolate cake. We critiqued Ann Arbor's oversupply of restaurants. Somebody heard something about a new supper club. Anna, our hostess, showed the pink winter cap and blue sweater she's knitting for two-year-old daughter Maya.

Neil, the man of the house, quietly jolted us back to conscience. "Wow, I haven't seen the TV in hours."

A few minutes later, my wife Monica and I left the crowd behind. We're usually hangers-on. She could feel a cold coming on. I needed rest. Of course, there is no rest. Five minutes into the ride home, I tuned to NPR.

"Well, let's see if we're attacking yet," I said.

Monica turned it up.

Personal Lessons

Gary Gach

As the world sorts through the rubble, internal and external, following September 11, I'm beginning to recover my own voice. For a while I was in shock. Frozen, almost. Numb.

Now I realize that personal psychic paralysis was also an aim of the terrorists. So, rather than contribute any opinion about the Big Picture, I am concentrating on personal reponse. Truth, as poet Sylvia Plath reminds, is white-hot and personal.

Well, a few days before the day our world changed, I'd played emcee for three Afghani American panelists, following a benefit screening of Iara Lee's new documentary film *Beneath the Borqa*, and so had a headstart on some of the seemingly alien terrain suddenly thrust into mass consciousness, the homeland of my new Afghani friends who long to rebuild their country to its former nobility and beauty. But still, even with my briefing on the Taliban and Afghanistan, it was like a chunk of the World Trade Center had fallen right on my head.

Now I can feel myself begin to thaw and let go. As the tide of words rises in my heart again, here are two lessons I know I've learned, arisen in my soul like lotuses blossoming out of muck.

Lesson One: It is okay to be genuinely afraid. To experience and live with one's personal fear.

Am I afraid? You betcha!

This was a terrorist attack. Terror strikes deeper than a bomb. Like a long, thin needle, it penetrates right into the human heart.

9/11. Someone noted it can be pronounced "nine-one-one," the national number for calling for help. Certainly, it inspires fear in many forms, on many levels. As for me, I know I was initially terrified to imagine what the horrific attacks must have been like. Then I felt greater fears of what might have happened were the target a nuclear installation.

As my thoughts raced, I tried understanding the murderers. What would compel human beings to commit suicide, to override the universal, instinctual, and tenacious will to live? Further, they lived in America for years, shopped at Wal-Mart, ate pizza, greeted neighbors, yet saw only a nation of Satan, not fellow human beings just like themselves.

This is all quite scary.

And it's natural to confess to feeling fear. Otherwise unrecognized fear turns to uncontrollable anger, a spark kindling a fuse of blind rage initiating cycles of tragic violence. (I admit I am also afraid just to say this, lest I seem unpatriotic. But isn't peace our ultimate agenda?)

Embracing my fear feels like holding a candle in an outdoor vigil among strangers. Whether agreeing or disagreeing, eventually we see the light we all radiate. We help keep each other's candles lit in the wind. Light begets the warmth of fellow feeling.

Staying with my own fear, I can see we're each no different in our suffering and our aspirations for peace. That moral clarity engenders compassion in me.

It doesn't take the destruction of countless lives to realize this. And still the tragedy remains.

Lesson Two: It's also okay to admit "I don't know." There's so much that's unknown.

Are we dealing with networks? Or a state? ("Who do we nuke?" "Or if we invade, what's our exit strategy?" "Or do we put them on trial?")

A terrorist mindset is alien to us. Plus, they're hidden.

And let's face it: so many Americans know so little of our global village.

And so the slaying on September 15 in Mesa, Arizona of Balbir Singh Sodhi, who immigrated from India ten years ago, father of three children, might be called a crime of ignorance as well as of hatred. Why? Because the murderer blamed the Sikh man for the terrorist attacks simply for being dark-skinned and wearing a turban like that of Osama bin Laden. (The Sikh religion has roots closer to Hinduism than to Islam.)

Mr. Sodhi was slain not by a white supremacist, by the way, but by a Latino. He drove up in a red pickup truck to where Mr. Sodhi worked at a gas station, rolled down his window, and shot him, three times, without leaving his seat, and drove off. This was, alas, the first of now hundreds of hate crimes reported across the U.S.

Terrorism attacks our democratic way of life.

Very scary.

No one knows where this will all lead. And it's okay not to know, and to be afraid. And to dwell in the honesty of such recognition.

Only from awareness can we dissolve fear and hatred with compassion, ignorance with wisdom.

One true thing about our modern era: we are evermore confronted with circumstances about which we can't be certain. That is deeply scary for most. Religion and much of politics have always offered the comfort of certainty and absolutes.

Myself, I am proceeding step by step in my immediate, personal, daily life, which somehow has suddenly become public. "We are all Americans," as one Frenchman put it.

I'm bearing witness to life around me. America's wounds and the waves of suffering flowing from them are very deep. Their presence is undeniable. They demand clarity and calm, wisdom and compassion—in my day-to-day life as a citizen, a family member, a neighbor, a workmate, a customer, and so on. Being kind to myself; being kind to others I interact with.

There is so much to be grateful for.

To be aware of something greater than myself, I need only think of the New Yorkers, the heroes of Ground Zero, who inspire me with many, many instances of the human hope for a better tomorrow amid the very, very worst of human blindness. Amid the evil, if you will, of ignorance.

And I am visiting my local mosque this week. I go to learn more, firsthand, about the community of my Islamic American brothers and sisters, aunties and uncles, and to pray in solidarity with their anguish at the betrayal of their faith and their hope for a better tomorrow for us all. (9/11 is a wake-up call on many levels.)

Personal matters of daily life might seem trivial and ineffectual. But I cannot find terrorists and bring them to justice, nor reunite any of the bereaved with the faces posted on the streets, MISSING (even in my neighborhood, in San Francisco). But I can take these small mindful steps with all my body, heart, and mind.

I nurture my healing.

And yours.

Within and without.

Remember: Peace is every step.

And out of the mud, grows the lotus.

The World's Fears Begin

Aung Zaw

While watching the horrific images of terror at the World Trade Center in New York and the Pentagon in Washington, the first question that comes to mind is: Why did this tragedy happen? Why were so many innocent people murdered in this brutal manner?

The terrorist attacks that struck America on Tuesday were politically motivated. The terrorists were not content with taking innocent lives: They also wanted to shatter the symbols of America's financial and military might.

The attacks were a wakeup call for America and the rest of the international community. World leaders and the United Nations must now make every effort to stem the tide of terrorism before it engulfs the entire world. Osama bin Laden, a millionaire from Saudi Arabia who is believed to be hiding in Afghanistan, is the prime suspect in the attacks, according to Secretary of State Colin Powell. Now the U.S. is sending fuel to its troops around the world, indicating that war is imminent.

"This is the first war of the 21st century," declared U.S. president George W. Bush, who is now facing the first great international challenge of his administration. While Washington girds for war, the rest of the world is watching anxiously, knowing that any action involving the United States is likely to involve every other nation as well.

Now we have to ask another question: War against whom? Who is the enemy? Afghanistan is high on the list of probable targets. There's little doubt that America's military might could inflict substantial damage on this extremely backward Central Asian country. But what would that accomplish, apart from aggravating tensions in the Middle East and setting off a spiral of reprisals that would leave no corner of the world untouched? At the moment, many U.S. citizens seem prepared to accept the high price of waging war, but we in the rest of the world are not quite so ready. Even if the conflict could be contained to Afghanistan—which is highly unlikely—the prospect of substantial civilian casualties among ordinary Afghanis is as unacceptable to us as the loss of life we have already witnessed in America.

What we expect from America at this time is not blind rage, but an appropriate response tempered by consultation with its allies and the United Nations. President Bush has already stated his intention of hunting down and punishing the culprits. We can only hope that in pursuing this goal, he will not inadvertently fulfill the wishes of the terrorists by legitimizing their message that America is indifferent to the suffering of the rest of the world.

In Thailand, a coalition of non-government organizations has called on the United States to rely on the rule of law rather than unilateral military action to bring to justice the perpetrators of Tuesday's terrorist attacks.

The Bangkok-based Asian Forum for Human Rights and Development (Forum Asia) joined the Coalition for the International Criminal Court (CICC) in citing the tragedy as an example of the need for an international criminal court.

"The failure of the most powerful nation with the greatest resources to prevent such a crime reinforces the need for massive co-operation throughout the international community in outlawing, investigating, prosecuting and bringing to justice those who commit these most serious crimes against humanity, which is what the International Criminal Court will do," they said.

The groups warned that "indiscriminate unilateral military retaliation, which has been the response to past terrorist attacks ... could result in more innocent deaths and a cycle of recrimination, revenge and terrorism."

It is doubtful, however, that the U.S. is ready to listen. Since taking power, the Bush administration has alienated even a number of America's closest allies by dispensing with the notion of forming an international consensus on important global issues. The U.S. has walked out of a recent racism conference in Durban, South Africa, refused to sign a global warming pact, and disregarded international misgivings about a proposed missile shield that is intended to defend America, but could end up setting off a global arms race.

Another blunder has been the administration's departure from the Middle East peace plan and taking of sides in the conflict between Israel and the Palestinians. By backing Israel and shielding it from censure in international forums, the US has angered Arabs, and not just the extremists. Many in the Arab world see America's stance in the Middle East as evidence of an anti-Islamic bias and blame it for the continuing bloodshed and conflict in their region.

Here in Asia, there are others who feel similarly victimized, and not without reason. Vietnam, Cambodia and Laos have all experienced the worst of America's determination to lead the world, while other countries have felt the double-edged sword of American hegemony. Even those who welcome the stability it has brought to the region worry that it could be their undoing. And while America is to be applauded for its current role in championing the cause of democracy and human rights in the region, it has not been forgotten that the U.S. has also sponsored some of Asia's worst dictatorships. Like most people around the world at this time, Asians feel immense sympathy for those in America who have fallen victim to a force they can scarcely begin to understand. Some may even pause to reflect upon their own experiences under such circumstances, when the incomprehensible menace was none other than the United States, ostensibly defending its own arcane way of life.

Few in the world are in a position to mitigate America's desire for revenge, and so it is up to Americans and those who share America's professed values to ensure that those values are not sacrificed in the name of avenging these recent heinous attacks. Human Rights Watch in New York has responded to these fears. In a statement, it called on the U.S. administration to make distinctions "between the perpetrators and the civilians who may surround them; between those who commit atrocities and those who may simply share their religious beliefs, ethnicity or national origin."

The statement continued: "There are people and governments in the world who believe that in the struggle against terrorism, ends always justify means. But that is also the logic of terrorism. Whatever the response to this outrage, it must not validate that logic. Rather, it must uphold the principles that came under attack yesterday, respecting innocent life and international law. That is the way to deny the perpetrators of this crime their ultimate victory."

If Americans want to feel safe again in their own country, they must begin to understand the insecurity many feel in theirs. More importantly, they must examine their nation's policies vis-à-vis the rest of the world, and ask themselves honestly if these policies have contributed in some way to this insecurity. Now that its own worst fears have been realized, America can no longer afford to ignore the fears of others.

"How about your country?"

Brian Calvert

From where I'm sitting, in a little office in a little corner of the world—Phnom Penh, Cambodia—the attack on the U.S. looks less like a day that will live in infamy, but more like a shot heard 'round the world. I watched the events unfold in a family-run Japanese restaurant with Japanese friends, alternating between CNN and the state-run news from Tokyo, just so everyone could understand what was going on. When I went to work the following day, Soda, a 19-year-old Cambodian woman who studies accounting, asked me, "So how about your country? How about your family?" Vietnamese bar girls are asking the same thing. They watch TV, too.

I was on the phone with a business source this morning, another Cambodian, who asked if all of my friends and family were all right. I told him, yes, they were, but we had two people working here that had lost old friends from college. After this attack, nearly everyone on the planet will likely know someone who knows someone who lost someone on September 11, 2001.

The effect of the attacks on Cambodia will likely be damaging almost immediately. There are just two industries here that until last Tuesday were the shining hope for employment of people here: garment manufacturing and tourism. Both of those will be hurt, as investors in the U.S. and the rest of the world balk at either purchasing orders of T-shirts or shoes, or getting on a plane to visit "the famed temples of Angkor Wat."

Everything has to be reassessed now. There is nothing

for the country to fall back on, no cushions, no reserves, no alternatives. People here will have to race themselves, struck yet another blow. But they're used to it, I suppose.

Even the international trial of top Khmer Rouge leaders will be delayed, as the UN in New York, where the trial law was being reviewed, adjusts to Tuesday's attacks. And now, I fear, world attention will be focused on whatever retaliatory, prolonged campaign the Bush administration decides to undertake.

As many as 5,000 people died in those attacks. The images—played over and over by 24-hour news stations looking to stretch their broadcasts—are startling, and will be properly entered and catalogued into this world's collective consciousness. Americans have a right to be outraged.

But to get pity from Cambodians? From a girl like Soda? This is a girl who is lucky to have made it out of high school. She'll be lucky to find a job when she graduates. Decades of war and chaos have left her country with little, and the ensuing corruption that came with peace took away even more.

"How about your country? How about your family?"

A startling question, coming from a gal whose countrymen underwent not just one day of terror, but years. Something in that question, spoken in a sweet, soft voice steeped with concern, knocked me off guard. It speaks volumes for most Cambodians—indeed for all people who have suffered. And perhaps we can take a lesson from that kind of passion.

Many Cambodians here are fully aware of the U.S. bombs that were rained upon their country in America's war with Vietnam. Most of them know that while they suffered silently—wilting under the Cambodian sun, scraping for food, drinking muddy water from the hoofprints of cattle—Americans and the rest of the world did nothing.

More than one million perished.

And now, after surviving the decades of protracted civil war that followed, the people here have emerged, quiet and stoic, eyes open to the world around them.

Cambodia is one of the countries farthest away from the United States when it comes to money and power. But after this week, they may be one of the closest in understanding and suffering.

These attacks have brought the United States closer to countries like Cambodia, closer to the pain that plagues much of the globe. If there is a lesson to be learned, if there is any sense to be made in any of this, any silver lining, it may be that.

There is likely to be more suffering in the wake of this potential cataclysm. There may be a full-on war, bombs may fall from the sky, Americans and others will fight and die, lose limbs, be crippled, burned, traumatized. And it could go on for a while.

But to cross that time of darkness, to emerge from it as Americans, as citizens of the world, with the same courage, innocence and compassion as Soda: that will be perhaps our greatest triumph.

Coyles Know What
Americans Are Going Through

Jeffrey Cohen

Wallingford, Connecticut, September 18—Janice and Matthew Coyle said they know the emotion that thousands of Americans are only beginning to feel. They know the anger, they know the frustration, they know the fear and they know the lack of confidence that follows when a loved one is lost to terrorism.

And they know it doesn't go away.

"It's just not going to happen," Janice Coyle said. "It's a glumness. I know I wouldn't have wanted to hear that early on, but you can't expect that all of the sudden there's magic.

"You have to be kind to yourself," she said. "You're going to feel emotions you never knew you had."

Matthew Coyle sat on the sofa beside his wife. "All kinds of things go through your person, they just do," he said. "And they don't just go away after a year. The veil is always there. Your happiness is not as full as it should be, and your sadness is sadder than it should be."

The Coyles lost their daughter Tricia, a Sheehan High School graduate and a 20-year-old sophomore at Boston College, to the Dec. 21, 1988, explosion of Pan Am Flight 103 over Lockerbie, Scotland. The attack killed all 259 on board and 11 on the ground, and was once known as the deadliest terrorist attack against American civilians.

Not anymore.

"Does it bring you back?" Janice Coyle asked of the terrorist attacks on Sept. 11. "Yeah, it brings you back. Way back. It brings you back to square one."

"You lose confidence in yourself; should I turn right or turn left?" she said.

"Should you go through the caution light, or should you not?" her husband quickly added. "My God, you can't make a decision. You're confident of one thing: that you're making the wrong decision all of the time."

Last Tuesday's attacks hit them hard, probably like it did every other person—American or otherwise—who watched the crashes, the collapses and the aftermath. But these emotions have been hitting them hard every day since the explosion over Lockerbie.

"We've lived in a world of terrorism for the past 12 years. We've had to deal with it," she said. "Twelve years ahead. That's exactly where we are, we're twelve years ahead of everybody else."

This isn't said with the spite of an angry "I-told-you-so," but with the emotion, frustration, and red eyes of parents who've been there, they said.

"We all should be knocked back," Matthew Coyle said. "To actually see the second plane hit, that's what Lockerbie must have been like." The planes that crashed on Tuesday, like Pan Am 103, were all filled with fuel for long flights. The difference this time is that there was video. "To see that fireball, now I know what ... the citizens of Lockerbie went through."

That's not the only parallel, Janice Coyle said. Her eyes focused on the people left with no other option but to jump from the flames to their deaths. "Our daughter fell 31,000 feet when that plane broke apart," she said. And then she turned to her husband. "Did you think of that?" He nodded he had.

A message still on their answering machine plays the voice of a friend living in Texas. The caller, an old friend, wanted to share her thoughts and one simple line: "Had they listened to you, we might not be here today."

"Are we upset? Yeah, we're upset," Janice Coyle said.

In December of 1988, Vice President George Bush had just been elected president. In the eyes of the Coyles, Bush and British Prime Minister Margaret Thatcher turned the Pan Am 103 investigation over to the United Nations because the suspected culpable countries—Libya and Iran—supplied most of Europe's oil. To attack them both was unthinkable, they said.

But this time it's different. "Afghanistan is nothing," Matthew Coyle said. "It's just dirt, there's nothing there. No one cares because it's just a bunch of hills." It therefore doesn't surprise him that an attack on Afghanistan is possible, he said.

"I guess we'll do whatever the Saudis tell us to do," he said. Perhaps, he added, had America taken a different, more aggressive tack towards terrorism, "we wouldn't be here today and the World Trade Center would still be around ... With a stronger resolve to handle terrorism, to attack it where it exists, perhaps the bin Laden apparatus might have been crippled."

Politics upsets them. So does political double talk, so do supposed terrorism experts, so do protracted legal proceedings.

"I'm angry it's twelve years later and we're still going through a process," Janice Coyle said. "It's always there. It's like pouring acid on an open sore."

But what soothes the anger just a bit is the nationwide response to this week's terror. The flags.

"I don't think they did that in 1988," Janice Coyle said. "There wasn't this kind of outrage like there is this time, and they should be outraged."

Amidst the memories and the outrage, the Coyle family is getting ready for a new arrival. Krisann Miller, Tricia's twin sister, is expecting her second child next week. This week, after visiting with Miller's two-and-a-half-year-old son, Janice Coyle remembered a short talk she and her grandson shared.

She had just finished telling him how she, Mimi, would come to Massachusetts to take care of him while his mother gave birth. He wanted to know who else would come.

"Grandpa?" he asked.

"Yes, Grandpa, too," Mimi said.

"Dad?" he asked.

"Dad, too," Mimi said.

"Tricia?"

At two and a half years old, he knows Tricia from the stories and the pictures: Almost every photo, like the one of Krisann and Tricia silhouetted in front of a low-hanging sun, shows them both.

What he doesn't know is how she died, or why she died, or even that she died at all. It is, the Coyles said, just another example of how the loss of their daughter is a daily thing. It's a reminder of the talks they've yet to have, and of the talks that the children of the attacks of September 11, 2001, have likely yet to endure.

"Of course I will be raped"

Lydia Lakwonyero

I wish to send my condolences to the people of America, especially the victims, friends and their families.

It was such a shocking tragedy on a great nation like America. I'm writing this because I heard that America has declared war. It really gave me a shock. War! In America! America has lost many innocent lives already, and I don't think they should be wishing for war now. Let us imagine all the people of America, the women, the children, the old. The men killed just because of a single tragedy.

It may be a very big issue to President Bush right now, but later, when the nation realizes how many innocent lives it has lost, it will become guilt for the people who ordered it, not just tragedy.

What goes straight to my nerves is the policy that you are either with or against us, but the question is how many countries everywhere have been hit with a ton of bricks and endured. Countries like Uganda. There's a war in the northern part, but I've never heard that other countries have allied with us to fight the rebel terrorists practically creating World War III.

Now the African countries of course are also expected to participate, but there are some which are really poor and can't even strike back. These countries have really tried to develop, but what I know is that a war will take them back to square one again.

If there's a war, it will definitely reduce the population. The wise people who would be governing the country will be dead.

I am just a 15-year-old girl who looks forward to a bright future. The question is, do I have any chance of living now, so helpless like this? You know, I had it all figured out. I wanted to be a musician and a lawyer, and maybe a good mother to my children if I were to have any and a good wife if I was to be married. But just like every cloud has a silver lining, mine vanishes before my eyes every time I think of war, and it hurts so bad.

We all know how brutal and immoral some soldiers are. What is going to happen to girls like me? Of course I will be raped. Many people have died from it, and I believe that no woman would want to be raped. If the thought and sight of it is sickening, then what of the act itself?

America should swallow this big blow just like any other country that has been hit. Let's use philosophy here; there's no foolish terrorist who can start such a war not knowing what next to do. Of course he had it all well planned. It may be just a matter of pride here, but even mighty ones sometime should humble down.

I don't know if this will help, but I've written from the bottom of my heart.

It Wasn't the Games That Mattered

Richard C. Crepeau

If there was any doubt about the significance of sport in American life, this past weekend should put those doubts to rest. The events of Friday night [September 21] in New York at Shea Stadium alone were a reminder of just how sport can bring a community together, sometimes to celebrate and sometimes to mourn. In this case to do both.

Pre-game ceremonies at Shea Stadium, like those in many baseball parks all through last week, paid tribute to those who died in the attacks of September 11 and to those whose heroism became nearly ordinary in the midst of the crisis. The twenty-one-gun salute and the other tributes were a moving reminder of what had transpired, and the fireman, policeman and rescue worker hats being worn by the Mets are a constant reminder of the heroism of those who put their lives on the line in public service. The singing of "Amazing Grace" once again showed why it is the most important song of hope ever written in the Western world.

Diana Ross sang the national anthem, and this too offered a reminder of just how much things had changed in less than two weeks. It was Ross who had sung an overblown version of the anthem at the U.S. Open Tennis Championship prior to the Saturday night historic women's final. In that rendition Ross was clearly the star, while Friday night the song itself, along with the occasion, was the center of attention. It has also been pointed out that many present that night at the U.S. Open were likely victims of the attack in New York.

The seventh-inning stretch rendition of "New York, New

York" by Liza Minnelli was a bit too rousing for some tastes, but again the backup dance line of firemen and policemen somehow saved the moment. Throughout the night the place was full of emotion as even Mayor Guiliani, a Yankee fan, took part in this communal ceremony of mourning and gratitude.

As if to underline the occasion, the game itself gave the fans everything they could have wanted and more. Trailing late in the game, Mike Piazza hit a two-run home run in the eighth inning to propel the Mets to a 3-2 win. It was better than the World Series, and according to Todd Zeile this game was more important than any World Series game the Mets have played.

Mets players donated their salaries for that night, no small sum indeed, to the fund to support the survivors of city workers who lost their lives in this catastrophe. Mets fans went home having experienced the joy of victory, but more importantly having taken part in a community exercise of hope in the face of disaster.

And of course it wasn't just baseball that provided the occasion for community expressions of unity and patriotism. The NFL is both very good and generally excessive in these moments of national patriotic expression. The opening of each game was the same with the singing of "America the Beautiful" televised into the stadiums and across the country from the streets of New York. This was followed by a moment of silence at each stadium and then the singing of the national anthem.

The size of the flag on the field seemed to get bigger at each venue, while the singing of the anthem evoked a variety of emotions among both players and fans. In the stands NFL fans who are experts in costume design outdid themselves as they dressed in as many forms of the red, white and blue as could be imagined. Despite this excess, it did seem that for the first time in memory the national anthem had the undivided attention of everyone in the stadium.

Perhaps the best tribute of all came in New England, where the Patriots' Joe Andruzzi was joined for the coin toss by his father and three brothers as Patriot co-captains for the game against the New York Jets. Andruzzi's father is a retired New York City detective, and his three brothers are New York firemen who were deeply involved in the events of September 11. It is now clear that in this crisis it is the heroism of firemen that is the worthiest role model for all Americans. It is they, and not our athletes, who need to be shown to the community for emulation. In New England on Sunday that was underlined.

In addition to the NFL and Major League Baseball, Saturday brought the return of college football. At hundreds of games involving hundreds of thousands of fans in an atmosphere that is unique to college football, there was another opportunity for the expression of community mourning and thanksgiving.

It wasn't the games that mattered so much over this past week and weekend, it was the opportunity for people to come together to express themselves as a community in thanks and in mourning. This of course has happened in churches, in community halls, in concert halls, and wherever people gather in numbers. However, none of these venues brought such large numbers of people together in person and united them with the nation via television as was done through sport over the past week and weekend.

Like it or not, sport is an integral part of our national community life and culture, and this past seven days showed that over and over again throughout the land.

© 2001 Richard C. Crepeau

The Long Way Back Home

Cynthia G. La Ferle

A little more than a week has passed since our country was attacked and brought to its knees.

A friend of mine says she is trying to wake up from what she calls Stephen King's worst nightmare. The rest of us still feel as though we've been wandering in a fog; unable to find our way home.

Home, it seems, has been completely redesigned by horrific acts of terrorism. Ever since last Tuesday, everything is different. Everything.

I have stopped assuming that home will ever be completely safe from disaster. This thought alone makes every wall, every window, every piece of oak, maple, brick, or concrete in my neighborhood, my world, seem all the more precious.

I've also stopped obsessing over the things I used to obsess about. I've stopped worrying about the fact that my refrigerator needs cleaning and the walls in the kitchen need repainting. Things like that don't matter now. My focus has changed.

It doesn't matter if my family leaves a mess on the breakfast counter every morning. And so what if I trip over somebody's shoes in the hallway? I am deeply grateful that there are people living here—eating breakfast and wearing shoes.

I imagine this is all part of the grieving process, and that someday things will seem normal again.

Right now, though, I feel a bit like Emily in Thornton Wilder's "Our Town." Emily is the character who, near the end of the play, returns to her hometown as a ghost and realizes how much she took for granted when she was alive. Emily recites a list of the simple things that made her days precious—things like the smell of freshly brewed coffee in the morning.

I know exactly what she meant. This week I'm savoring the taste of summer's last tomatoes. I'm taking time to watch the sun set behind the trees in our yard, and to listen to the sound of church bells just a few blocks away.

But I can't think of anyone who is appreciating the comforts of home as much as Norma Gormly of Troy, Michigan.

Norma is the friend I mentioned in last week's column—the friend whose plane was diverted back to London's Gatwick Airport immediately following the terrorist attacks on the World Trade Center and the Pentagon.

Norma and her daughter, Jan, ended up stranded at a B&B in London until the airways were cleared for their return to the United States. Theirs was the first Northwest flight to leave last Friday. As Norma told me, it was quite an experience.

"We had to go through four checkpoints and check in all bags," she recalled. "We were allowed our purses with personal stuff only. Following a body search, we were admitted to the lounge area."

None of the passengers complained, though, even though their wait was long. Another three hours passed before their flight left Gatwick.

"We felt good that they had done all that they could for our safety," Norma said. "We had the same flight crew from our diverted plane."

That crew, Norma recalled, wore black ribbons around the gold wings on their uniforms. Some were fighting tears, "but they all promised to do their best to make our trip as normal as possible. Our captain was informative and soothing."

Norma and her fellow passengers clapped and cheered loudly as their plane finally took off. They cheered again when the plane passed over Canada.

And it was, as Norma remembers, a tremendous relief to arrive back home in America. "We cheered and clapped, then cheered and clapped again upon landing at Metro Airport. We were home at last!"

No matter what shape it's in, Norma added, there's no place like home. Home is a word every American cherishes—more than ever, now.

Israel's New York Road

Blake Lambert

The small blue street sign recently posted at an intersection in downtown West Jerusalem managed to capture Israel's feelings of solidarity with the United States in three words. It says New York Road, the new temporary name for Jaffa Road, a major artery that stretches across the western part of the city. The decision by municipality officials to rename the street is anything but coincidental, I believe, for Jaffa Road is Israel's ground zero for terrorist attacks.

Two suicide bombers blew themselves up on crowded buses at opposite ends of the street during a seven-day span in 1996, killing a total of 45 people. More recently, a suicide bomber blew himself up in the Sbarro restaurant at a Jaffa Road intersection in August 2001, killing 15 people. A nondescript memorial along the street near the former central bus station serves as a reminder of the deadly events, but blink once and you might miss it.

Many Israelis consider themselves to be quite experienced in dealing with surprise attacks such as car bombs or suicide bombings. Enough have suffered through the horrific feeling of being unable to get in touch with a loved one or friend when a blast occurs because panicked customers swamped the cellular phone services with calls. Yet the scope of the attacks on the U.S. simply shocked Israelis, even the experts.

"This is the most spectacular attack ever. There's no question about it," Yoram Schweitzer, a researcher at the International Policy Institute for Counter-terrorism in Herzliya, told me hours after it happened. "It makes the

Popular Front for the Liberation of Palestine's attempt to hijack four airplanes in the 1970s look like a joke."

While many Israelis offered their condolences to the American people, attended solidarity rallies in Jerusalem and Tel Aviv, and flew U.S. flags, some felt a sense of vindication. Israel, these voices said, is on the front line in the war against Islamic extremism, and the Western world ignored the threat to our country until it struck the U.S. The message, spoken by the people and echoed by the politicians, was clear: Terrorism is the common enemy of Israel and its chief ally, the U.S. "Now the Americans will understand," many Israelis said. "They will know what we've been going through for the past twelve months."

Since last October, Israelis have indeed conducted their lives with greater apprehension to deal with the threat of an attack. Bombs have exploded everywhere over the last year: on the street, beside a bus, at a train station, in a sherut or taxi van, in a car, in a market, in front of a bar and in a restaurant. For me, this fear has become personal: Since August, two suicide bombers blew themselves up in separate, well-populated locations within a ten- to fifteen-minute walk of my apartment since August.

Israeli Prime Minister Ariel Sharon sensed the attacks on the U.S. provided him with a window of opportunity to crush his nemesis, Palestinian leader Yasser Arafat. Seizing the moment, Sharon described Arafat as Israel's Osama bin Laden. He even blasted Arafat at a special Knesset session held in solidarity with the American people on September 16. "It was Arafat who—dozens of years ago—legitimized the hijacking of planes. It was Palestinian terrorist organizations who began to dispatch suicide-terrorists," said Sharon.

Several hawkish cabinet ministers invoked the "Arafat is our bin Laden" comparison as they questioned why the U.S. and Secretary of State Colin Powell urged Israeli Foreign

Minister Shimon Peres to meet with Arafat in the wake of the attacks on America. Should Powell now meet with bin Laden, asked Public Security Minister Uzi Landau and Communications Minister Reuven Rivlin. While Arafat's hands are not clean—nor are Sharon's for that matter—and his rule is imperfect, he is not bin Laden. Israeli politicians once again ignored that Arafat did receive 88 percent of the vote in the presidential election of the Palestinian Authority in January 1996.

The anti-Arafat rhetoric, post-New York and Washington, D.C. terrorist attacks, was a novel manifestation of the perennial Israeli debate surrounding the Palestinian leader. Israelis moderates felt Arafat was their partner, if an imperfect one, to achieve a peace deal, but they changed their tone after he rejected former prime minister Ehud Barak's offer at Camp David in July 2000. Leftists still believe that Arafat, for better or worse, is still Israel's partner.

Right-wingers never believed Arafat was a peace partner, even after he signed the Declaration of Principles with the late Yitzhak Rabin in September 1993, since they thought Arafat's intention was to liberate all of Palestine. Landau described Arafat in June 2001 as a "cruel and anti-democratic despot" who is the partner of Iraqi leader Saddam Hussein, the ayatollahs in Iran and bin Laden.

Yet the U.S. rejected Israel's crude "Arafat is our bin Laden" slogan. It still sees Arafat as Israel's partner for dialogue in the continuing efforts to stop the violence in the region. The Bush administration needs a calmer Middle East in order to enlist moderate Arab states in its international anti-terrorism coalition, which requires senior Israeli politicians to hold cease-fire talks with Arafat. At the same time, Israel will probably be asked to sit on its hands and do nothing if and when the U.S. launches its "war" on terrorism, as it did during the 1991 Gulf War.

Israelis are already worried about what they think will happen next: The U.S. attacks Afghanistan or somewhere, and Iraq fires Scud missiles at Tel Aviv. Thousands have visited the Israeli Army's Homefront Command to update or pick up their gas masks. No one I know is trusting the reassurances of Israeli Intelligence that the country will not be attacked. I don't have a gas mask yet, even though all but one of my friends apparently do. But the good news is that there's a chemically-permeable bomb shelter right in front of my apartment just in case.

It's no wonder some Israelis are already disappointed. "I think it is very ironic that the U.S. is wooing two of the most prominent sponsors of terrorism [Iran and Syria] in its so-called war against terrorism," said my friend Larry Ramer, an American-Israeli. "The U.S. is then forcing Israel to talk to another terrorist [Arafat]."

A Complex God

Stanley Hauerwas

Even if the culprit is Osama bin Laden, and we track him down, and we kill him and destroy his network, he's won.

That's because he is ready to die, and the people who support him are ready to die. Americans aren't ready to die. Under those circumstances, you begin to see some of the cracks in a determinedly bourgeois civilization, which is basically about securing safety rather than securing goods. This situation holds a deep moral challenge for us.

The events of September 11 have brought home to America that war is about dying. I'm not quite sure how that will be received. I suspect it will produce a more repressive politics than we already experience. Americans have no sense of how it is that we can be this hated. It never occurs to them that our country's actions have terrible results for other people around the world, and that they blame us. I have a friend who pointed out that September 11 is the anniversary of the overthrow of Salvador Allende in Chile and the beginning of a regime of torture there, and of course that was U.S.-sponsored. Why shouldn't people be mad at us?

We are willing to worship a God only if God makes us safe. Thus you get the silly question, How does a good God let bad things happen to good people? Of course, it was a rabbi who raised that question, but Christians took it up as their own. Have you read the Psalms lately? We're seeing a much more complex God than that question gives credit for.

Toward the "New Normal"

Edward T. Linenthal

This event is so painful, and the scale is beyond anything in American history.

One of the things I've been thinking about today is: Somewhere down the line, when we are engaging and struggling with this event without the visceral immediacy of now, I think it is going to be very difficult for those people who deal with cultural representations—aesthetic, historical, or whatever.

We already have films that have imagined these sorts of scenarios, but those always have happy endings, and this didn't.

What has happened is imaginatively unmapped terrain, and we are likely to fall back on familiar narratives, story lines, slogans, rhetoric -- none of which will be able to approach the magnitude of this catastrophe.

I'm reminded of a phrase that people use in Oklahoma City, and there the phrase works (it's not going to work in New York or Washington for a long time yet); they talk about the "new normal." There's a sense in my mind that we live now in a kind of alien, foreboding, frightening landscape, and we're searching for the resources with which to deal with it. And I find myself uncomfortable with the understandable but, I think, problematic narrative of civil or national renewal that's already begun to be formed. "Yes, it was horrible, but ... it will bring us together." "Yes, it was horrible, but if it results in a, b, and c ..." That is so false to the horror and evil of the event. It's obscene rhetoric to me.

This is a time to be silent and filled with awe in the face of the power of evil and the enormity of mass death, and not to begin to extract redemption from it. To wriggle out of this horror in redemptive ways is false to the power of the event and dishonors the dead.

Obviously, there are tremendous differences from Oklahoma City—particularly the scale of death. September 11 was a day of mass death that far surpassed Oklahoma City, Pearl Harbor, or other attacks on the United States. It was a qualitatively different event from anything that has ever happened. And I think it's going to be a while before we get a sense of the new landscape. This has created a psychic, social, cultural earthquake of such massive proportions that we aren't going to know for a very, very long time—maybe, it would be better said that we will know only little by little, in different nooks and crannies of the culture—what the "new normal" is going to look like.

I never, ever will use the word "closure" again, except to talk about it in angry ways, because there is no such thing. I think it's a horrific pop-psychology term. There are events to be endured, not resolved, and I think that is something Americans have a very difficult time with. People sometimes— not all the time—integrate violent loss into their lives. One thing we know is that the lives created after such events are new lives; they are not the old lives. That is what we are now facing, as individuals, as cities, as states, and as a culture. The "new normal" in America, what America is, is going to be redefined by this event.

When the rubble is gone, months down the road, and there's this toxic, haunted place, transformed by the deaths of thousands of people, is that, in fact, going to be a site where you can go back to business as usual? That will be a tremendously interesting, contentious, vexing question, I suspect.

Even after Oklahoma City, the impact of that bombing on the wider culture, and even across the world, was absolutely stunning. I think largely because of the media, people felt enfranchised, sending in thousands of memorial ideas, writing family members of the casualties, acting as if survivors and family members were friends, sending money, sending statues, in some cases, in a darker way, even stalking mothers of the murdered children, whom they had seen on television, and becoming infatuated with them. So this kind of pseudo-intimacy—media-intimacy is a perhaps more nonjudgmental term—is going to be re-created here on an even larger scale.

It's a very complex business, because people who have lost loved ones not only are used by the media, but also use the media. I don't mean that negatively; it's a form of public eulogy for loved ones. The deaths in Oklahoma City and the deaths here—these are now very public deaths. They are not the anonymous deaths of the violence that we've all learned to live with. They are not the anonymous deaths of business as usual on the nation's highways, or the deaths of those distanced by caricature and stereotype, like the people who died at Waco—cult members, fanatics, zombies, people who are not like us and whose deaths do *not* count in the same way. The fact that these deaths are public, and their scale, will make dealing with them incredibly challenging.

I think the next few months are going to be some of the most turbulent months we have ever, ever lived through, in terms of setting foreign policy and trying to get some semblance of the fabric of everyday life restored. Because we're going to be living with the images of rescue and recovery for a very long time.

Why We Shouldn't Call It War

Christopher Phelps

Since the initial disbelief and shock, I have been
meditating about how many of us on the left—I consider
myself a socialist historian—were mistaken in discounting the
seriousness of the problem of terrorism.

I can recall a certain sniggering in the 1980s about
"terrorism," as if it were merely a pretext for U.S.
interventionism—almost an invention of the military-
industrial complex. I have a sinking sense that we were wrong
on some elemental level about how the matter should be
treated, as if it were sufficient to minimize it by listing the
more egregious contrary cases of state-sanctioned violence,
from the Nicaraguan contras to Israel. I do not deny that
terrorism has been used, like communism before it, to justify
endeavors that had more to do with the assertion of American
state power than with anything else. Just as Stalinism was
no bugaboo, however, the practical and moral reality of the
phenomenon should have been confronted.

Still, I have deep reservations about the way the news
media are casting the issue as well as about the direction of the
administration's response. To call what we are experiencing
"war" speaks to the acts' aspects of aggression, force, terror,
and violence—all features of war. However, this rising "war
on terrorism," strikes me as rife with danger and unintended
consequences.

I worry that such talk gives advantage to the perpetrators.
To me, what is significant about the attacks is precisely that
they did *not* follow definitions of war. Pearl Harbor was a

sneak attack, but it was by a hostile regime on the key U.S. naval installation in the Pacific. The attack on the World Trade Center, unlike Pearl Harbor, can have no military rationale whatsoever. The Pentagon is a military command center, but to use commercial airliners full of civilians as weapons makes it not an act of war but a crime against humanity. The attacks have been claimed by no state. To speak of those assaults on human life and liberty as "war" legitimizes the terrain sought by the perpetrators. I fear that it will inadvertently mean an open invitation to destroy innocent American civilian lives, with every casualty a "victory."

To repeatedly emphasize the "Attack on America," as the news media are doing, I also worry, risks inflaming the very sort of particularistic and ethnocentric sentiments that motivate the groups willing to do this sort of thing. The moral significance of the conflict is the indiscriminate murder of innocent people. Nationality, from a moral point of view, is beside the point, especially since we now know the tremendous variety of nationalities represented among the victims. The answer to bigotry and barbarism is insistence upon international solidarity, democracy, and humane principles, not jingoism.

As an American historian, I am wary of wars framed for freedom, which in general have produced the exact opposite effect. During the cold war, the "Communist menace" became the basis for hysterical McCarthyist attacks on civil liberties. Woodrow Wilson's "war for democracy" resulted in the crushing of the left and, with it, liberal reform. Watergate, which threatened American democracy itself, grew directly out of Vietnam. Even during World War II, which resulted in the defeat of the fascist powers, Japanese-Americans were confined to internment camps and Trotskyist dissenters imprisoned without basis. Those domestic violations are matched by the history of American interventionism abroad, which often resulted in human-rights catastrophes, from Hiroshima to Chile.

I find myself torn a bit between myself as a citizen and as a trained historian. I have felt unspeakable revulsion about the acts and admiration for those engaged in rescue operations, but on the other hand I have a resistance to lines that I have often heard spoken on the radio that before September 11 we were all safe. Forgotten are Oklahoma City, the postal attacks, Columbine, the crime scares of the 1970s and 1980s, the shootings at Kent State and Jackson State, the massacre at Wounded Knee -- a long list could be constructed. Loss of innocent civilian life is nothing new to this country. To recognize this is important for historical memory; it should not diminish the horror and importance of the events. This is violence of a new *magnitude* and *type*. But Americans are forever losing their innocence in ways that their historians may find a bit disconcerting. It reflects the weakness of historical knowledge—or, to be more precise, historical understanding— that people can speak in such oblivious ways about a national innocence when, along with our many finer qualities, our history is shot through with violence and terror.

Giving Meaning to Survival

Robert Jay Lifton

The greatest danger in our present situation would be to resort to extreme measures to deny our vulnerability and reassert a sense of superpower invulnerability. That tendency is all too consistent with a larger sense of American exceptionalism.

A healthier reaction, in my judgment, would be to take in, and attempt to absorb and recognize, our vulnerability. To do that would entail combining our compassion for the thousands of victims with a kind of survivor mission—because we are all, to some degree, survivors here—that would seek to diminish violence and avoid an escalation of violence in the world.

I'm talking about the ways in which we translate our psychological responses into public and political policy. The country is suffused with rage, and, unfortunately, almost all of our leaders are joining in and limiting their rhetoric to warlike images and warmaking. I believe that the rage and calls for justice must be responded to, and that there must be measures to track down the terrorists and bring them to justice; but those approaches should be restrained and discriminating. I'm also talking about a dynamic of terrorism, in which terrorist acts can bring about extreme countermeasures that, in turn, can result in an escalation in terrorism and a continuing vicious circle.

The psychological and the political are inevitably combined. For instance, political statements could have a constructive impact on our psychological responses. I think much wisdom would lie in giving Americans perspective on terrorism and its sources, on recognizing terrorism as a longstanding process that must be countered not just militarily, but also in diplomatic and political ways. That's very much the opposite of what we're hearing from our leaders; it's what we desperately need.

Survivors of any event need to give form and meaning to their survival. They need to find significance in it that can help them bring significance and meaning to the rest of their lives. Otherwise, they are stuck in the terrible suffering and mass killing, and it's meaningless. Now, the kinds of meaning we can give, as a form of collective survival, can take two forms (or a combination of both): either the form of the most aggressive military behavior, or the form of a more thoughtful approach to preventing a recurrence of this kind of terrorism, which would include a focus on nonviolent approaches. That would be a more healthy, in my view, kind of survivor mission, translated into political policy.

This disaster has an apocalyptic quality. It felt to many people close to it, in New York and Washington, like some version of the end of the world. That is how people in Hiroshima felt. (It is interesting that some of those who witnessed the recent disaster have associated it with nuclear weapons and Hiroshima. The explosions looked like a mushroom cloud, and there were large populations fleeing from "ground zero.")

I first developed the themes of how survivors react in my work on Hiroshima, and I and others have used them as a kind of phenomenology or psychology of survivors. In Hiroshima, people's responses were accompanied by a sense of threat to the human chain, the great chain of being, a lasting image of the end of the world. In New York and Washington, that initial sense of the world ending can be altered and transformed into various expressions of rebuilding and reconstruction, physically, and in other ways as well. That occurred in Hiroshima, too. Despite the lasting sense of threat to human existence, there developed over many years among people in Hiroshima considerable energy toward rebuilding, finding some kind of survivor mission that would give the city's experience meaning for the world. That has strongly taken the direction of warning the world of the danger of nuclear weapons.

In this case, especially in New York, where the devastation is greatest, the survivor mission is bound up with individual and collective feelings about America's role in the world. Although there are parallels with Hiroshima, there are differences -- most notably, that New York still stands, while most of Hiroshima was destroyed. One bomb, one city. In New York, the disaster is both more limited and more complicated.

That allows room to unleash the energies of rebuilding—and to give thoughtful responses to what has occurred.

This article is based on a telephone interview.

A Radically Different Set of Questions

Susie Linfield

"Where were you?"
"How did you hear about it?"
"Did you see it?'
"What did you do?"
"Did you know anyone who worked there?"
"How far downtown do you live?"

These are the questions we obsessively ask, and re-ask, each other. Because we are human, we want to know these things—we want to re-live those incomprehensibly terrible first moments of finding out, as if the re-living will lessen the horror. It doesn't. We will, no doubt, continue to tell these personal stories of "the event," "the attack" or "the tragedy," as it is now euphemistically called, for a long time to come-- perhaps, in some cases, forever. But this is, I would suggest, among the last things writers should be writing about now.

A different set of questions needs to be asked, and the endless reiteration of our personal stories prevents us from asking them. In fact, I suspect a major function of that endless reiteration is precisely to shield us from further difficulty. Here's what I'd like to know: How do we understand this massacre? What is the connection between understanding, judgment and action? Where does our understanding cease? How do we as a nation (and hopefully as many nations) react to this atrocity without pretending that we are, or can be, simply reactive? How do we connect this horror to the past and to the future, and to the many horrors that preceded it and will surely follow? (It is connected; the only question is to what extent we are willing and able to see that.) And where do we go from here?

We are stunned and grief-stricken; we stagger; we swirl in a vortex of confusion. None of that will cease. But that grief and that confusion should be only the starting-points of our stories, not their conclusion. Certain understandings of (or assumptions about) the world have ceased—violently and suddenly—for many of us. But personal narratives will not help us to reconstruct those old understandings (they're gone), nor create new ones, nor even figure out what can and should and does remain. Only by asking a radically different set of questions will we begin to gain the knowledge that we so desperately need. And we must ask those other questions *with* others, both within our country and outside it—not as a form of therapeutic activity but as a social, moral and political one.

Contributors

Humera Afridi is a freelance writer who recently moved to New York City to pursue an M.F.A. degree in fiction at New York University. She is working on a book of fiction.

Helga Ahmed is a social worker and environmental activist based in Islamabad, Pakistan.

Gene Albertelli lives in New York.

Nuno Andrade is a journalism student at New York University.

Anna Arutunyan is a journalism student at New York University.

Derrick N. Ashong is a musician and actor currently residing in Cambridge, Massachusetts.

Aung Zaw, a former student activist from Burma, is now a journalist living in Thailand. He has been covering Burma and regional affairs for almost 10 years. He has contributed opinion pieces, articles and stories to the Bangkok-based daily newspaper *The Nation*, the *Bangkok Post*, and other international publications, and is the founder and editor of the magazine *Irrawaddy*.

Kevin Barber, a flight attendant for a domestic airline, has written articles, short stories, consumer product reviews and editorials for various Web sites, newspapers and newsletters.

Grant Barrett is a lexicographer, a writer, an information technology consultant and a returning student at Columbia University studying French.

Aman Batheja is a senior in the Department of Journalism at New York University and a Resident Advisor in the Water Street dormitory.

John Bebow is editor-in-chief of *Michigan Live* (www.mlive.com), the leading online news and information service in the state. Before jumping to the Internet, he was an award-winning investigative reporter for *The Detroit News*, *Ann Arbor News*, and other newspapers in Michigan.

Kate Bolick is a graduate student in New York University's cultural reporting and criticism program. Her essays, interviews, and reviews have appeared *in The Atlantic Monthly*, *DoubleTake*, and *Newsday*, among other publications.

Brian Calvert is an economic reporter at the *Cambodia Daily* in Phnom Penh and contributes a fortnightly column, "Chasing Cambodia," to the Blue Ear Forum. The *Daily* is the only daily English-language newspaper in the country and is widely considered Cambodia's paper of record.

Father Julian Cassar is a Catholic Priest from the island of Malta, serving the Archdiocese of New York, presently as a Parochial Vicar in St Stanislaus Parish, Pleasant Valley, New York. He came to New York in 1981 and has worked in four different parishes so far.

Jeffrey Cohen is a New Orleans native with a graduate degree in journalism from Columbia University. He is the Wallingford reporter for *The Record-Journal* of Meriden, Connecticut.

Richard C. Crepeau is author of *Baseball: America's Diamond Mind, 1919-1941*, and professor of history at the University of Central Florida.

Constance Daley, originally a New Yorker, now lives on St. Simons Island, Georgia, where amongst other things, she is a regular columnist *for TheAmerican Reporter*, producing the ever popular "Hominy & Hash" column.

William Davis is a staff writer at the Jacksonville, North Carolina *Daily News*.

Betsy de Lotbiniere worked as a journalist for ten years in her hometown, New York, then Rome, Paris and finally in London. It was while interviewing the Mexican film director, Alejandro Jodorowski, that she realised she was in the wrong business. Two children and twenty-years-with-the-same-man later, she writes poetry and fiction.

Alex M. Dunne has edited and published *digittant*e, a magazine for creative writing and art (www.digittante.com) since 1998. He regularly contributes reviews, columns and commentary to Blue Ear, and recently completed his first novel, "Good Love Robots."

Niamh Early is a Languages and Marketing graduate of Dublin City Universityand has a Business post-graduate qualification from the Queens University ofBelfast. She now calls New York home and works on Wall Street.

Mindy Diane Feldman is a specialist in emerging market investment. She lives in midtown Manhattan.

Caleb Frazier is a journalism student at New York University.

Gary Gach is author of *The Complete Idiot's Guide to Understanding Buddhism* and editor of *What Book!? - Buddha Poems from Beat to Hiphop* (American Book Award, 1999) . He's been weaving a web site of spiritual responses to 9/11, http://awakening.to/peace.html, an online active anthology of vows and prayers, analyses and poetry.

Karmann Ghia is a New York-based freelance journalist. An anthropology graduate, she has written for the *Los Angeles Times*, *New York Post, Your Flesh* and *Behutet*. She is also a freelance book editor at Inside.com. She specialises in entertainment and lifestyle features and human-interest stories.

Todd Gitlin is a professor at New York University and the New York editor of openDemocracy.net, where his piece in this collection originally appeared.

Monica Haim is a student in New York University's graduate program in magazine journalism.

Larry Hartsell, a translator and traveler with a day job as an office worker, is a recent transplant to New York from Seattle.

Stanley Hauerwas is Professor of Theological Ethics and of Law at Duke University. His many books include *Resident Aliens: Life in the Christian Colony* (1989) and *The Hauerwas Reader* (2001). In September 2001, *Time* magazine called him "contemporary theology's foremost intellectual provocateur."

Donna Headrick is a researcher, writer and social worker in Portland, Maine. She has lived, worked and traveled extensively (compared to most U.S. citizens anyway) outside the United States.

Karen Houppert is adjunct professor in New York University's graduate journalism department and a freelance journalist who has written for *The Village Voice*, *The Nation*, *Salon*, *New York Newsday*, and *Ms. Magazine*, among others. She is also the author of *The Curse*, a cultural history of menstruation, published by Farrar, Straus & Giroux in 1999. She lives in Brooklyn, New York with her husband and 4-year-old son.

Aisha Khan is a graduate student in New York University's joint journalism/Near East studies program. She is writing her thesis on Islamic revival in Central Asia.

Cynthia G. La Ferle is an award-winning, nationally published columnist based in Royal Oak, Michigan. Visit her Web site at www.laferle.com. In addition to her weekly "Life Lines" column in *The Daily Tribune*, her columns and essays have been published in *Reader's Digest*, *Writer's Digest*, *The Christian Science Monitor*, *The Detroit Free Press*, *Cleveland Plain Dealer*, and others.

Lydia Lakwonyero is 15 years old and attends Iganga Girls Secondary School in Kampala, Uganda. She writes Christian songs for her school choir and poems for her school paper.

Blake Lambert is a Canadian journalist on the staff of Jerusalem Post Radio, an Internet radio station owned by *The Jerusalem Post*. He contributes a fortnightly "Jerusalem Diary" to the Blue Ear Forum.

Steve Lanier is Director of American World Services Corporation (AWS), a consulting company that assists non-U.S. organizations in their U.S. trade and inward investment promotion activities, and publisher and co-founder of BlueEar.com: Global Writing Worth Reading.

J. R. Lankford, author of the mystery-thriller *The Crowning Circle*, was the first woman to staff a Secretariat in the International Electrotechnical Commission.

Carol Lee is a graduate student in New York University's Department of Journalism.

Robert Jay Lifton is a professor emeritus of psychiatry and psychology and director emeritus of the Center on Violence and Human Survival at John Jay College of Criminal Justice, City University of New York.

Edward Linenthal is the author of *The Unfinished Bombing: Oklahoma City in American Memory*, and is a professor at the University of Wisconsin-Oshkosh.

Susie Linfield, a book critic for the *Los Angeles Times*, teaches in the Cultural Reporting and Criticism program in New York University's Department of Journalism.

Robert Manoff, formerly managing editor of *Harper's* magazine and editor of the *Columbia Journalism Review*, is Director of the Center for War, Peace, and the News Media at New York University's Department of Journalism and Mass Communication.

Challiss McDonough is the Southern Africa Correspondent for the Voice of America. She has worked in more than a dozen countries on three continents. She has five sisters and a mother who worries a lot. She wishes they would come visit her in Johannesburg.

Scott McLemee is a staff writer on the humanities *at The Chronicle of Higher Education*. His reviews and essays have appeared in the *New York Times*, the *Washington Post*, *Lingua Franca*, *Feed*, *Newsday*, and numerous other journals.

Leonard T. Miller is a pilot for United Airlines.

David T. Z. Mindich is a native New Yorker, a graduate of New York University, and chair of the Journalism Department at Saint Michael's College, Vermont. He is the author of *Just the Facts: How "Objectivity" Came to Define American Journalism*. His articles have appeared in the *Wall Street Journal*, *New York* magazine, the *Christian Science Monitor*, and elsewhere. He visits New York City as often as he can.

Doug Nairne is the Deputy Technology Editor of the *South China Morning Post*.

Shanty Nambiar is a global emerging markets reporter for BridgeNews in New York, covering both international financial and political events in developing countries, prior to which she worked for Dow Jones in New York and Malaysia. She has worked as a journalist and photographer in the Middle East (Jordan and Israel) and in Africa (Uganda, Kenya and Tanzania), and is a graduate of Columbia University's Graduate School of Journalism.

Robin O'Brien works in Human Resources for Brown Brothers Harriman, a Wall Street investment bank. He lives in Manhattan with his wife, cat, and 64 teenaged ballet dancers.

Conor O'Clery is the International Business Editor of *The Irish Times*.

Jaclyn O'Malley is a staff writer for the *Garden City Telegram* in Garden City, Kansas.

Preston Peet is a freelance journalist living in Manhattan's Lower East Side. He is a contributing editor at disinfo.com, contributes regularly to *High Times* magazine and website, writes a monthly column for the New York Waste, and has an article in the recently released *You Are Being Lied To* from Disinformation Publishing.

Bill Pfeiffer is founding director of the Massachusetts-based environmental nonprofit organization Sacred Earth Network. He LOVES sea-kayacking.

Christopher Phelps, assistant professor of history at Ohio State University, lived in New York City at three different points in his life. He is the author *of Young Sidney Hook: Marxist and Pragmatist* (Cornell University Press), a biography of that New York intellectual.

Paula Porter is an Iowa farm girl currently living and writing in Ashland, Massachusetts and is a Senior Web Editor with Cahners Business Information. Two of her co-workers were on American Flight 11. She was married to a Vietnam vet who died as a result of his exposure to Agent Orange and is writing a book about her experiences as a young widow.

Brian Pride is an artist, designer and creative consultant in New York, whereby he was graced to have worked alongside many of the World Trade Center victims, decorating for their holiday celebrations, corporate affairs, and benefits.

Mary Quigley is a professor of journalism at New York University and co-author of *And What Do YOU Do: When Women Choose to Stay Home*. She worked as a special correspondent for *Newsday* for 13 years, and now writes for *Forbes*, *Good Housekeeping*, and *Women's Day*, specializing in women's, children's and educational issues.

Jeff Rigsby is a writer based in New York City. He has worked and traveled extensively in East Asia and is currently preparing for an extended visit to the Middle East.

M.J. Rose is the author of the novels *Lip Service* and *In Fidelity*.

Jay Rosen is chair of the Department of Journalism at New York University and author of *What Are Journalists For?* (Yale University Press, 1999).

Andrew Ross is Professor and Director of the Graduate Program in American Studies at New York University. He is the author or editor of ten books, including, most recently, *The Celebration Chronicles: Life, Liberty, and the Pursuit of Property Value in Disney's New Town*.

Peter Shankman is CEO of The Geek Factory, a public relations company in New York serving the entertainment, high-tech, consumer, and corporate sectors.

Robyn Shepherd is a junior at New York University, majoring in journalism.

Laurel Sheppard is president of Lash Publications International and lives in Columbus, Ohio. She is currently a contributing editor *for Society of Women Engineers* and writes for several other publications.

Dawn Shurmaitis is a freelance writer who lives in Jersey City, New Jersey and works in the New York metropolitan area.

Mitchell Stephens is a Professor of Journalism and Mass Communication at New York University.

Natalie Stevens, a native of St. Joseph, Missouri, is a student in New York University's graduate program in magazine journalism.

Roger Tatoud was born in Grenoble, France in 1967. He moved to the UK after obtaining a Ph.D. in Molecular and Cell Biology in 1996 in Paris, has been working in Cancer Research for the past ten years in Paris, Norwich (UK) and Dundee (UK), and will soon join the UCL in London.

Alexandra Walker is an aspiring writer with a background in working to prevent rape and domestic violence. She lives in Washington, D.C.

Jade Walker is the overnight producer of the *New York Times* on the Web (www.nytimes.com) and the editor of *Inscriptions* (www.inscriptionsmagazine.com), the weekly e-zine for professional writers. She writes a weekly column called Jaded Writings, a monthly column for *Cyber Age Adventures*, freelances for various online and print magazines, and runs The Written Word quote service for publishing professionals. Her new book, *Sex, Death and Other...* will be published in the late fall with Metropolis Press.

Wei Gu is a graduate student of Business and Economic Reporting at New York University. She has published stories in the Chinese edition of *Fortune* and *Global Finance* magazine, among other publications. She also freelances for CNN Financial News in New York and has won awards from the New York Financial Writers' Association and the Foreign Press Association.

Hali Weiss is the founder of RemembrancePlace.com and an architect in New York City.

Ellen Willis directs the Cultural Reporting and Criticism program in the Department of Journalism at New York University and is a fellow of the Nation Institute. Her latest book is *Don't Think, Smile! Notes on a Decade of Denial*.

Peter Wong, Vice President & Chief Trader of a Singaporean bank, worked in the World Trade Center for 15 years.

Bonnie Zimmer is a photographer and a writer, recently retired from a position as a staff scientist for the State of New Jersey Department of Environmental Protection.

Publisher's Note:

The outpouring of support from survivors, witnesses and their families has been so tremendous that we have not been able to include all the stories we would have liked to include in this book. The second volume will be available Thanksgiving 2001, with more first-hand accounts and information about this unfolding historical drama and its effect on the world. To pre-order your copy, please visit www.booksurge.com/Volume2

We thank you for helping us keep alive the stories that have touched us all.

This book was produced as an on-demand paperback, an innovation in book printing and distribution that breaks down many of the conventional barriers to reaching readers with worthwhile content. No paper is wasted- books are printed and bound as they are sold, on high quality acid-free paper.

For more information on this revolution in publishing, writers and readers can visit www.imprintbooks.com or www.greatunpublished.com.

NOTES

NOTES

NOTES

NOTES

NOTES